B1
25 Great Philosophers

The SCM Briefly series

Anselm's *Proslogion* (with the Replies of Gaunilo and Anselm)
Aquinas' *Summa Theologica Part 1* (God, Part I)
Aquinas' *Summa Theologica Part 2* (God, Part II)
Aristotle's *The Nicomachean Ethics*
Ayer's *Language, Truth and Logic*
Bentham's *An Introduction to the Principles of Morals and Legislation*
Descartes' *Meditations on First Philosophy*
Fletcher's *Situation Ethics: The New Morality*
Hume's *Dialogues Concerning Natural Religion*
Hume's *An Enquiry Concerning Human Understanding*
Kant's *Critique of Practical Reason*
Kant's *Groundwork of the Metaphysics of Morals*
Kant's *Religion within the Boundaries of Mere Reason*
Kierkegaard's *Fear and Trembling*
Mill's *On Liberty*
Mill's *Utilitarianism*
Moore's *Principia Ethica*
Nietzsche's *Beyond Good and Evil*
Plato's *The Republic*
Russell's *The Problems of Philosophy*
Sartre's *Existentialism and Humanism*

Other books by David Mills Daniel published by SCM Press:

SCM AS/A2 *Ethics and Moral Philosophy*
SCM AS/A2 *Revision Guide: Ethics and Religious Ethics*
SCM AS/A2 *Revision Guide: Philosophy of Religion*

Briefly: 25 Great Philosophers from Plato to Sartre

David Mills Daniel,
Dafydd E. Mills Daniel
and Megan Daniel

scm press

Published in 2011 by SCM Press
Editorial office
13–17 Long Lane,
London, EC1A 9PN, UK

SCM Press is an imprint of Hymns Ancient & Modern Ltd
(a registered charity)
13A Hellesdon Park Road,
Norwich, Norfolk, NR6 5DR, UK

www.scmpress.co.uk

British Library Cataloguing in Publication data

A catalogue record for this book is available
from the British Library

978-0-334-04212 9

Originated by the Manila Typesetting Company
Printed and bound by Lightning Source UK

Contents

vi

For Jenny and Edmund

Introduction

Readers of this book may already be familiar with the existing books in the *Briefly* series, which the SCM Press has been publishing since 2006, and which now number 21. The aim of these 'classic text' books is to help students and general readers to acquire knowledge and understanding of key texts in philosophy, philosophy of religion, theology and ethics. So, their focus is on a particular piece of writing by a philosopher, ethicist or theologian.

The aim of this book is rather different: to provide an outline of the lives of 25 Great Philosophers from the Western tradition, from Plato to Sartre, and to discuss two of their key ideas, which have contributed to the development of Western thought and society.

How have the philosophers and key ideas been chosen? That is a fair question. Inevitably, any selection involves a subjective element, and not everyone will agree with it. While few students of philosophy would quibble over the inclusion of, for example, Plato, Aristotle, Descartes, Locke, Kant, Hume or Mill, there will be those who would argue that Pascal, Schopenhauer or Hegel should have been included instead of Aquinas, Butler or Paine. And, there is no denying the legitimacy of such preferences. However, it can certainly be claimed that all the philosophers chosen and their ideas have played a significant part in the development of the Western philosophical tradition and/or Western society: although it is certainly not maintained that their impact has been equally significant, or (wholly) beneficial in every case. Further, the ideas selected are central to the philosophical approach of the philosophers concerned.

This book is part of the *Briefly* series, so it does not provide a full biography of each philosopher, or exhaustive analysis and assessment of his ideas. Each chapter is not more than 2,800 words long, and contains a context section, an outline of the philosopher's life, discussion of the key ideas, an indication of their impact and some suggestions for further reading, including resources available on the internet. The context section is not intended to give a complete account of all the philosophical ideas associated with a particular philosopher. Its purpose is to outline those aspects of the philosopher's thinking that shed light on the key ideas, and to put them into context. The impact section gives a brief indication of how the key ideas have influenced the development of Western thought and society.

The book also tries to highlight contrasting approaches to philosophical issues, such as rationalism and empiricism, different and differing treatments of particular issues, such as the nature and role of government, and areas where the thinking of the various philosophers overlaps, or has influenced, or been influenced (one way or another) by the ideas of others, as with Plato and Aristotle, Locke and Berkeley or Bentham and Mill. The book has two glossaries. The Glossary of Philosophers and Thinkers provides brief information about other philosophers and thinkers who are referred to in the text. The Glossary of Terms contains brief definitions of specialist philosophical and other terms used in the book. There is also an index.

This book is not a complete history of Western philosophy. It therefore offers an invitation to those who find its contents thought-provoking and horizon-expanding: please do not stop at what you find here! Philosophy is for everyone, not just the few who study it at university. The Great Philosophers wrote about the big issues of life. Studying their lives and exploring their ideas can help us to answer some of the questions we face today. At least, it can help us to understand the questions more clearly.

So, find out more about these Great Philosophers. Read some of their books. The main texts referred to for each chapter are listed in the suggested reading sections. And, of course, you can use the classic text *Brieflys* to help you. There are *Brieflys* available for texts by 15 of the 25 Great Philosophers featured in this book.

Finally, there is a question that may well occur to a number of readers. What about female philosophers? The reason why none appears in this book is not because there are no female philosophers today, but because, in the past, women have not been given the same opportunities as men to develop and publish their philosophical ideas. Through history, however, there have been women who have taken a keen interest in philosophy, and some of these are referred to in the text, such as Princess Elizabeth of Bohemia, the critical correspondent of Descartes, Damaris Masham, whose home at High Laver in Essex was a place of refuge for John Locke in his declining years, and Simone de Beauvoir, the feminist philosopher and companion of Jean-Paul Sartre.

I would like to thank my two younger children, Dafydd and Megan, for their invaluable contribution to his book; my wife, Jenny, and my other son, Edmund (to both of whom this book is dedicated), for their tireless encouragement and assistance; the previous editor at the SCM Press, Barbara Laing, who commissioned the *Briefly* series in 2005, and took a keen interest in its development; and the present editor, Dr Natalie Watson, for her continuing support.

David Mills Daniel

I

Plato
(c. 429–347 BCE)
The theory of forms, the form of the good and philosopher–rulers
The role of women in government and society

Context

Why did the Cambridge philosopher Alfred North Whitehead say that the Western philosophical tradition was best described as a series of footnotes to Plato? It is because of the range of ontological, epistemological and ethical issues which Plato addresses and which have dominated philosophy and metaphysics ever since: What is the nature of ultimate reality? How do we discover it? What is knowledge? What is the difference between knowledge and opinion? What is the basis of morality? How do we distinguish between right and wrong? What is justice? How should a state be governed? Who are the best people to rule it?

Plato also provides some interesting answers. However, as Whitehead acknowledges, they are not ones which every subsequent philosopher has accepted. Whereas we, living in a scientific age, tend to be empiricists, believing that knowledge comes through experience and observation of the empirical world and how it operates, Plato is a philosophical rationalist, believing that only through our minds, by the use of reason, can we discover truth and penetrate the nature of ultimate reality.

Why did he think this? For Plato, the world we experience through our senses is in a continual state of flux and so cannot give us certain knowledge. He believes that individual things, or particulars, in the ordinary, visible, ever-changing world, which we experience through the senses, acquire their identity by being, in some way, copies of the unalterable, indivisible forms or essential natures of these things, which exist in a transcendent, eternal, unchanging world to which only our minds can gain access. Thus, a particular thing is beautiful or just by being a copy of or participating in what Plato calls the form or essential nature of beauty or justice. This view of reality, expressed in Plato's theory of forms, is dualistic: it holds that there are two orders or levels of reality.

Plato's writings take the form of dialogues, in which such philosophical issues as what exists, how do we know what exists and what is right are discussed. There is a principal speaker, usually Plato's teacher Socrates, whose views seem to emerge victorious. For example, in *The Republic*, Socrates acknowledges the difficulty of determining the nature of justice. He then interrogates and debates with those who hold differing views. He dismisses the conventional view, that it is giving everyone his or her due and helping friends, and the cynical approach, which identifies morality or justice with the interests of the powerful. He also rebuts the contention that people practise justice unwillingly, because it is the middle ground between what they see as most desirable, doing wrong and getting away with it, and least desirable, being the victims of others' wrongdoing.

Socrates then considers what justice is in the state, concluding that it involves the three classes in society (wealth-creators, the professional soldiers who defend it and the rulers) concentrating on their own role and not meddling with that of the others. He argues that the situation is the same with people. The individual personality consists of three elements: reason, the irrational appetite and reason's ally, spirit or indignation. Here, justice involves each of the three elements performing their particular function, with reason, supported by spirit, ruling and thus controlling the irrational appetite, leading to a well-disciplined person. Thus, justice or morality, in the state or the individual, is an appropriate division of responsibilities among the elements that constitute it, and the integration, self-discipline and effective functioning that this produces.

Plato's view of the nature of ultimate reality led him to believe that only those who dedicate their lives to the long process of philosophical reflection will be able to understand the essential nature of things. Therefore, states must be ruled by philosophers, who, after rigorous intellectual training, will understand the true nature of goodness and justice and thus govern well and in their subjects' interests. In Plato's eyes, government by philosophers stands in contrast to democracy, an anarchic system which treats people as equal when they are not. Plato's theory of forms and views about the need for philosopher–rulers is one of the key ideas discussed below. The other is whether or not women are capable of participating in government.

However, although we naturally regard these views as Plato's own, there is no unambiguous declaration that they are. For example, he discusses his fundamental doctrine of the forms in a number of his dialogues, including *The Republic*, *Phaedo*, *Timaeus* and *Parmenides*; but, in the last-mentioned, it is robustly challenged. In his exchange with the young Socrates, the philosopher Parmenides subjects the relationship between particular instances of things in the empirical world and their forms to searching criticism: how can many particulars participate in one form, when the forms are held to be indivisible; and are there forms of, for example, mud and dirt, as well as beauty and justice?

Life

The son of Ariston and Perictione, Plato was born into a leading aristocratic Athenian family at a critical period in the history of the Greek city-state. Under Pericles' leadership, Athens had become not only Greece's cultural heart, but also had developed democratic institutions, while its formidable navy, which had played a crucial part in defeating the Persian invasions of Greece, had enabled it to build up a large empire. However, Athens' success produced tensions with other Greek states, notably Sparta, Greece's leading military power.

In 431 BCE, the Second Peloponnesian War between Athens and Sparta broke out, and Plato may have taken part in the successful naval battle of Arginusae in 406. But, generally, the war went badly for Athens. The failure of an expedition against Syracuse (415–12 BCE) discredited the democratic politicians, resulting in political instability and violence. Following Athens' eventual defeat, in 404 BCE, Sparta supported a successful oligarchic revolution, but this brutal regime was short-lived and democracy was restored.

As a young man, Plato had been taught by the philosopher Cratylus, a follower of Heraclitus of Ephesus, who maintained the impossibility of attaining certain knowledge from the ever-changing world of the senses. By the end of the Peloponnesian War, Plato had become a pupil of Socrates, who devoted his life to the pursuit of truth, particularly in ethics. From Socrates, Plato learned that certain knowledge is only attainable through the reason. However, some Athenians resented Socrates, finding his constant challenges to conventional ideas offensive. He was accused of undermining belief in the gods and corrupting young people. Plato was appalled when, on top of all the other terrible events he had witnessed, Socrates was tried and executed in 399 BCE.

Plato had been considering a political career, but now became disenchanted with politics and all existing forms of government, particularly democracy, which he felt forced political leaders to do what they think will please the majority, rather than what they judge to be right. He left Athens for Megara, where he stayed with the philosopher Euclid. He developed the view that states must be ruled by philosophers, who will know the true nature of goodness and always govern in their subjects' interests.

Back in Athens, Plato founded his Academy, the world's first university, around 386 BCE. Designed as a place to train future philosopher–rulers, through study of a range of disciplines, culminating in philosophy, it was attended by students from all over Greece, including Aristotle. Plato devoted the rest of his life to teaching and to writing books, in which he first recorded and then developed Socrates' thought and his own ideas.

Unfortunately, Plato's attempts to put his political theories about philosopher–rulers into practice were a failure. He had visited Syracuse in Italy in the early 380s BCE and made friends with Dion, the brother-in-law of its ruler, Dionysius I. In 367, Dion invited Plato to Syracuse, to help with the education of its new ruler, his nephew Dionysius II. However, Dionysius II proved to be a cruel and oppressive tyrant, who forced Dion out of Syracuse and confiscated his estates.

Plato (c. 429–347 BCE)

It is possible to trace the development of Plato's thought through his dialogues, all of which have survived, and fall into three stages: the early dialogues (such as *Protagoras*, *Crito* and *Euthyphro*), the middle dialogues (such as *The Republic*, the *Symposium* and *Phaedo*) and the late dialogues (such as *Statesman* and *Laws*).

Key ideas

The theory of forms, the form of the good and philosopher–rulers

In *The Republic*, Plato argues that the problems of states and their citizens will only end if philosophers become rulers, or if existing rulers become philosophers, as only philosophers are fit to govern. Why does he hold this controversial and elitist view? The reason is his theory of forms and belief in two orders of reality. As things in the ordinary visible world are not perfectly just or beautiful, but only approximate to the beauty or justice of beauty-in-itself or goodness-in-itself in the intelligible world, those who know only particular things, such as beautiful objects or just acts, and not beauty or justice itself, do not really know these things, but merely have opinions about them. Only those who have penetrated to the true nature of ultimate reality and know the essence of goodness are capable of ruling well.

And the essence of goodness, the form of the good, is not just one form among many, but presides over all the other forms in the intelligible world. In the striking simile of the sun, Plato likens its relation to the other forms or essences to that of the sun to visible objects in the empirical world. The form of the good is not only the source of the intelligibility of the other forms or essences, but also of their being and reality.

Indeed, it is the source of all reality, truth and goodness. Only those philosophers who have seen it will know what is good in itself and which things and actions really are good, right and just. Plato uses another famous simile, that of the cave, to illustrate the ascent of the mind from the visible world to the intelligible one, where it finally sees the form of the good. It is possession of this vital moral knowledge that equips those philosophers who have acquired it to govern the state.

This knowledge will not just fall into their laps. To attain it, philosopher–rulers (Plato calls them 'Guardians') must undergo a course of advanced studies, which will enable them to see the form of the good and gain access to moral truths. Study of mathematics will shift their focus away from the world of change, while dialectic, an intense programme of philosophical enquiry and discussion, will enable their minds to penetrate to the essential nature of things. Those who reach the final stage and see the form of the good will become their states' rulers, reluctantly taking turns to govern the state and train their successors, while devoting the rest of their time to their preferred occupation of philosophical study.

Is there a world of forms or essences, which transcends the ordinary, empirical world? Philosophers such as Bertrand Russell have been attracted by Plato's theory, which would account for our concept of universals: the properties, such as whiteness of triangularity, which particular things have in common. However, most people, including Plato's famous pupil Aristotle, do not agree that there are two orders of reality or that the ordinary world, experienced through the senses, is less real than an invisible, intelligible one. Plato's theory is speculative metaphysics, which runs counter to common sense and sense experience, and Plato does not explain how the intelligible and visible worlds relate to each other.

Plato (c. 429–347 BCE)

The role of women in government and society

What about women? Are they capable of becoming philosopher–rulers or Guardians? Rejecting the view that women belong in the home as wives and mothers, Plato identifies the key question in relation to their role. This is not the one always put by opponents of female equality: are there any differences between men and women? It is: are there any relevant differences between them, which should preclude women from positions of responsibility? There are obvious natural differences between the two sexes, but the issue is not about differences in an unqualified sense, but about those relating to suitability for particular roles and responsibilities.

Plato argues that, in relation to being philosopher–rulers, the relevant factors are intellect and physical capacity. As the major difference between male and female is that the one sex begets children, while the other bears them, there are no relevant differences disqualifying the latter from traditional male occupations. No administrative or other role is suitable only for men as men or women as women. Natural capacities are similarly distributed in each sex, so there are women capable of defending the state and doing philosophy to the level of understanding the essential nature of things. Therefore, women should receive the same intellectual and physical training as men, and play their part in government.

However, becoming Guardians will not give women lives of privileged ease. Plato believes that philosopher–rulers must give up private and family life, in order to serve the state. They should not have their own households or own private property. Sexual partners and children should be held in common, so that parents and children do not know each other. Children should be taken to state nurseries at birth and weak or defective children disposed of. Female Guardians should be allowed to breed between the ages of 20 and 40, males from 25 to 55. In Plato's view, these are the optimum ages for producing healthy children with leadership potential. To prevent incest, Guardians would regard all children born within ten months of their mating as sons and daughters, their children as grandchildren, and so on.

Such arrangements would ensure that the state's rulers and subjects regard each other as fellow citizens and prevent the dissension that arises when rulers accumulate wealth for themselves or promote their own family interests. Unity among the philosopher–rulers would be guaranteed by their regarding themselves as members of one family. However, who, male or female, would wish to belong to a ruling class at such a cost? Moreover, even if the benefits were as clear-cut as Plato claims and his system produced rulers who were models of integrity, would a state be well governed by those who were as personally unhappy as Plato's Guardians were likely to be?

Impact

- Plato's influential theory of forms has led philosophers to seek a level of reality which transcends the ordinary, empirical world and established the rationalist tradition in Western philosophy: the view that it is reason, not the senses, that gives us access to fundamental philosophical truths.
- His view that only philosopher–rulers, who know what good itself is, and who will lead lives guided by reason and knowledge, are fit to rule the state, has led to scepticism about the suitability of democracy as a system of government,

and fostered the notion that states are best governed by specially trained elites.

- Plato's ethical theory highlights the demanding nature of moral philosophy and has helped even those philosophers who reject his view that there is an essence of goodness, located at a different level of reality, to recognize that discovering or deciding what is good or right requires intense intellectual effort and careful philosophical enquiry.
- Despite numerous examples of what women can achieve (from Elizabeth I to Jane Austen), Plato's insistence that there are no relevant intellectual or physical differences between men and women that disqualify the latter from participating in government, generally fell on deaf ears until the twentieth century.

Further reading

J. Annas, *An Introduction to Plato's Republic*, Oxford and New York: Oxford University Press, 1981.

T. Brickhouse and Nicolas D. Smith, 'Plato' (updated in 2009), in J. Fieser and B. Dowden (eds), *Internet Encyclopedia of Philosophy*, at www.iep.utm.edu.

G. M. A. Grube, *Plato's Thought*, Indianapolis: Hackett Publishing Company, 1980.

R. Kraut, 'Plato' (revised 2009), in E. N. Zalta (ed.), *Stanford Encyclopaedia of Philosophy*, at http://plato.stanford.edu.

D. Mills Daniel, *Briefly: Plato's Republic*, London: SCM Press, 2006.

Plato, *Five Dialogues: Euthyphro, Apology, Crito, Meno, Phaedo*, trans. G. M. A. Grube and revised J. M. Cooper, second edition, Indianapolis: Hackett Publishing Company, 2002.

Further reading

Plato, *Parmenides*, trans. B. Jowett, at http://classics.mit.edu/Plato/parmenides.html.

Plato, *The Republic*, trans. H. D. P. Lee, second edition (revised and reissued with new Further Reading), London: Penguin, 2003.

Plato, *Timaeus and Critias*, trans. H. D. P. Lee, revised edition, London: Penguin, 1977.

Bertrand Russell, *History of Western Philosophy*, London: Routledge, 2004.

Bertrand Russell, *The Problems of Philosophy*, reissued second edition, with Introduction by John Skorupski, Oxford and New York: Oxford University Press, 2001.

2

Aristotle
(384–322 BCE)
The foundations of logical thinking
Virtue ethics, cultivating the moral
virtues and *eudaimonia*

Context

Who was regarded as *the* Philosopher during the Middle Ages?
It is Aristotle, whose philosophical ideas had an immense influence on such thinkers as Thomas Aquinas. Indeed, like his
teacher Plato, Aristotle has had a central role in philosophy for
almost 2,500 years. He is also the inventor of 'metaphysics' as
the term for the study of ultimate reality, which goes beyond
physics and cannot be pursued by ordinary empirical methods. Unfortunately, though we seem to have a lot of Aristotle's
writings, it is only a small proportion of his original output,
most of which has been lost. Those we know about came into
Western philosophy through the translation of commentaries
on Aristotle by such Muslim scholars as Averröes.

Though a student of Plato's for many years, Aristotle became
a critic of his belief that only reason can yield philosophical
knowledge. What is his alternative? He thinks we discover philosophical truths, including what is the good for human beings,
and what they ought to aim at, by observing the world, life and

human beings themselves. They will not be found in a transcendental or intelligible realm, set over against the empirical one, to which only professional philosophers can gain access. While he does not reject the use of reason for philosophical speculation, he also emphasizes the importance of experience and of an empirical approach to the acquisition of philosophical knowledge.For the rationalist philosopher Gottfried Wilhelm Leibniz, Aristotle's approach may accord with popular ideas of philosophy, but this makes him a less profound thinker than Plato.

Aristotle explicitly rejects Plato's theory of forms and his view of the form of the good as the source of reality, truth and goodness. For Aristotle, every individual substance that exists in the world is a unity of matter and form. Matter is the indeterminate material out of which everything is made; its form is the principle which determines what the essential nature of each thing will be (although there are different and differing interpretations of Aristotle's theory of substance). Thus, he does not believe that the particular things we experience in the empirical world are copies of their forms or essences, which exist independently of them in an intelligible world. Rather, each particular thing in the empirical world is an instance of one or more universals, which exists in or as part of it. This fits in with the common sense view that to talk of universals is to identify or refer to features which certain particular things have in common.

Although he holds that our senses generally give us reliable evidence about the external world, and that there is no need for scepticism, Aristotle considers that the information we receive through them is not always unambiguous and straightforward. So, we engage in philosophy in order to resolve issues which we find difficult to understand or interpret. Thus, he emphasizes a painstaking approach to observation and thorough analysis of concepts.

But, if we are going to think and argue successfully, we also need rules. And, Aristotle is the inventor of logic, which is the science of drawing inferences and, specifically, of the syllogism. This provides a formal structure for argument and makes it possible for a conclusion to be inferred from two premises. Aristotle's view of logical thinking is one of the key ideas discussed in this chapter.

The other key idea is Aristotle's ethical theory, from which the normative ethical theory of virtue ethics originates. He had a teleological view of the world. Everything has a *telos* or end, which is determined by its nature or function. The supreme or highest good for all things, including human beings, is to fulfil this *telos*, so it is both what they ought to aim at, and also what they actually do aim at. The task of ethics is to identify human beings' supreme or highest good. This has an important bearing on how we lead our lives, as we are more likely to achieve our aim with a definite target to aim at. He links ethics to politics, which seeks to determine what we should and should not do in society, reflecting the fact that we do not exist in isolation, but as members of communities.

Aristotle acknowledges that ethics and politics are not exact sciences. We must not look for more precision in these subjects than their nature permits. His concern is not with the ethical qualities of individual acts, but with development of the virtues that will enable people to lead good lives. The function of a good person is to lead his or her life well. Such an individual will then be happy throughout it as he or she will spend it in virtuous conduct and contemplation. However, it is only when a person's life is complete and it is clear how that life has been spent, that he or she can rightly be called happy. Popular belief, which holds that the happy person lives well, supports the philosophical analysis of happiness. Aristotle also notes that people need material goods to practise the moral virtues, as fine deeds cannot be performed without resources.

Life

The son of Nicomachus, a court physician to the kings of Macedonia, Aristotle was born in Stagira in Macedonia. At 17, he went to Athens to study at Plato's Academy, staying there, as student and teacher, for 20 years and gaining a reputation as a hard-working student with a wide range of interests. In 347 BCE, following Plato's death, changes at the Academy, together with Athenian hostility towards Macedonia, led Aristotle to move to Assos in Asia Minor, where he married Pythias, the niece and adopted daughter of the ruler Hermias, who was keen to encourage education. During this period, he engaged in philosophical reflection and carried out scientific research with the botanist Theophrastus of Eresos.

In 343 BCE, King Philip II, who ruled the country from 359 to 336 BCE and whose military skill had enabled him to make Macedonia supreme in Greece and to become leader of the Greek federation, invited Aristotle to tutor his son, the future Alexander the Great (356–323 BCE). However, it is not clear for how long Aristotle performed this role or how much influence he had on Alexander's development.

In 335, the year after Alexander succeeded Philip, Aristotle returned to Athens, where in 334 he established his own school, the Lyceum, just outside the city. It was also known as the 'Peripatetic School', due to Aristotle's practice of walking around, as he talked with his students. He taught there for 11 years, engaging in a wide range of studies, including philosophy, metaphysics, logic, ethics, history, politics, the different branches of science and medicine. He also established a large library of manuscripts and a museum of natural objects.

When Pythias died, Aristotle formed a relationship with Herpyllas, with whom he had children, including a son, Nicomachus, traditionally regarded as editor of Aristotle's *Nicomachean Ethics*. In 323 BCE, after Alexander's death in Babylon, following his conquest of the Persian Empire, Aristotle, fearing an anti-Macedonian reaction in Athens, and perhaps mindful of what had happened to Socrates, left for Chalcis, dying a year later. Theophrastus of Eresos took charge of the Lyceum, which survived for another 500 years.

Aristotle's interests extended well beyond what are now regarded as philosophical subjects, embracing science and natural history, and his books show his enormous intellectual range. There are treatises on logic, including the *Categories* and *De Interpretatione*; metaphysics, *The Metaphysics*; ethics, the *Nicomachean* and *Eudemian Ethics*; politics, the *Politics*; physics, biology and psychology, including the *Physics*, the *Historia Animalium* and *De Anima*; and poetry and rhetoric, *Rhetoric* and the *Art of Poetry*. However, the texts pose problems because they are not all complete works but collections of lecture notes which contain inconsistencies and repetitions. This is why Aristotle's literary style is often compared unfavourably, and unfairly, with Plato's.

Key ideas

The foundations of logical thinking

In his *Critique of Pure Reason*, Immanuel Kant declares that the science of logic, the formal laws of all thought, has not needed further attention since its complete elucidation by Aristotle. Kant's statement precedes the major developments in modern logic associated with Frege, Peirce and Russell. However, the fact that Aristotelian or traditional logic held the field until just over a century ago, testifies to the thoroughness of Aristotle's treatment.

He devised three of logic's most fundamental principles, known as the 'laws of thought'. This does not mean that they describe how people actually think; they prescribe how they should think, in order to do so logically. First, there is the law of the identity: 'x is x', with x as any entity. So, if x is a flower, but y is not a flower, then y is not x. Next is the law of non-contradiction: an entity cannot be both x and not-x. It cannot be both a flower and not a flower. Finally, the law of the excluded middle states everything is either x or not-x: x is either a tree or it is not a tree.

Taken together, these rules of thought are necessary conditions of any logical thinking; they ensure consistency in the way propositions are formulated. Indeed, it can be instructive to apply them to metaphysical or theological works or to experimental writing. Their failure to make sense may arise from breaches of these rules. A further point is that these rules are not themselves provable. They are self-evident logical principles, which must simply be accepted for any argument or proof to be possible.

To be convincing, a philosophical argument needs structure, so that the conclusion reached follows from the premises: that is, the proposition or propositions from which it starts. Addressing this issue, Aristotle introduced the syllogism, or the syllogistic inference. In this form of argument, a proposition is inferred from two premises, a minor and a major premise: for example, 'All human beings have eyes; all things with eyes are animals; so all human beings are animals.' Here, the first premise is the minor one and the second one the major premise. Both premises have one term in common with each other and one in common with the conclusion. Thus, it is possible to make a valid or logically sound inferential move from premises to conclusion.

Aristotle identifies four types of proposition that can be generated from syllogistic reasoning. They are universal affirmatives (known as A propositions), such as the example above; universal negatives (E propositions); particular affirmatives (I propositions); and particular negatives (O propositions). As the syllogistic form of argument is deductive, the conclusion follows necessarily from or is entailed by the premises. Thus, if the premises are true and the process of syllogistic reasoning is performed correctly, the conclusion will be true necessarily. It would be self-contradictory to deny it, this breaching one of the laws of thought.

According to Kant, logic's advantage over other branches of philosophy is the narrowness of its field: it has not needed further development, because its concern is with purely formal rules of logic. Although this is not the case with modern logic, which expands the possibilities, and where there can be valid and invalid arguments, depending on the pattern of inference used, it does apply to Aristotelian logic. As the syllogism involves purely deductive reasoning, the conclusion must follow necessarily from the premises: there cannot be an invalid syllogism.

Virtue ethics, cultivating the moral virtues and eudaimonia

How do we decide what is good or right and what we ought to do? Deontological ethics and consequentialist ethics are two of the most important normative ethical theories. The first concentrates on what duties we have as human beings, and to whom; the second on what is good, or 'the' good, for human beings and the kind of actions which will achieve it. Both focus on what we do, or ought to do, rather than on who does it: on actions, rather than the agent who performs them.

Is this the best approach? Or do right actions flow almost automatically from people of high moral calibre? Perhaps, we should concentrate on developing in ourselves those qualities or virtues which will lead us to conduct ourselves well instinctively, so that we will always behave appropriately towards others and ourselves.

This is virtue ethics. It emphasizes development of virtues, that is, admirable character traits or moral excellences, such as justice, prudence and courage, which lead people always to behave well. It is particularly associated with Aristotle, who describes virtues as dispositions to behave in ways that will benefit the individual and the wider community. He believes they are like crafts and are acquired by habit. People become good builders by building well and just by performing just acts. So, how we behave from the earliest age will determine our moral tendencies: for example, we will become temperate by refraining from, not indulging in, pleasures.

Further, right conduct is incompatible with excess or deficiency in feelings or actions, which destroy our moral qualities just as eating or drinking too much or too little destroys health. We must also appreciate that a virtuous act is not virtuous because of its external quality, but only if the agent knows what he is doing, chooses to perform the action for its own sake and does so from a permanent disposition towards it.

The moral virtues involve Aristotle's famous doctrine of the mean. We can and do feel fear, anger, pleasure and so on, too much or too little. The right way is to avoid excess or deficiency and to have or do them to an intermediate or appropriate degree. This is the mean. For example, the mean in relation to anger may not always be a moderate degree of anger. It will vary according to the situation. The doctrine of the mean does not provide a clear-cut rule; it is a general guiding principle.

Aristotle believes that those who live a virtuous life will achieve perfect happiness or *eudaimonia*. This is not a life of pleasure and endless self-gratification. Perfect human happiness is to be found in the activity which is proper to human beings, and which fulfils their essential nature. This is not, as we might expect, engaging in philanthropy and doing good works, but intellectual activity. Why is this? For Aristotle, the intellect is the highest thing in human beings, apprehending the highest forms of knowledge, such as philosophical and scientific truths. Leading a life of thought or a contemplative life is how human beings fulfil their *telos* or purpose. Thus, the happiest human beings will be those who think. However, human beings are not just minds, so moral activity, which relates to our common humanity and the fact that we lead our lives as members of society, also brings happiness but at a lower level.

Impact

- Aristotle's rules of thought are essential conditions of any logical thinking or argument: it is only by following them that any consistency in the formulation of propositions can be ensured.
- Philosophical arguments need structure, so that the conclusion reached follows from the premises: the syllogism, which dominated logic until a hundred years ago, makes possible valid inferential moves from premises to the conclusion.

- Aristotle's ethical ideas, which emphasize development of virtues, or admirable character traits, which will lead people always to behave well, still command wide respect and are embodied in the normative ethical theory of virtue ethics.
- Aristotle's concept of *eudaimonia*, with people achieving happiness through leading lives which combine cultivation of their intellects and moral activity, continues to be very influential.

Further reading

J. Ackrill, *Aristotle the Philosopher*, Oxford and New York: Oxford University Press, 1981.

Aristotle, *Metaphysics*, trans. H. Lansson-Tancred, new edition, London: Penguin, 1998.

Aristotle, *The Nicomachean Ethics*, trans. J. A. K. Thomson (Notes and Appendices by H. Tredinnick, Introduction and Further Reading by J. Barnes), further revised edition, London: Penguin, 1976.

Aristotle, *Selections from the Organon of Aristotle*, ed. J. R. Magrath (1868), Whitefish, MT: Kessinger Publishing, 2009.

J. Barnes, *Aristotle*, second edition, Oxford: Oxford University Press, 2000.

IEP Contributors, 'Aristotle' (2005), in J. Fieser and B. Dowden (eds), *Internet Encyclopedia of Philosophy*, at www.iep.utm.edu.

Immanuel Kant, *Critique of Pure Reason*, ed. V. Politis, London: Everyman, 1993.

D. Mills Daniel, *Briefly: Aristotle's The Nicomachean Ethics*, London: SCM Press, 2007.

Bertrand Russell, *The Problems of Philosophy*, reissued second edition, with Introduction by John Skorupski, Oxford and New York: Oxford University Press, 2001.

C. Shields, 'Aristotle' (2008), in E. N. Zalta (ed.), *Stanford Encyclopaedia of Philosophy*, at http://plato.stanford.edu.

R. Smith, 'Aristotle's Logic' (revised 2011), in E. N. Zalta (ed.), *Stanford Encyclopaedia of Philosophy*, at http://plato.stanford.edu.

3

Marcus Aurelius
(CE 121–80)
Living in accordance with nature
Leading a virtuous life

Context

Is philosophy primarily about knowledge and trying to understand the nature of ultimate reality or about discovering
how to lead a good and happy life? We would probably agree
that it should address both questions and others besides. For
many ancient Greek philosophers, questions of the first kind,
the metaphysical ones, though important in themselves, were
even more important as a means of answering the second
kind. The three giants of ancient Greek philosophy, Socrates,
Plato and Aristotle, posed a range of metaphysical questions
with which philosophers still grapple, and offered answers
which their successors continue to debate. They also have an
overriding concern with ethics and the principles according to
which we should live. This philosophical preoccupation with
moral and practical questions and with achieving *eudaimonia*
continued in subsequent centuries with Stoics and Epicureans
offering different answers.

Stoic philosophy originated with the fourth-century BCE
philosopher Zeno of Citium, who gained respect in Athens for

applying the teaching he gave in his own life. His work was carried on by Cleanthes of Assos and then Chrysippus of Soli. The name of this school of philosophy comes from the *stoa poikile*, the painted colonnade in Athens, where Zeno and his followers met. Although all three of its founders (particularly Chrysippus) wrote many books, none of these has survived. Therefore, knowledge of their teaching comes from information provided by later writers, such as Arrian, who recorded Epictetus' teachings, Diogenes Laertius, who wrote about the lives of the famous Greek philosophers, and the writings of such Roman followers or students of Stoicism as Seneca, Cicero and Marcus Aurelius.

The Stoics taught that the world was created and is directed by an active, rational principle, the *logos spermatikos*. The precise relationship between this rational principle and matter, the other part of ultimate reality, can be understood in different ways. From one perspective, the *logos spermatikos* can be identified with God or Zeus and thought of as separate from the world. However, this suggests a dualism, as in Plato or the Judaeo-Christian tradition, between an intelligible world on the one hand and the empirical world on the other; or between a transcendent creator and a created world which is dependent on, but wholly distinct from, God: which the Stoics rejected. Rather, the Stoics believed that God is also material, and thus they subscribed to a form of pantheism. God is the intelligent, active principle or (material) soul within the world, who acts upon matter; who can be identified with nature (or Nature); and who determines everything that occurs. Thus, under the direction of this rational principle or God, the world operates in an orderly, harmonious and pre-determined fashion; so everything that occurs in it happens necessarily. It also goes through an unceasing series of cycles; at the end of each cycle, the world is consumed by divine fire and the process starts again, with the next world following an identical pattern to the previous one.

Through their reason, human beings, who are at the top of the scale of living things, are able to understand the fundamental character of the world they inhabit and the rational principle which animates it; and their instinct for self-preservation leads them to cultivate their reason, in order to do so. This will enable them to realize that, as everything that happens is pre-determined, they must lead their lives in accordance with nature, which means acceptance of what befalls them, as it cannot be otherwise. An essential element in this is ensuring a correct perception of things. The Stoics were empiricists, as they believed that we acquire knowledge through the senses. However, we are not neutral recipients of this information. As we receive impressions of things outside us, we form judgements about them. This colours our perceptions, so that they do not correspond (precisely) to reality and may prevent us from accepting the inevitability of what takes place. We must use our reason to develop the feeling of inner certitude, which will accompany and be the guarantee of accurate perceptions.

Epicurus taught that pleasure and/or the absence of pain is the sole good, as it is the one we know about through our senses. He was not advocating self-indulgent hedonism, though, but a simple life, which achieves a balance between the needs and pleasures of mind and body, leading to happiness. Aristotle held that *eudaimonia* is achieved through a life devoted primarily to cultivation of the intellect, together with moral activity, which reflects our obligations to other members of society, and satisfaction of our material needs. For the Stoics, the practice of virtue is the only good and the only route to happiness; and the virtuous life is one that is lived in harmony with nature.

Crucial elements of such a life are recognition that other human beings are our brothers and sisters, towards whom we have responsibilities and whom we should treat benevolently and justly. We must also appreciate that many of the concerns which exercise human beings, including the pursuit of wealth, power or fame, are matters of indifference. This even applies to personal suffering and death, which are just part of how the world is, and must be accepted. By liberating ourselves from the baggage of ordinary human preoccupations, ambitions and fears, we achieve a degree of imperturbability in the face of, and detachment from, the ups and downs of existence, and learn to live in accordance with nature.

Life

Originally called Marcus Annius Verus, Marcus Aurelius Antoninus (Emperor, CE 161–80) was born in Rome, the son of a former consul, Annius Verus, and Domitia Calvilla. Brought up first by his grandfather, he was then adopted by his uncle, Titus Antoninus Pius (Emperor, CE 138–61), after his father's death. Antoninus Pius, whom Hadrian (Emperor, CE 117–38) had named as his successor, gave him a thorough education in the principles of Stoic philosophy, which taught him the importance of hard work, steadfastness in the face of adversity and consideration for others. He married Faustina, Antoninus Pius' daughter.

Although Antoninus Pius named Marcus Aurelius as his sole successor, the latter chose to share the government with Antoninus Pius' other adopted son, Lucius Verus, who was joint Emperor until his death in 169. Marcus Aurelius' reign got off to a difficult start, with natural disasters at home, threats of revolt in Britain and military defeat by the Parthians in Armenia. These problems set the scene for the rest of his reign, most of which he spent fighting the barbarian tribes who challenged Rome's power and threatened to invade Italy itself. A dedicated public servant, who paid careful attention to the details of public administration, such as maintaining roads, and a keen supporter of education and the study of philosophy and rhetoric, Marcus Aurelius reduced unnecessary public spending and tried to establish high moral standards in public life and society generally.

From 169, Marcus Aurelius had to spend most of his time in the north, fighting the Quadi, Marcomanni and Vandals. His decisive victories over them were followed by a revolt in Asia, led by the military commander Avidius Cassius. The revolt was defeated, but Marcus Aurelius showed mercy to Avidius Cassius' family. In the late 170s, he was forced to return to Germany, where he enjoyed military success, but died there at the age of 59. He is said to have succumbed to disease, but there are also allegations that he was poisoned in order to ensure the succession of his son Commodus (Emperor, 180–92).

Unlike his immediate predecessors, Marcus Aurelius was an active persecutor of Christians, for which he has been strongly criticized. However, he had little knowledge of Christianity and Christian teaching, while he believed that the rapid expansion of Christianity endangered the role and standing of the Emperor, which were inextricably bound up with traditional Roman religion and ritual, and also challenged Stoic beliefs and principles.

Key ideas

Living in accordance with nature

While most philosophical ideas are presented in tightly argued treatises, this is not the case with the *Meditations*. They lack structure and appear to be notebooks in which Marcus Aurelius recorded his thoughts for personal reference. In fact, the Romans were more interested in philosophy as a source of practical guidance about how to lead a virtuous life and to cope with its vicissitudes, than in speculative metaphysics. Stoic principles, which they learned about through the writings of such philosophers as Epictetus, were popular and influential with them. In the *Meditations*, Marcus Aurelius shows the value he attaches to Stoicism, with its emphasis on living in accordance with nature, as a means of providing him with encouragement and solace as he contended with the intense difficulties and challenges of ruling the Roman Empire.

Marcus Aurelius ponders alternative theories about the universe and how it operates. Either every event that occurs in it is caused by an intelligent being (and happens necessarily), or the universe consists only of atoms and everything happens randomly. As he believes that the universe is directed by an intelligent being, it is pointless to complain about the course of events. We should not ask for things to be other than they are, but pray for the capacity not to be afraid of what happens or will happen: it is a matter of indifference, and we should be capable of treating it as such.

We must develop the right attitude to change, neither resisting nor resenting it. An inescapable feature of life, it reflects the ultimate character of the universe, which goes through its endless, repetitive cycles. We must not be dissatisfied with its outcome, but resign ourselves to it, accepting that we are part of the process. We must cultivate detachment from the things of this world, all of which, including ourselves, decay and die. We need to come to terms with death, which is just another aspect of change, and regard it and whether it comes to us when we are young or old with indifference: either way, we will quickly be forgotten.

Of course, people do fear death, as they do suffering, and Marcus Aurelius suggests a way of making it more bearable. If, at any point, we think back over our lives, we can see that we have experienced many changes: from childhood, through youth to old age. They all seemed frightening at the time, involving a kind of death to the previous stage, as we entered the next. But, in retrospect, we can appreciate that there was nothing terrible about any of them; and it will be the same with death. We should always be prepared for the separation of the soul from the body; but our resignation does not mean that we should seek death or be eager for it. That would be as much of a failure to accept the way things are as trying to avoid it. Willingness to face death should flow from our rational judgement about the ultimate reality of the universe; it should not arise from an obstinate defiance of life: his view of the Christian attitude to death.

Marcus Aurelius stresses the importance of recognizing that everything in life is predetermined and so must be accepted. People who pursue pleasure as (the sole) good and seek to avoid pain as something evil are questioning nature. While we cannot control what happens, we can control our attitude to events. The key characteristic of the rational individual is that he sees things as they are, inevitable and under nature's government, and so has eliminated illusions and erroneous judgements. Thus, he will live in accordance with nature; be satisfied with things as they are, which will make them endurable; and be happy when anything, however insignificant, goes well.

Leading a virtuous life

How do we lead a virtuous life? As nature has made rational beings for the sake of one another and for mutual assistance and support, those who hurt others do not live according to nature; instead of being guided by reason, they are at odds with it. Marcus Aurelius points to the crucial difference between words and actions. Some people declare their good intentions towards others, but what matters is not discussion about what a good person ought to be, but being one. We should not need to tell people we are going to treat them justly: our actions should prove it.

When we wrong our neighbours, treat them unjustly or behave anti-socially, we diminish ourselves morally and show that we are not (as we ought to be) useful members of society who contribute positively to it. We should be continually asking ourselves whether our actions serve the common good; their doing so will be a reward in itself. Where people separate themselves from the rest of society in order to pursue their own selfish interests, they are like a branch that has been severed from the rest of a tree. This is what people do when they despise or avoid other members of society. But, society is part of the world we inhabit, with which we must re-engage, if we have separated ourselves from it, however tough it may be to do so.

Marcus Aurelius suggests precepts to guide our conduct towards other people, including those who offend or harm us. Yes, we can point their errors out to them. But we must bear in mind how hard it is to judge whether others are doing wrong or not, particularly when we do not know all the circumstances. But, whatever they do to us, our concern must still be for their welfare and we must treat them tolerantly. Instead of condemning their actions and judging them harshly, we should reflect on our own shortcomings. How often have we done wrong ourselves, as when we pursue pleasure or money or seek other people's good opinion? When we encounter hostility, disapproval or vilification, there is no cause for anxiety; it should be a matter of indifference to us. We should respond with friendliness and patience.

If we practise injustice, we will be the main victims, because we are failing to live in accordance with nature. Our aim should be to lead a life which is free of dishonesty and hypocrisy. If, as will inevitably happen, people try to prevent us from being guided by reason, we must refuse to be provoked by their words or actions or to be indignant with them. Above all, we must acknowledge justice as the root of all the other virtues. However, we will be distracted from practising it if we are anxious about things that we should treat with indifference, or fail to be well-disposed towards others.

Impact

- Although Marcus Aurelius is not in the first division of philosophers, his presentation of Stoic principles and how to lead a rational and virtuous life have appealed to readers of his *Meditations* over the centuries.
- The Stoic virtues of endurance, detachment and fearlessness in the face of death have been widely admired and valued, particularly in times of adversity, such as war or persecution.
- Although Marcus Aurelius persecuted Christians, there are important parallels, as well as significant differences between

the Stoic pantheism and Christian monotheism; while many of the virtues he commends, such as justice, tolerance and not judging others, are also prized in Christianity.

• There is common ground between Stoic ethics, as set forth by Marcus Aurelius in the *Meditations* with its focus on the use of reason in order to live a virtuous life in harmony with nature, and Aquinas' exposition of natural law ethics in the *Summa Theologica*, with human beings using their reason to discern the natural law within the God-given order of the universe, upon which they can base their ethical principles and decisions.

Further reading

Marcus Aurelius, *Meditations*, ed. D. Clay, London: Penguin, 2006.

Marcus Aurelius, *The Meditations*, trans. G. Long, http://classics.mit.edu/Antoninus/meditations.html.

A. R. Birley, *Marcus Aurelius: A Biography*, second edition, London: Routledge, 1993.

A. S. L. Farquharson, *Marcus Aurelius: His Life and His World*, Oxford: Basil Blackwell, 1951.

B. Inwood (ed.), *The Cambridge Companion to the Stoics*, Cambridge: Cambridge University Press, 2003.

R. Kamtekar, 'Marcus Aurelius' (2010), in E. N. Zalta (ed.), *Stanford Encyclopaedia of Philosophy*, at http://plato.stanford.edu.

G. H. Rendal, 'Marcus Aurelius Antoninus', in James Hastings (ed.), *Encyclopaedia of Religion and Ethics*, Vol. 8, Edinburgh: T & T Clark, 1930.

J. M. Rist, *Stoic Philosophy*, Cambridge: Cambridge University Press, 1977.

F. H. Sandbach, *The Stoics*, second edition, Cambridge/Indianapolis: Hackett Publishing Company, 1994.

J. Sellars, 'Marcus Aurelius' (updated 2005), in J. Fieser and B. Dowden (eds), *Internet Encyclopedia of Philosophy*, at www.iep.utm.edu.

W. O. Stephens, 'Stoic Ethics' (updated 2004), in J. Fieser and B. Dowden (eds), *Internet Encyclopedia of Philosophy*, at www.iep.utm.edu.

4

Anselm
(1033–1109)
God as that than which nothing greater can be thought
The ontological argument as a proof of God's existence

Context

How can a medieval monk, writing almost a thousand years ago, have produced a philosophical argument which has fascinated and divided philosophers ever since? It seems hard to believe, but is nonetheless the case with Anselm's ontological argument for the existence of God. In the preface to his *Proslogion*, in which he puts forward the argument, Anselm tells us he wrote the book to provide a single proof of God's existence, rather than the complex of arguments he had put forward in an earlier book, the *Monologion*. And it is a startlingly concise argument. Unlike the cosmological or design arguments, which start from experience or interpretations of it, it is an *a priori* argument. It does not depend on experience, but moves with remarkable brevity from the idea of God to his existence.

But, why should a monk like Anselm, who has devoted his whole life to God's service, be interested in proving God's existence philosophically? Surely, he has all the knowledge of God he requires from God's revelation of himself, in particular through the life and work of Jesus, as recorded in the New Testament. However, medieval philosophers and theologians, such as Anselm and Thomas Aquinas, did not see revelation and reason as mutually exclusive sources of knowledge about God, with the religiously committed discarding reason. God gives human beings an intellect so that they can use it for his service. Anselm wants to use all the means at his disposal to increase and deepen his knowledge of God and to get as close as he can to God so that, as thinker, teacher and religious leader, he will be able to serve God better.

So, what about the various arguments for the existence of God? Do they prove God's existence or merely assert it? The main traditional ones are the ontological argument, which originates with Anselm and is the first key idea discussed in this chapter; the cosmological argument, put forward by Aquinas; and the design and moral arguments. When we think about these arguments for God's existence, we tend to discuss them in terms of philosophical arguments that are intended as objective proofs that God exists. The idea seems to be that, once they have understood the argument(s), even sceptics and outright atheists will be persuaded to believe in God: understanding precedes and creates belief. This is how the arguments have been regarded in the past and how some still view them.

But, it does not seem to be the position Anselm takes. For him, belief not only precedes understanding, but is essential to it. He does not seem to have expected that his argument would persuade atheists to set aside their disbelief and embrace theism, or even to mean much to anyone who does not have a pre-existing belief in God. However, it will help those who already believe in God, through faith, to achieve a deeper understanding of him. And, following the criticisms of Immanuel Kant, who first called this type of argument ontological, and David Hume in particular, Anselm's understanding of the role of the arguments for God's existence is the one generally taken today. They are not seen as philosophical heavy artillery, which will pound away at atheism, but as explorations of God's nature and his relationship to creation and human beings, which will help to clarify thinking about God and may strengthen faith. Criticism of the ontological argument, particularly by Immanuel Kant, is the second key idea explored in this chapter.

In the *Proslogion*, Anselm discusses the attributes that a being than which none greater can be thought, which is how God is conceived in his argument, must possess. As nothing good can be missing from the highest good, through which every good thing exists, they include omnipotence, mercy and justice, which are all the attributes of the Christian God. However, even if Anselm's argument worked, it would only prove the existence of a being than which nothing greater can be thought, not the specifically Christian God. However, for Anselm, who already believes in him, it is the Christian God whose existence he has now clearly established by the single argument he was seeking.

Life

Anselm was born in Aosta, in the north of Italy. His father Gundulph, a nobleman and landowner, who is said to have been harsh and overbearing, opposed his desire to enter a monastery, and after a period of illness Anselm abandoned pursuit of his vocation for a time. However, following the death of his mother Ermenberga, a devoutly religious woman, Anselm decided to leave home. In 1059, he made his way through France to Normandy. There, he joined the Benedictine Abbey of Bec, where the distinguished scholar Lanfranc was prior and ran a celebrated school.

After Lanfranc moved to Caen as abbot, in 1063, Anselm, through his outstanding abilities, succeeded him as prior. He became abbot in 1078, following the death of the abbey's founder Herluin. During his time as abbot, Anselm encouraged study and research at Bec and also wrote books himself. These included his two important philosophical works, the *Monologion* and the *Proslogion*, which were completed between 1075 and 1078. Both contain arguments for the existence of God.

Following William Duke of Normandy's (William I) conquest of England in 1066, the Abbey of Bec had received extensive English lands. As a result of his visits to these, Anselm came to be well regarded in England. In 1093, after the death of Lanfranc, who had become Archbishop of Canterbury in 1070, William's son, William Rufus (William II), persuaded a reluctant Anselm to succeed him.

As William Rufus had taken over the assets of the archdiocese, acceptance involved Anselm in disputes with the monarch about church lands, which he sought to recover, and the rights of the Church, including the question of whether Anselm would be allowed to travel to Rome to receive his archiepiscopal *pallium* (worn around the neck as a symbol of ecclesiastical authority) from Pope Urban II (1088–99). Although this difference was resolved, by the *pallium* being sent to England, further issues arose. In 1097, Anselm travelled to Rome to confer with Urban and was well received. However, William, who had been unwilling to give permission for Anselm's visit, took the opportunity of his absence to take over church revenues and would not allow him back into the country.

William was killed in 1100 and William's successor, his brother, Henry (Henry I), invited Anselm to return. However, disputes about church lands and privileges continued and Anselm was forced to make another visit to Rome, to seek support from Pope Paschal II (1099–1118). Henry then declared that Anselm would only be permitted to come back to England if he submitted to the king. Anselm was not allowed back into the country until 1107, after an absence of four years, and then only after he threatened to excommunicate Henry. For the remaining two years of his life, he was able to discharge his duties as archbishop without interference. He was canonized by Pope Alexander VI in 1494. Anselm's other writings include *De veritate* and *De sacramentis ecclesiae*.

Key ideas

God as that than which nothing greater can be thought

Is it possible to establish God's existence by the use of reason and argument, as opposed to revelation? In his *Proslogion*, Anselm argues that it is. As a Christian, Anselm believes that human beings are made in God's image with a God-given intellect to use in God's service. However, Anselm does not regard philosophical arguments as an alternative route to establishing the existence of God, nor does he see them as a means of strengthening faith or reassuring doubters. Rather, faith and reason go hand in hand. They are part of the same endeavour to extend and deepen knowledge and understanding of a God in whom he already believes.

For Anselm, faith precedes and is an essential prerequisite of understanding. Anselm also wants a single argument for God's existence, as this would be more appropriate for the one God who depends on nothing, but on whom everything else depends, than a series of connected arguments, such as those Aquinas later put forward as his 'five ways'. Anselm believes that what is now called the ontological argument, which argues from God's essential nature to his existence, rather than from the world to God, provides it.

Anselm asks God to help him to understand that he is, as Anselm believes him to be, something than which nothing greater can be thought. This, he thinks, is a concept which even the fool mentioned in Psalms 14 and 53 would understand. However, Anselm argues that if this concept exists in the understanding, it could also be thought to exist in reality, which would be greater. And, if that than which nothing greater can be thought exists only in the understanding, something greater than it can be thought. But this is impossible. Therefore, something than which a greater cannot be thought exists in both the understanding and in reality.

Anselm goes on to contend that that than which nothing greater can be thought exists so truly that it cannot be thought not to exist, because something that cannot be thought not to exist is greater than something which can be thought not to exist. If it can be thought not to exist, it is not that than which a greater cannot be thought, which would be a contradiction. Therefore, it exists so truly that it cannot be thought not to exist. This being is God, and to understand that God is that than which nothing greater can be thought is to understand that he exists in such a way that he cannot fail to exist, even in thought.

39

So, by treating existence as an attribute or perfection, which it is better or greater to possess than not, Anselm considers that he has proved not only that God exists in reality, but that he has necessary existence, because there is a contradiction involved in thinking that that than which nothing greater can be thought does not exist. Anselm now goes on to discuss the attributes that the greatest of all beings must possess. As nothing good can be missing from the highest good, through which every good thing exists, they include omnipotence, mercy, impassibility and justice: in fact, all the attributes of the Christian God.

The ontological argument as a proof of God's existence

Not everyone was convinced. In his *Reply on Behalf of the Fool*, the monk Gaunilo maintains that even a being than which nothing greater can be thought, can be thought not to exist, as even God can be thought not to exist. Further, Anselm's argument could define anything into existence. He uses the example of a supposedly perfect lost island. As it exists in the understanding, and existence in reality is better, it must exist in reality. Gaunilo's point is that whatever we can conceive as existent, we can also conceive as non-existent, so there is no being whose non-existence implies a contradiction.

In response, Anselm clarifies his idea of that than which nothing greater can be thought possessing necessary existence. Such a being has this type of existence because, not consisting of parts, he cannot be thought of as beginning to exist. Only things with a beginning or an end, and which do not exist always and everywhere as a whole, can be thought of as not existing.

But, how persuasive is this? It seems possible to have the concept of such a being, but still to think that it does not exist. Anselm also dismisses Gaunilo's perfect island argument, on the grounds that his own argument applies uniquely to that than which nothing greater can be thought. However, Thomas Aquinas also rejects the ontological argument. He distinguishes between things that are self-evident in themselves and also to us, such as 'Human beings are animals', and things that are self-evident in themselves but not to us. As God is his own existence, subject and predicate are the same, and as we do not know God's essence, the proposition 'God exists' is not self-evident to us. Nonetheless, the ontological argument continued to fascinate philosophers and was reformulated by Descartes in his *Meditations*. Descartes argues that, in the case of God alone, existence cannot be separated from essence, any more than three angles can from the essence of a triangle.

Immanuel Kant provides the fundamental criticism of the ontological argument in his *Critique of Pure Reason*. Its first weakness, Kant maintains, is that it confuses logical necessity and necessary existence. If we suppose that a triangle exists, three angles must necessarily exist in it, as part of its definition. To exclude them is self-contradictory. But, to suppose the non-existence of both triangle and angles is not. If our *a priori* concept of God includes existence (we make existence part of our concept of God), denying his existence is self-contradictory. However, if we simply deny the concept, together with all its predicates (including existence), no contradiction is involved.

Second, it wrongly treats existence as a predicate or perfection. Existence is not a concept of something that can be added to the concept of a thing. To say, 'God is', adds no new predicate to the concept of God, but just affirms the existence of the subject, God, with all its predicates. A hundred real pounds contains no more money than a hundred possible pounds. If they did, the concept and its object would not correspond exactly. Existence is not another (and greater) attribute that something has. Rather, to say that something exists, is to say that there exists in reality an object that corresponds to our concept.

The Christian concept of God is of an infinite being, and, if he exists, he exists in a completely different way from everything else. But, such a being can be thought not to exist, and there is no contradiction involved in doing so.

Impact

- The ontological argument is a remarkably bold and concise argument for the existence of God, which argues not from the existence or nature of the world to God but from the idea of God to his existence, and philosophers have returned to and debated it ever since.
- Even if Anselm's argument fails as a philosophical proof of God's existence, it encapsulates an important aspect of the Christian concept of God: as that than which nothing greater can be thought.
- Anselm seems to accept that belief not only precedes understanding, but is essential to it, so his own position is the modern one: that the role of his argument is to help those with a pre-existing religious belief to explore and understand the nature of the Christian God, in whom they already believe on the basis of faith.
- Kant's cogent criticisms of the ontological argument pinpoint the distinction between logical necessity and necessary

existence, and highlight the philosophical pitfalls of treating existence as a predicate or perfection.

Further reading

Anselm, *Monologion and Proslogion with the Replies of Gaunilo and Anselm*, trans. T. Williams, Indianapolis/Cambridge: Hackett Publishing Company, 1996.

Anselm, *Proslogion with the Replies of Gaunilo and Anselm*, trans. T. Williams, Indianapolis/Cambridge: Hackett Publishing Company, 2001.

Basic Writings of Saint Thomas Aquinas, Vol. I, ed. A. C. Pegis, Indianapolis/Cambridge: Hackett Publishing Company, 1997 (contains *Summa Theologica*, Part I).

René Descartes, *Discourse on Method and Meditations on First Philosophy*, trans. D. A. Cress, fourth edition, Indianapolis/Cambridge: Hackett Publishing Company, 1998.

Immanuel Kant, *Critique of Pure Reason*, ed. V. Politis, London: Everyman, 1993.

W. Kent, 'St Anselm' (1907), in *The Catholic Encyclopedia*, New York: Robert Appleton Company, at www.newadvent.org/cathen/01546a.htm.

N. Malcolm, 'Anselm's Ontological Arguments', in J. H. Hick (ed.), *The Existence of God*, New York and London: The Macmillan Company, 1972.

D. Mills Daniel, *Briefly: Anselm's Proslogion*, London: SCM Press, 2006.

New World Encyclopedia contributors, 'Anselm of Canterbury', *New World Encyclopedia,* 15 April 2008, at www.newworldencyclopedia.org/entry/Anselm_of_Canterbury?oldid=692451.

G. Sadler, 'St. Anselm of Canterbury' (updated 2006), in J. Fieser and B. Dowden (eds), *Internet Encyclopedia of Philosophy*, at www.iep.utm.edu.

R. W. Southern, *St Anselm: A Portrait in a Landscape*, Cambridge: Cambridge University Press, 1990.

T. Williams, 'Saint Anselm' (revised 2007), in E. N. Zalta (ed.), *Stanford Encyclopaedia of Philosophy* at http://plato.stanford.edu.

5

Thomas Aquinas
(1224/5–74)
Arguing from the existence of the world
to the existence of God
The natural law approach to ethics

Context

Surely, Thomas Aquinas is a theologian not a philosopher? He is
certainly a theologian; and, for the Roman Catholic Church, the
pre-eminent one, who was proclaimed a 'Doctor of the Universal
Church', alongside Gregory the Great, Ambrose of Milan, Augustine of Hippo and Jerome, in 1567. However, Aquinas held that
philosophy also addresses religious issues and truths – but from a
different perspective. Theology's concern is with religious truths
known through revelation: what God chooses to disclose of himself to human beings, through the Bible, for example; and which
are believed on the basis of faith. The concern of philosophy, or
(more precisely) natural theology, is with discovering religious
truths for ourselves, through the use of reason. However, there
should be no conflict between the two approaches. In his encycli-
cal letter *Aeterni Patris* (1879), designed to revive interest in the
study of scholastic philosophy, and particularly that of Aquinas,
within the Roman Catholic Church, Pope Leo XIII distinguished

between 'true' and 'false' philosophy: what the reason discovers in pursuit of true philosophy cannot contradict the truths of revelation, as taught by the Roman Catholic Church.

But, if human beings can discover religious truths through reason, why is revelation needed? Aquinas answers this question in his *Summa Theologica*. Reason and revelation are not mutually exclusive sources of knowledge about God. Although we can discover some religious truths, such as God's existence, by means of our reason, there are others, such as the Trinity, which have to be revealed to us. And, even those truths which can be known through reason can also be known through revelation and believed on the basis of faith: religious truths, which could only be discovered through reason, would not be accessible to those who cannot understand philosophical arguments. On the other hand, in addition to being a means of discovering some religious truths through philosophical enquiry, reason also has an important role to play in exploring and understanding what God has revealed. Theology is, after all, an intellectual activity.

God is infinite, and Aquinas acknowledges that there is an infinite distance between God and human beings' created intellects. Further, he is an empiricist, accepting that, in relation to knowledge of the world around us, there is nothing in the mind which is not first in the senses. However, as natural knowledge starts with the senses, this means that it can only extend to things which can be known through them; so, in this life, our intellects cannot penetrate to God's essence. This is why Aquinas rejects attempts, such as Anselm's, to prove God's existence by arguing from his essence to his existence. But, although we cannot know God's whole power from sensible things, this does not mean we cannot obtain any knowledge of him in this life. Sensible things depend on God as their cause, and from them we can at least know that

God exists and that he is the first cause of all things, who is much greater than and completely different from everything he causes. Aquinas' attempt to argue from the world to the existence of God is one of the key ideas discussed below.

But, Christians believe that God is very different from human beings. They believe that he created everything that exists from nothing, and is omnipotent and omniscient, while we have limited powers. So, how is it possible for us to talk about God? Any language we use about God will be inadequate and will fail to capture his full reality. Aquinas explains that, although we cannot know God's essential nature in this world, we do know something about him as the cause of the things that he has created, such as ourselves. Therefore, we can talk about God by basing the language we use about him on his creatures and talking about him analogically. But, when we do so, we must distinguish between the attributes and perfections referred to and the language used to express them. Perfections, such as goodness and wisdom, exist more excellently in God than in creatures, and apply primarily to him. However, the terms themselves are applied primarily to creatures, because we know creatures first.

Further, as God has created the world as the environment in which we can develop spiritually and morally, its natural order, including human nature, indicates God's purpose for human beings and the way that we should live our lives and behave towards others. This natural law approach to ethics is the second key idea discussed below.

Life

Thomas Aquinas, the son of Landulf, Count of Aquino, was born at the castle of Roccasecca, near Naples, and educated at the Benedictine Abbey of Monte Cassino and the University of Naples, where he began his studies at the age of 14. While a student, he was attracted to the order of Dominican Friars, which he entered in 1244. This was against his parents' wishes. They wanted him to become a Benedictine monk and to rise to high office in the Church. Despite being kidnapped and held prisoner by his family for a year, Aquinas refused to change his mind, and after his release the Dominicans sent him to the University of Paris in 1245.

Aquinas was a student there for three years, studying under Albert the Great, the Dominican philosopher and theologian, and going with him to the University of Cologne in 1248 to establish a Dominican house of studies. Albert encouraged Aquinas' appetite for knowledge, and his interest in adapting the ideas and writings of Aristotle for the purpose of expressing and expounding Christian teaching had a tremendous influence on his pupil's intellectual development. Aquinas returned to Paris in 1252, eventually becoming Dominican professor of theology there.

He moved to Rome in 1259, where he taught theology at the papal court for the next nine years. Due to his growing reputation as philosopher, theologian and reconciler of Aristotelian philosophy with Christian teaching, he became an adviser to a succession of popes (Alexander IV, Urban IV, Clement IV and Gregory X), while continuing to teach and write prolifically. In 1268, he returned to Paris, where he taught until 1272, and then went to Naples (1272), where he established a Dominican house of studies.

During his life, Aquinas engaged in a number of disputes with opponents of religious orthodoxy. These included, among others, those who challenged the role of the religious orders and the adherents of Averroism, which derived from the work of the Muslim philosopher, Averröes, who taught that human beings share a single soul.

In 1274, Pope Gregory X, who had become pope following a three-year interregnum, invited Aquinas to participate in the Second Council of Lyons, which he summoned shortly after his election, to address such issues as the conquest of the Holy Land and the union of the Western and Eastern churches. However, during his journey from Naples, Aquinas died at the monastery of Fossanuova, near Rome. He was canonized by Pope John XXII in 1323, and declared a Doctor of the Universal Church by Pius V in 1567. In 1879, Pope Leo XIII declared that his setting forth of Roman Catholic teaching was definitive. His books include the *Summa Contra Gentiles* (1258–64), intended as a defence of Christianity for use against its critics, and the massive *Summa Theologica* (*Summa Theologiae*, 1265–72), which provides a complete exposition of Christian theology and philosophy.

Key ideas

Arguing from the existence of the world to the existence of God

Can God's existence be proved by reason? Aquinas believes so, but not by *a priori* arguments, such as Anselm's ontological argument. In the *Summa Theologica*, he explains that there are two kinds of proof: those that start with God and those that start with his effects. With the limitations of finite existence we do not know God's essence, so cannot start there. But, we are familiar with God's effects, the world he has made, so we need to use *a posteriori* arguments, which start from this experience.

Aquinas' cosmological argument argues from the world to God. But, will this approach give us knowledge of God? It will not be perfect knowledge, because effects (the finite world) and cause (infinite God) are not in proportion. However, as every effect depends upon its cause, if there is a cause, there must be an effect. So, the existence of the cause, God, can be proved.

Aquinas puts forward five proofs, 'the five ways', which move from (alleged) features of the world to God's existence. They are motion (whatever is moved must be moved by something else), the nature of efficient causality (nothing is its own efficient cause), possibility and necessity (the difference between things that can not-be and necessary things), the gradation to be found in things (things are more or less good, implying an absolute standard by which they are measured) and a version of the design argument (the way that natural things appear to be subject to intelligent direction).

Aquinas considers that these arguments show the inadequacy of a naturalistic account of the world. Natural things cannot be explained by nature or human decisions by human reason. Both natural events and the outcomes of human reason must be traced back to a higher cause, a self-necessary first principle: God. However, many Thomists regard the third way, which distinguishes between finite or contingent things (the world and its contents, which depend on something else for their existence) and an infinite, necessary being, God, on which the contingent things depend, as the key argument. It focuses on the point that the very existence of finite beings is puzzling and clearly expresses the central idea of all *a posteriori* arguments for God's existence: that the finite must depend on the infinite.

But, is the cosmological argument any more convincing to the non-believer than the ontological argument? David Hume thinks not. First, he denies that it is an *a posteriori* argument. It is an *a priori* one. It presupposes God's necessary existence, which it contrasts to the contingent existence of everything else, and the impossibility of God not existing. Therefore, it is vulnerable to the same kind of criticisms as the ontological argument. Perhaps, God is a necessarily existent being, and, if we knew his essence, we would see that he is the kind of being who cannot not-be. However, with our limited faculties, we are not going to. So, God, like every other being, can be thought of as non-existent, because no contradiction is involved.

Further, if we require something to be necessarily existent, why not the material universe itself? The universe may contain qualities, which, if we knew about them, would make its non-existence seem as great a contradiction as twice two being five. So, the arguments relating to God's necessary existence can be applied just as convincingly (or unconvincingly) to the universe. Again, in a series of objects, each is caused by the preceding one. To state the chain of causes is to provide a full explanation of how each individual object comes into existence. It is pointless to seek a single cause of the objects (that is, all the things in the universe) as a whole.

The natural law approach to ethics

For Aristotle, everything in the world, including human beings, has an end or purpose, determined by its nature or function, and the highest good for all things is to fulfil this purpose. In his *Summa Theologica*, Aquinas fits these ideas into a framework of Christian belief. Human beings have a purpose which is determined by their God-given human nature. Within the natural order of the universe which God has created, human beings, through the use of their God-given reason, are capable of discerning a natural law which shows how they should behave in order to fulfil their purpose. By following this natural law, human beings can participate in the eternal law, by which God governs the universe; and, by basing their ethical principles and decisions on it, which they are naturally inclined to do anyway, they can fulfil their proper purpose as rational beings, made in God's image, and achieve happiness.

For Christians, and those who believe in an all-powerful creator God, this is a persuasive approach to morality. Ethical principles, derived from natural law, are ultimately grounded in God, through his eternal law. Further, they are not divine impositions, running against the grain of human nature. On the contrary, they fit the nature of human beings, not just as rational beings, but also as living beings, who seek to preserve their lives, and as sentient beings, who share many inclinations and instincts, such as the desire to reproduce, with other animals. This is why the natural law approach is also attractive to secular (non-religious) ethicists, as it relates ethical principles to the actual nature of human beings and their needs and wants.

However, there are problems with the natural law approach to ethics. It is one thing to say that the natural order and human nature should guide our adoption of ethical principles; quite another to say that they should determine it. To define what is good or right as what is 'natural' would be to commit the naturalistic fallacy. As G. E. Moore points out, 'good' does not mean 'what is natural', and it is always an open question whether what is natural is good; and Aquinas concedes that, even with the basic principles of natural law to guide us, it will not always be easy to apply them in specific and possibly complex situations. Indeed, especially for those who are not religious, it may be hard to achieve consensus about what the basic principles are, or even what is natural.

For example, Aquinas says that natural law includes such ends as sexual intercourse and having children, which are to be encouraged. However, homosexuality, which he dismisses as unisexual lust, is unnatural and to be condemned. But, advocates of gay rights would argue that same-sex inclination is a natural inclination and is certainly not to be condemned, as it is the way of life freely chosen by a substantial minority of people. Supporters of birth and population control would argue that, although the desire to reproduce is a natural one, there are situations in which it needs to be restrained, in the interests of individuals and/or society. A great danger with the natural law approach is that it can confine moral decision-making within a straitjacket of what the majority considers to be 'natural' and therefore necessarily good or right.

Impact

- Aquinas' insistence that God's existence can only be proved by an argument to God from his effects, the world he has made, has led natural theologians to prefer *a posteriori* arguments for God's existence, which are based on experience, to *a priori* ones, such as the ontological argument.
- Aquinas' cosmological argument may not work as an objective proof of God's existence, but it may help those who already see the world as finite, contingent and dependent, and who are well on the way to believing in God, to relate their perception of the nature of the world to its creator and cause.

- For Christians, the natural law approach to ethics is persuasive, because it holds that ethical principles are ultimately grounded in God, as natural law is the way that human beings, through the use of their reason, can participate in the eternal law, by which God governs the universe.
- However, it is difficult, particularly in societies which are both multi-faith and increasingly secular, to achieve consensus about the basic principles of natural law, or even what is natural: for example in relation to homosexual inclination and practice.

Further reading

Basic Writings of Saint Thomas Aquinas, Vol. I, ed. A. C. Pegis, Indianapolis/Cambridge: Hackett Publishing Company, 1997 (contains *Summa Theologica*, Part I).

F. Copleston, *Aquinas*, Harmondsworth: Penguin, 1955.

Frederick Copleston, *A History of Philosophy*, Vol. 2, Part II (Medieval Philosophy), New York: Image Books, 1962.

A. P. d'Éntreves, *Natural Law*, second edition, London: Hutchinson, 1970.

David Hume, *Dialogues Concerning Natural Religion*, ed. R. H. Popkin, second edition, Indianapolis/Cambridge: Hackett Publishing Company, 1998.

D. Kennedy, 'St Thomas Aquinas' (1912), in *The Catholic Encyclopedia*, New York: Robert Appleton Company, at www.newadvent.org/cathen/14663b.htm.

R. McInerny and J. O'Callaghan, 'Saint Thomas Aquinas' (revised 2009), in E. N. Zalta (ed.), *Stanford Encyclopaedia of Philosophy*, at http://plato.stanford.edu.

D. Mills Daniel, *Briefly: Aquinas' Summa Theologica* (God, Part I), London: SCM Press, 2006.

D. Mills Daniel, *Briefly: Hume's Dialogues Concerning Natural Religion*, London: SCM Press, 2006.

A. Nichols, *Discovering Aquinas: An introduction to his life, work and influence*, London: Darton, Longman and Todd, 2002.

6

Thomas Hobbes
(1588–1679)
The evils of human beings in a state of nature
The need for the absolute power of the ruler

Context

What do people know about Thomas Hobbes? They may have heard a phrase, which they associate with his name, about life being nasty, brutish and short. And, if that is all they know about him, they will conclude that his outlook on human existence must have been extremely bleak. Others, vaguely recalling history lessons, may think of him as a rather sinister figure, an advocate of despotism and apologist for the kind of absolute monarchy that successive Stuart monarchs attempted vainly to establish in England during the seventeenth century, and which Louis XIV succeeded in setting up in France. This picture contains elements of truth, but is misleading. In *Leviathan*, Hobbes does describe life as nasty, brutish and short; but he is not talking about life as such. The statement refers to how miserable life would be (and in England during the Civil War and its aftermath often was) without an effective government. Given the nature of human beings, unless there is a strong government to keep them in check, life will, indeed, be nasty, brutish and short. And, Hobbes did not glorify absolute power for its own sake. He simply believed that any government capable of enforcing order, however repressive, was better than the anarchy resulting from there being no government or a weak one. Hobbes' views about the evils of human beings in the state of nature and the need for the absolute power of the ruler are the key ideas discussed below.

So, what was Hobbes' approach to philosophy? An empiricist, he believed we acquire knowledge through the senses, rejecting the continental rationalism of Descartes, which holds that the first principles of philosophy can be known intuitively, and that propositions deduced from them will be certainly true. We gain our knowledge of general principles inductively, by arguing to them from observed effects. Hobbes was also a materialist or physicalist, believing that nothing exists apart from bodies. He holds that, contrary to what we like to think, human beings are material beings, and mental events and passions are explicable as motions occurring in the brain, which in the latter case are transmitted to the heart. Depending on whether these motions are affected favourably or unfavourably, we experience pleasure or pain, the keys to what we regard as good or bad.

This physicalist outlook shaped Hobbes' view of philosophy, which is concerned with bodies and causes. We learn about causes from their effects, and about effects from reflection on their causes. For Hobbes, a cause is the sum of all the factors, both in the agent and the object, which concur to produce a particular effect. So, when the cause is present, the effect always necessarily follows, making necessary causality the only kind of causality, and ruling out human freedom in the libertarian, Kantian sense. He does not deny that human beings deliberate, but he defines it in terms of passions. The last appetite is the act of willing, and the action performed follows from it. Hobbes maintains that liberty, in the sense of absence of causal necessity, is not to be found in the will of either humans or animals. Like Locke and Hume, he is a soft determinist: in the absence of external compulsion, we are free to do as we please, and this is what human freedom means; but we do not have the power to will as we please.

What about such metaphysical concerns as the existence and nature of God? Hobbes accepts that God exists, but believes no more can be said. Human beings, desiring to argue from the order they see in the world to its causeless cause, try to go further. However, while Hobbes rejects natural theology, as an attempt to gain knowledge of God's nature, which he considers unattainable, it is not entirely fair to say he was an atheist, the charge traditionally brought against him.

In keeping with his materialistic and deterministic view of human beings, Hobbes believes we are naturally egotistical, self-centred and selfish. At best, we can comply with a negative version of the Golden Rule and refrain from doing to others what we would not wish them to do to us. In a state of nature, without organized society or government, there are no moral distinctions or rules. Left to ourselves, we are in a state of war with each other. The rational pursuit of self-preservation is what drives us to make a covenant or social contract with each other and to create societies within which we relinquish our right to take whatever we can get and accept as much freedom against others as they will permit to us. Hobbes prefers monarchies to republics as likely to produce greater unity and authority in the state, but does not advocate the divine right of kings. All that matters is the sovereign's ability to enforce his will and deliver peace and security, leading to his being reviled by both republicans and royalists.

Life

Thomas Hobbes was born near Malmesbury, in Wiltshire. His father, a rather down-at-heel Church of England clergyman, had to leave the area following a brawl, so Hobbes' uncle, Francis Hobbes, supported him through Magdalen Hall, Oxford (1603–8). Hobbes then became tutor to the son of Sir William Cavendish (first Earl of Devonshire) and travelled with him in France and Italy (1608–10). This association with the Cavendish family continued throughout Hobbes' life, giving him access to books, opportunities to travel on the Continent to meet leading contemporary thinkers and time for philosophical reflection. His first book, an English translation of Thucydides' *History of the Peloponnesian War*, was published in 1629.

In 1628, Hobbes left the Cavendish family, following the death of the second earl, his former pupil. During a second visit to the Continent (1629–31), as tutor to Sir Gervase Clifton's son, his interest in mathematics, geometry, science and the problems of sense perception developed. Re-employed by the Cavendish family, he was on the Continent again in the mid 1630s, where he is believed to have met Galileo and the philosopher and mathematician Marin Mersenne. He also put forward pre-publication objections to Descartes' *Meditations*, which were published with the book in 1641.

Increasingly interested in political issues, he wrote *The Elements of Law, Natural and Politic* in 1640, which did not appear as a whole until 1889, and *De Cive*, which was published in both Latin (1642) and English (1651). Growing fear of conflict between king and parliament, and concern for his own safety in view of his royalist principles, led him to leave England for France, and he remained abroad while civil war (1642–51) raged in England. For a time, he tutored the exiled Charles Stuart (the future Charles II) and also met Descartes, though the two did not get on particularly well. Hobbes wrote his most famous and controversial work, *Leviathan*, in Paris between 1647 and 1650. It was published in 1651.

Hobbes then became concerned about his safety in France. He was hostile to Roman Catholicism, while the ideas expressed in *Leviathan* were unpopular with many royalists, especially following Charles I's execution in 1649, as they did not identify monarchy as the only legitimate form of government. Further, the English Civil War, the reason Hobbes had gone abroad, was over. In 1651, he returned to England and made peace with the republican government. As Lord Protector from 1652, Cromwell could provide the kind of strong and effective government in which Hobbes believed.

Hobbes returned to the Cavendish family, engaging in disputes with such opponents as John Wallis, John Bramhall and Robert Boyle, and publishing his *De Corpore* in 1655 and *De Homine* in 1658. After the monarchy's restoration in 1660, Hobbes was treated kindly by Charles II, and given a pension. However, there was criticism of the alleged atheism of *Leviathan*. Hobbes wrote a history of the civil wars, *Behemoth; or, The Long Parliament*, which was published after his death. In 1679, he died at Hardwick Hall, one of the Cavendish family properties in Derbyshire.

Key ideas

The evils of human beings in a state of nature

What would life be like with no government, social structure or laws? Those who believe human beings are naturally benevolent and disinclined to violence may think they would live together peacefully and co-operatively. Locke, though accepting that there are good reasons why people prefer an organized society, does not think the law of the jungle would prevail. The state of nature would be governed by reason, which shows human beings their duty not to harm others. For Hobbes, conscious of how little people are guided by reason or a sense of responsibility to others when their country is wrecked by civil strife, as England was in the 1640s, the state of nature means a state of war. People are incapable of living peacefully and harmoniously with others, unless forced to do so. Without a government capable of imposing order, there can be no personal safety or security.

Why is this? Human conflicts arise naturally from competition for resources, while nature has made us so nearly equal in mental and physical abilities that no individual is immune from harm. Even the weakest can kill the strongest, particularly with the wisdom that comes from experience. Equal abilities give rise to equal hope of attaining our ends, so, when two people want the same thing, but cannot both have it, they try to crush each other. Again, fear drives people to use force to master one other. We also want to be valued, but are easily slighted, leading to resentment. According to Hobbes, competition, fear and the desire to be valued are the three main causes of human conflict. The first makes us attack each other for gain, the second for safety and the third for reputation.

Without a common power to restrain them, people are in a state of war with each other. They may not actually fight, but their disposition to do so removes any assurance of peace. Without any security, except that of their own strength, they lack the incentive to work, having no certainty of being able to keep the fruits of their labour. There is no point in trying to farm, establish financial institutions or develop an education system. Their situation will be characterized by continual fear and danger of violent death, and life will be solitary, poor, nasty, brutish and short.

Is Hobbes too pessimistic? He urges those who reject his bleak view of human nature to consider their own conduct. If they doubt people's natural inclination to attack and destroy one other, why do they take care to protect themselves when travelling, even in a country with laws and public officers to enforce them? Perhaps, there was no period in the past, when people actually were in a state of war with each other, but Hobbes points to the America of his day. The native tribes live in exactly such a brutish manner. International relations furnish further examples. Rulers with sovereign power, who are not subject to the laws of society in their dealings with each other, often fight and invade each other's territories.

In the state of nature, nothing is unjust, because there are no laws to make it so, and ideas of right and wrong have no place. There is no settled title to property, only what each man can get for himself, for as long as he can keep it.

The need for the absolute power of the ruler

Hobbes believes that the human longing for peace derives from fear of death, a desire for the comforts of property and the hope of being able to obtain it through industry. However, this state of affairs is only achievable if people are controlled by a strong government. The central authority's role is to deliver peace and security to its subjects. His account of how a state, and the relationship between government and governed, is created involves a social contract, although there is no need to regard it as an actual historical event.

The state is formed when its members covenant with each other to accept the actions and judgements of the individual or group to whom the majority has given the right to exercise authority over them. From this covenant, all the rights and powers of the sovereign originate, although he or she is not a party to it. Despite his royalist background, Hobbes does not stipulate that the sovereign power must be exercised by a hereditary monarch. All that matters is that the sovereign power should provide strong, effective government.

However, once they have decided on their type of government, subjects cannot chop and change. If they chose monarchy, they cannot repudiate it, return to a state of anarchy, or transfer the government to others, without the sovereign's permission. They are bound to regard themselves as the author of all their sovereign does. Again, as the covenant conferring sovereignty was made, not between the sovereign and the people, but between the people with each other, the sovereign cannot breach the covenant, nor can his subjects free themselves from subjection to him. Further, their covenant means they have no right to protest against any of the sovereign's actions, however unjust they may appear, nor have they any right to punish him.

As the purpose of instituting sovereignty is the peace and defence of all, the sovereign decides laws and punishments, the political and other opinions his subjects may hear, what property they may enjoy and what actions they may perform. The sovereign settles all controversies, determines issues of war and peace with other nations and chooses ministers. These are the essential rights of sovereignty, and there is no room for the view that the sovereign, though having more power than his subjects individually, has less than they do collectively.

What do subjects get from this apparently very one-sided arrangement? What about personal freedom and individual rights? Hobbes admits the subjects' situation seems miserable; they have a ruler with unlimited powers. There is nothing to stop him harming them, although he should leave them alone, as long as they do not harm others. Apart from the freedom to refuse to injure themselves or others, subjects' liberty relates only to those things which the sovereign permits, such as buying and selling, choosing where to live, or raising children.

But, for Hobbes, this matters more than liberty. Any government, however tyrannical and oppressive, is better than none or the harm the majority suffers when people do not obey it. Oppressive government is preferable to the miseries and disasters of civil war, or the terrible condition of those without laws or a ruler to prevent plunder and revenge. Thus, there can be no competing powers in the state: the sovereign must control civil, military, judicial and ecclesiastical powers. However, the subjects' obligation to their sovereign is understood to last as long, and no longer, than his ability to protect them.

Impact

- Though we may not share Hobbes' pessimistic view of human nature, his depressing picture of the state of anarchy that exists when human beings are not subject to external control, reinforces our appreciation that there are always those who will prey upon, and exploit, others, if given the opportunity.

- For many people around the world today, who (like Hobbes) inhabit countries wracked by civil war, or religious/ideological conflict, it is understandable that their first priority is to have any government that is capable of enforcing public order and ensuring personal security.
- Hobbes' view that the ruler must have absolute power has been widely rejected, due to its being considered only in the context of seventeenth-century autocracies like Louis XIV's France: but Hobbes identifies the essence of the nation state and national sovereignty, as was the case in Britain, where parliamentary sovereignty ('king-in-parliament') was supreme and unchallengeable, until accession to the European Community in 1972/3.
- Hobbes makes the point that, as sovereignty is indivisible, it cannot be shared with competing sources of power and authority, or jurisdictions, within the state: there can only be one government and only one legal system.

Further reading

Frederick Copleston, *A History of Philosophy*, Vol. 5, Part I (Hobbes to Paley), New York: Image Books, 1964.

S. Duncan, 'Thomas Hobbes' (2009), in E. N. Zalta (ed.), *Stanford Encyclopaedia of Philosophy*, at http://plato.stanford.edu.

Thomas Hobbes, *Leviathan*, ed. J. C. A. Gaskin, Oxford: Oxford University Press, 1998.

Thomas Hobbes, *The Elements of Law, Natural and Politic*,

Chestnut Hill, MA: Adamant Media Corporation (Elibron Classics), 2005.

John Locke, *Second Treatise of Government*, ed. C. B. Macpherson, Indianapolis/Cambridge: Hackett Publishing Company, 1980.

A. P. Martinich, *Hobbes: A Biography*, Cambridge: Cambridge University Press, 2007.

A. P. Martinich, *The Two Gods of Leviathan: Thomas Hobbes on Religion and Politics*, Cambridge: Cambridge University Press, 1992.

New World Encyclopedia contributors, 'Thomas Hobbes', *New World Encyclopedia*, 10 September 2008, at www.newworld encyclopedia.org/entry/Thomas_Hobbes?oldid=804100.

J. W. N. Watkins, *Hobbes' System of Ideas*, London: Hutchinson, 1965.

G. Williams, 'Thomas Hobbes: Moral and Political Philosophy' (updated 2005), in J. Fieser and B. Dowden (eds), *Internet Encyclopedia of Philosophy*, at www.iep.utm.edu.

7

René Descartes
(1596–1650)
Cartesian or systematic doubt
The rationalist foundation of knowledge

Context

Does knowledge require an absolutely certain foundation? Not for empiricists, like Locke, Hume and Mill; but, for Descartes, the first principles of knowledge need to be indubitable truths, so that all the propositions deduced from them will also be certainly true. He rejects the empiricist view that we acquire knowledge through the senses. Immersed in sense experiences, we just assume that they are its source, thus failing to appreciate that knowledge comes from intellectual perception. In his major philosophical work, the *Meditations*, Descartes describes a process of withdrawing from the senses through a method of systematic doubt, which will enable us to realize that knowledge comes from our reason, and that the criterion of truth is an intellectual perception of something which is so clear and distinct that it cannot be doubted.

In his *Discourse on Method*, published four years before the *Meditations*, he describes his approach to philosophy. As generally accepted opinions are merely probable, and are unsupported by objective proofs, they are likely to be further from the truth than the findings of an enquirer who thinks for himself and is guided by reason alone: he must rid his mind of them altogether. He resolves to adhere strictly to four rules: never to accept anything as true that he does not definitely know to be such, and to avoid hasty judgements; to break down complex problems into small parts, so as to solve them more easily; always to think in an orderly fashion, starting with the simplest issues; and to list and review everything, so that nothing is overlooked.

He decides to treat as false everything about which he has the slightest doubt, to see if anything indubitable remains. While not adopting the comprehensive scepticism of the *Meditations*, he regards everything in his mind as no more true than the illusions experienced in dreams. What is the outcome? Even as he tries to think that everything is false, it necessarily has to be the case that he, the one who is thinking this, is something. Here is an indubitable truth, *Cogito ergo sum*: I think, therefore I am. This tells him that he is a substance, the whole essence of which is simply to think, and which, in order to exist, does not depend on anything physical. The 'I', the soul through which he is what he is, is entirely distinct from his body, and, even if he had no body, would not cease to be, and so is immortal. But, what makes the proposition, 'I think therefore I am', so certain and true? It is the clear intellectual perception that, in order to think, it is necessary to exist. So, as a general rule, he can take it that the things that the mind perceives clearly and distinctly are true: although, as the senses can mislead us, it may be hard to decide what they are.

In the *Meditations*, Descartes provides a full exposition of his rationalist theory of knowledge, and Cartesian or systematic doubt and the rationalist foundation of knowledge are the key ideas discussed in this chapter. Descartes invited objections to his book from other philosophers, including Thomas Hobbes and Antoine Arnauld, and it was published with these objections and Descartes' replies. In the *Meditations*, he puts forward two *a priori* arguments for the existence of God, neither of which works. What he considered his principal proof, which appears in the third *Meditation*, is discussed with the key ideas below. His version of the ontological argument, in the fifth *Meditation*, holds that God's existence is inseparable from his essence: God is supremely perfect, so it is contradictory to think he lacks the perfection of existence. This explicit treatment of existence as one of the perfections that a supremely perfect being must possess makes his version of the argument even more vulnerable to Kant's criticisms than Anselm's.

For Descartes, mind and body are different and distinct: the essence of the mind is that it is an unextended, indivisible, thinking substance; the body is unthinking and extended, and consists of one type of matter, which is infinitely divisible and can exist on its own. As well as rejecting Aristotelian and scholastic theories about the relationship between matter and form, this mind–body dualism raises serious questions about how the two can relate to each other, being dismissively characterized by Gilbert Ryle as the 'ghost in the machine'. As for the senses, their role is to acquire detailed scientific knowledge, for which observation is needed.

Despite being a pioneering mathematician and scientist, Descartes was deeply attached to the Roman Catholicism in which he was brought up. Though considering revealed religious truths to be beyond human understanding, he believes that philosophers need to demonstrate God's existence and the soul's immortality, because non-believers will not accept what God has revealed in the Bible. However, despite the respect that Descartes expresses for the Roman Catholic Church and its teachings, his philosophical ideas were considered too radical, and his work was banned in 1663.

Life

Descartes was born in La Haye, now Descartes, in Touraine. As his mother, Jeanne, died while he was very young, and his father, Joachim, a lawyer, was often absent, he was brought up by his grandmother and later his uncle, who was also a lawyer. From about 1606, he attended the Jesuit college of Henri IV at La Flèche for about eight years. His family wanted him to become a lawyer, and he studied at the University of Poitiers, completing his degree in 1616, but he never practised. Instead, in 1618, he became a soldier in the army of the Protestant Prince Maurice of Nassau, the son of William the Silent, who was continuing his father's crusade against Spanish rule in the Netherlands.

Descartes' aim was to travel and widen his experience, rather than to follow a military career; and his time as a soldier gave him the opportunity to think. While in the Netherlands, he met the Dutch scientist and mathematician Isaac Beeckman, and worked with him on problems in natural science and mathematics. During this time, he developed the techniques of analytical geometry and Cartesian coordinates, which make it possible to represent geometrical figures numerically. Mathematics had a strong appeal for Descartes, because it offered certainty. In 1619, he joined the army of the Duke of Bavaria, and, being overtaken by severe winter weather, was forced to stay in the little town of Ulm, near Munich, where, as he tells us in the *Discourse*, shut up with his thoughts in a stove-heated room, he resolved to transform knowledge, starting with philosophy.

For the next few years, Descartes seems to have led a peripatetic existence in France and Italy. In 1628, he settled in Holland, where he lived for the next 20 years, and, in 1635, had a daughter, Francine, who died five years later, by his housekeeper, Helena Jans. Descartes concentrated on philosophical and scientific study, keeping his address secret, due to fear of how his ideas would be received. He did not complete his first work, *Rules for the Direction of the Mind*, which set out his methods for conducting intellectual enquiry and research, and, in 1634, he decided to suppress his treatise on science, *The World*, which was designed to explain all natural phenomena, fearing that the Roman Catholic Church would condemn its Copernican ideas, just as it had Galileo's.

He published his *Discourse on the Method to Rightly Conduct the Reason and Search for the Truth in Mathematics* (the *Discourse on Method*), with the essays, *Dioptrics* and *Meteorology*, in 1637, and the work for which he is best known, the *Meditations on First Philosophy*, in 1641. *The Principles of Philosophy*, setting out philosophical and theological ideas, was produced in 1644, and *The Passions of the Soul*, dealing with the issue of how soul and body interact, in 1649.

Descartes corresponded extensively with Princess Elizabeth of Bohemia, the grand-daughter of James I, particularly about mind–body dualism. In 1649, Queen Kristina Wasa invited Descartes to Sweden, to teach her philosophy, but he developed pneumonia there and died in 1650.

Key ideas

Cartesian or systematic doubt

Descartes' overriding desire is to find an absolutely certain basis of knowledge. But, where should he begin? It is no good building on shaky foundations. He accepts that many of his beliefs are based on sense experience, but his senses sometimes deceive him. For example, although it seems impossible to doubt the existence of his own hand when he is looking at it, in his dreams, he seems to do all sorts of things that he is, or thinks he is, not doing. He can find no absolute criterion for distinguishing what he sees in dreams from what he sees when awake.

How convincing is this point? People do not find it hard to tell the difference between dreams and reality, as events in dreams do not follow a predictable pattern. But, there is room for doubt, putting a question mark over all sense experiences. What about mathematical truths? Two and three always add up to five. However, an all-powerful God may have so arranged matters that, although the earth and its contents do not exist, they appear to. The belief that God is supremely good is not reassuring, because this suggests he would not allow people to be mistaken at all, but they are.

The common sense response is to ask what difference such a comprehensive delusion would make. If everything looks the same, and the world still seems to function, why worry? However, for Descartes, the possibility of his being deceived is not compatible with the certainty he is seeking. Until he has removed this possibility, he must withhold assent from all his former beliefs, however probable they seem. He will conduct himself as if an evil demon is deceiving him, treating external objects as illusions and regarding himself as having neither body, nor senses.

Here, we have Cartesian doubt, a comprehensive doubt that embraces everything that can possibly be doubted, including the existence of the external world. It was not a new idea, as it can be traced back to the writings of the Greek sceptic, Pyrrho of Elis. But, why should such a doubt arise? It seems an extraordinary attitude to adopt. However, it picks up a feature of human experience. We have no direct knowledge of other people's minds or thoughts, so it is possible, though pointless, to maintain that only ours exist. Is it sustainable? It seems unlikely. Somebody who claims to hold such a view would belie it every time he behaves as if people and objects in the external world actually exist.

Having put himself in this position, how can Descartes move forward? Although our senses sometimes deceive us, we use the information we receive from them to correct our mistakes. However, total doubt makes progress impossible. One approach is to accept that it is possible to doubt everything, but to recognize that this need have no practical effect on the way we lead our lives and the use we make of sense experience.

But, this will not do for Descartes, who wants absolute certainty.

The rationalist foundation of knowledge

But, as he expresses his all-embracing doubt, he identifies a point of certainty: he is thinking. Even if an all-powerful God is deceiving him, to be deceived, he must exist; and must do so as long as he is conscious of himself as something that thinks. Thinking cannot be separated from him: it is the only thing that belongs to his essence. Thus, knowledge starts with consciousness or thought and the mind (rationalism), not sense experience (empiricism). He uses the way a piece of wax changes when heated to illustrate the point that he understands himself better than external objects. His realization that wax can change does not come through his senses, but through mental inspection and judgement, so there is nothing he perceives with less difficulty than his own mind.

Intellectually, he now clearly and distinctly perceives that he is a thinking thing, and feels that he can take it as a general rule that what he clearly and distinctly perceives in this way is true. But, where does he go next? His instinct tells him that his ideas of things come from external objects. However, having chosen to doubt the existence of the external world, there is no way that he can discover, from the experiences themselves, whether or not they have an external source. He is locked inside his own thoughts.

But, there is no evidence that God is a deceiver: it was his idea to suppose that God was deceiving him. Further, his idea of an infinite and omnipotent creator God seems more real than those of finite things. An effect (his idea of God) cannot come from nothing; its cause cannot be less perfect than the idea itself. As this is of an infinite God, it cannot have originated in his own mind, as he is finite. It must have come from an infinite being. As a finite being, he is aware of the defects of his own finitude by contrasting them with his idea of an infinite being and its perfections.

This is his most clear and distinct idea. He could not exist, or have the idea of God, unless God exists. Aware of his own defects, he recognizes his dependence on a thinking thing that possesses all perfections, as his cause. Therefore, God must exist and is no deceiver, because deception is a defect. Thus, he can re-establish his faith in the evidence of his senses. As

74

God has strongly inclined him to believe that his perceptions relate to external objects, they must do so.

However, mind and body are completely different and distinct: whereas the mind is indivisible and immortal, the body is divisible and mortal. As human beings consist of distinct minds and bodies, with the mind receiving information via the senses, which, though generally reliable, can give misleading information, they are bound to make mistakes. However, as God is no deceiver, Descartes can dismiss his extreme doubts, and take it that all he clearly and distinctly perceives intellectually is true.

What should we make of these arguments? Descartes never satisfactorily explains how, if mind and body are completely different and distinct, they can relate to each other. Again, God is the ultimate guarantor of the truth of what he clearly and distinctly perceives, but his principal proof of God's existence is unconvincing. Can the idea of a supremely perfect being only come from such a being? Instead of agreeing that we become aware of our own imperfections by contrasting them with our (God-given) idea of an infinite being and its perfections, we may think that we develop the idea of an infinite being from imagining ourselves as immortal and free of the limitations of physical existence.

Impact

- Descartes is called the father of modern philosophy because, by refusing to operate within the constraints of Aristotelian philosophy, he revolutionized philosophical enquiry and developed a radically different theory of knowledge and of the mind–body relationship.

- His insistence that knowledge comes from intellectual perception, not through the senses, had a tremendous impact on other philosophers, particularly his fellow rationalists Spinoza and Leibniz, and the *Meditations* continue to be the most influential statement of the rationalist approach to philosophy.
- Cartesian doubt laid down a starting-point for philosophical enquiry, which has been extensively followed since: to withhold assent from all existing beliefs, until they have been subjected to rigorous scrutiny.
- Descartes' *a priori* arguments for the existence of God continue to be widely studied and debated.

Further reading

J. G. Cottingham, *Descartes*, Oxford and Malden, MA: Blackwell Publishers, 1986.

René Descartes, *Discourse on Method and Meditations on First Philosophy*, trans. D. A. Cress, fourth edition, Indianapolis/Cambridge: Hackett Publishing Company, 1998.

René Descartes, *Meditations, Objections and Replies*, eds R. Ariew and D. A. Cress, Indianapolis/Cambridge: Hackett Publishing Company, 2006.

René Descartes, *Meditations and Other Metaphysical Writings*, trans. D. M. Clarke, revised edition, London: Penguin, 2000.

G. Hatfield, 'René Descartes' (2008), in E. N. Zalta (ed.), *Stanford Encyclopaedia of Philosophy*, at http://plato.stanford.edu.

A. Kenny, *Descartes: A Study of His Philosophy*, New York: Random House, 1968.

Further reading

D. Mills Daniel, *Briefly: Descartes' Meditations on First Philosophy*, London: SCM Press, 2006.

G. Ryle, *The Concept of Mind* (Introduction by D. C. Dennett), London: Penguin, 2000.

J. Skirry, 'René Descartes Overview' (updated 2008), in J. Fieser and B. Dowden (eds), *Internet Encyclopedia of Philosophy*, at www.iep.utm.edu.

T. Sorrell, *Descartes*, Oxford and New York: Oxford University Press, 1987.

8

John Locke
(1632–1704)
Government by consent
The tolerant society

Context

Why is John Locke so important in British history? It is not just because he was a great philosopher and the founding father of British Empiricism. He was also the philosophical articulator and exponent of the Whig principles, promulgated by his employer and associate, the Earl of Shaftesbury (Anthony Ashley Cooper), during the reign of Charles II. At a time when, in philosophy, continental Europe was dominated by Descartes' rationalism, which held that the mind is capable of apprehending truths about the world directly, and without the use of the senses, Locke was insisting that the source of our knowledge is experience. In politics,during this period, continental Europe was dominated by the repressive absolutism of Louis XIV's France, which both Charles II and James II sought to reproduce in England, and where, following the revocation of the Edict of Nantes in 1685, religious dissent was banned and religious minorities were persecuted. However, Locke was advocating government by consent, insisting that governments have a duty to respect the life, liberty and property of their citizens, and calling for religious toleration of all those who are themselves tolerant.

Thus, Locke can be regarded as the intellectual architect of Western, democratic, pluralistic society, among whose chief characteristics are constitutional government, the rule of law, freedom of opinion and speech, and religious toleration. The key ideas discussed in this chapter relate to his political philosophy, and come from his influential *Two Treatises of Government*, in which he makes the case for the rights and liberties of citizens against governments and for government by consent, and his *Letter Concerning Toleration*, in which he argues compellingly for religious toleration.

But, what about Locke's empiricism? His *An Essay Concerning Human Understanding* is the classic statement of British Empiricism, where he expounds a philosophical position that is completely opposed to Descartes'. His epistemology is based on sense perception or representationalism. What we perceive are sense-data, which arise from objects in the external world; although Locke distinguishes between the secondary and primary qualities of these objects. It is their secondary qualities, such as their smell, colour or taste, which produce sensations in us and which we perceive. Their primary qualities, such as extension, shape and motion, underlie the secondary ones and do not relate to a specific sense. The mind combines the simple ideas we receive through our senses into complex ones, and compares them. General ideas are then arrived at through a process of abstraction. From our experience of particular instances, such as a particular human being or horse, we form a general idea of a human being or horse. We then take our general ideas of a human being and a horse and form another, more general, idea of an animal, which includes human beings and many other living creatures. Eventually, we reach such universal ideas as substance, being and thing.

Locke rejects the theory of innate ideas: there is no evidence for them. All knowledge is based on and derives from experience. However, reason does play an important role in acquiring knowledge as we reflect on our experience. Further, Locke maintains that reflection on how we think shows that our minds sometimes perceive the agreement or disagreement of two ideas immediately by themselves; and it is on this intuitive knowledge that the certainty of all our knowledge depends. Even if we doubt everything else, doing so makes us perceive our own existence and will not allow us to doubt it. Thus, we have an intuitive knowledge of our own existence; other things we know about through our senses.

A deeply religious man, Locke argues that our knowledge of God's existence derives from knowledge of our own. We did not always exist, but it is no more possible for nothing to produce something than for it to be equal to two right-angles. Therefore, there must be something which has existed from eternity, and this eternal, all-powerful and all-knowing being is God; and by reflecting on this concept of God we will be able to deduce his other attributes. Locke believes that we have a more certain knowledge of God's existence than of anything we do not immediately perceive through our senses. However, in relation to revelation, Locke insists that nothing that is contrary to reason should be assented to as a matter of faith. As for our moral principles, these derive from experience. We regard things as good or evil on the basis of the pleasure or pain they produce. Locke also believes that a thorough exploration of the idea of the supreme being and of ourselves as rational beings should provide a basis for working out our moral duties and rules of conduct in detail. However, he accepts that the complexity of morality and ethics makes this difficult.

Life

Born in Wrington, Somerset, John Locke was the son of a lawyer and small landowner who supported the parliamentary side during the English Civil War. He was educated at Westminster School and then at Christ Church, Oxford, which he entered in 1652. In 1658, he became a senior student (fellow) of the College and subsequently a lecturer in Greek and Rhetoric. At this point, Locke's sympathies seem to have been royalist and he welcomed Charles II's restoration to the throne in 1660. As the majority of Christ Church fellowships were reserved for Church of England clergy, ordination would have helped Locke's academic career. However, there were also fellowships available in medicine, and he chose to pursue that route, studying science and medicine with Robert Boyle, the leading Oxford scientist at the time. He was also influenced by Descartes' philosophical ideas.

In 1666, Locke met Anthony Ashley Cooper, later first Earl of Shaftesbury, then one of Charles II's ministers, and in 1667, he became his physician and political adviser. Locke was also appointed secretary to the newly created Board of Trade, which reflected Ashley Cooper's keen interest in overseas trade, and to the Lords Proprietors of Carolina, one of his commercial interests.

However, as well as being an advocate of religious toleration and a critic of the Clarendon Code, the laws that excluded Protestant Nonconformists from public office and certain forms of employment, Shaftesbury opposed Charles' policy of closer relations with France and the promotion of Roman Catholicism. He feared that the result would be curtailment of individual liberty. Shaftesbury became the leader of the anti-Roman Catholic Whig party, which sought to limit the monarch's powers and exclude Charles' brother James, who was openly Roman Catholic, from the throne in favour of Charles' illegitimate son, the Protestant James, Duke of Monmouth. Shaftesbury looked to Locke to provide the theoretical arguments for revolt against a despotic monarch.

In 1674, Locke returned to Oxford, where he received his medical degree, and then travelled in France. Shaftesbury exploited the anti-Roman Catholic feeling produced by Titus Oates' revelations of a plot to murder the king, leading to the Exclusion Crisis. However, Shaftesbury's efforts to prevent James' succession failed, and, after a period in the Tower and being tried for treason, he fled to Holland on his acquittal in 1681, dying there in 1683.

Meanwhile, the exclusionist cause was further discredited by the Rye House Plot (1683), a conspiracy to assassinate Charles and James. Locke was conscious of the dangers to the opponents of Charles and James (who became king in 1685) and left for Holland. During this period, he wrote *Two Treatises of Government* (published in 1690), which subsequently provided the theoretical basis for the 'Glorious Revolution' of 1688–9, which ousted James II in favour of his Protestant daughter Mary and her husband, William of Orange (William III). Though written a few years earlier, Locke's arguments for people's rights and liberties took on added significance in the light of James' oppressive government, his disastrous efforts to impose a Roman Catholic regime on England, and Louis XIV's revocation of the Edict of Nantes in 1685, which had allowed a degree of toleration to French Huguenots (Protestants).

After returning to England with William and Mary, Locke lived at the home of Sir Francis and Lady (Damaris) Masham, the daughter of the philosopher, Ralph Cudworth. A Commissioner of Trade from 1696 to 1700, he was also involved in the recoinage of 1696, which introduced silver coins with milled edges to prevent illegal clipping. Locke's most important work, *An Essay Concerning Human Understanding*, was published in 1689. His other works include *Letter on Toleration* (1690) and *The Reasonableness of Christianity* (1695).

Key ideas

Government by consent

Should the ruler be absolute, as Hobbes argues? Or is it more important for subjects to have some rights? Locke explains that, to appreciate the proper limits of political power, we need to understand the state of nature, human beings' situation before the creation of any government. Locke's more optimistic view of human nature yields a different account from Hobbes'. The state of nature is not one of anarchy and conflict, but of freedom and equality in which no one has power over anyone else. The law of reason enables people to understand that they ought not to violate others' natural rights to life, health, liberty and property; and that transgressors should be punished.

But, if human beings enjoy unlimited freedom, complete equality and absolute control of their persons and possessions in the state of nature, why would they choose to give it up and subject themselves to the restrictions of an organized state with its government and laws? It is because, in the state of nature, too many people disregard reason and prey on others, making even their survival uncertain. So, they agree to contract with others to form a society for the mutual preservation of life, liberty and property. Civil government provides laws which are generally accepted as the standard of right and wrong, impartial judges who can resolve differences between citizens, and the means of enforcing the judges' decisions. In exchange for the security of society, human beings accept the rule of law, and relinquish their individual power of punishing wrongdoers.

Is any government, however tyrannical, better than none? Locke thinks not. People only relinquish the total freedom and equality of the state of nature to improve their situation. They do not do so to make themselves worse off. For Locke, the power that society, in the legislative, executive and judicial branches of government, can legitimately exercise over its members can never go beyond what serves the common good. Those who govern the state are bound to do so according to properly enacted laws. They should only employ force at home or abroad, in order to enforce the law, or to protect the community against invasion. Their ultimate objective should always be their citizens' peace, safety and welfare. No government is entitled to wield despotic power over its people, or to end their lives arbitrarily. Such tyranny is an abuse of power, imposed for the ruler's advantage, not the good of those he rules.

Even a monarch, such as Charles II or James II, receives his authority from the laws which have been enacted for the benefit of all members of society, and he must not breach them. When a ruler claims an absolute power over the lives, liberty and property of the people, he or she puts him- or herself into a state of war with them. Through his breach of trust, he forfeits the authority the people gave him for a quite different purpose and it returns to them. They have a right to resume their original liberty, and to resist him, in order to ensure their safety and security, which is the reason why they consented to the creation of society in the first place.

The tolerant society

Locke maintains that religious toleration, which accords with both the teachings of Jesus and what reason tells us is right, is the chief characteristic of true Christianity. He considers it monstrous that people not only overlook this truth, but also try to justify harsh treatment of those with differing religious views on such grounds as public good, loyalty to their ruler or sincere worship of God. Opponents of toleration, who want state persecution of religious dissidents, fail to recognize that the proper role of civil government does not include controlling people's religious beliefs and practices. The state is a society of human beings, established for the purpose of advancing civil interests. A civil government's responsibility is to ensure its people's rights to life, liberty, health and property, and to punish those who try to violate these rights. Its jurisdiction is limited to the issues of this world and does not extend to the care or salvation of their souls.

Why not? God did not give any government the right to compel its citizens to conform to a particular religion. Locke dismisses as absurd the idea that individual salvation could be the responsibility of a civil authority. The appearance of belief, which is all the state could secure, would not deliver the inner conviction about religious truths which alone would be acceptable to God. People join religious groups because they believe their teachings are acceptable to God and will lead to eternal life. As Christ did not decree any particular form of church organization, the New Testament contains nothing that justifies state persecution in order to compel people to embrace a particular doctrine or to join a particular religious group.

However, as religious groups are free and voluntary societies, the fact that they operate in a tolerant society does not oblige them to retain members who refuse to comply with their rules. But excommunication from a religious group, or belonging to one rather than another, does not entitle the state to deprive someone of his civil rights or property. Officers of the state have no role in the direction of religious affairs. Further, a civil government cannot legitimately confer rights on members of a particular religious group over non-members, nor can the authority of the clergy extend beyond ecclesiastical jurisdiction into civil affairs.

The law should not prohibit religious practices, unless, like the sacrifice of infants, they are damaging or dangerous to society. Society should apply a simple test to religious organizations: activities that are unlawful in the ordinary course of life should not be permitted in religious communities either, while those that are lawful in society should be permitted in religious communities. Civil government's concern is the temporal good and material prosperity of society. In religious matters, the right to liberty entitles all to believe and practise whatever their consciences tell them is acceptable to God. It is not diversity of opinion but refusal of toleration that has produced all the religious conflicts that mar the Christian world.

Impact

- Locke's insistence that governments have a duty to respect their citizens' lives, liberty and property has played a vital role in the establishment of Western, democratic, pluralistic society, characterized by constitutional government, the rule of law, freedom of opinion and speech, and religious toleration.

- His view that government is based on consent, and that the authority to rule is entrusted to a government by the people, who can withdraw this authority if it is used to oppress or persecute them, has inspired those resisting tyranny and is enshrined in the American Declaration of Independence (1776).

- Locke draws a clear boundary between the legitimate responsibilities of civil governments and the rights of individuals to freedom of religious conscience: civil governments should not enact laws to prohibit or regulate religious practices, unless they damage or threaten society.

- Locke's powerful case for religious toleration is reflected in the United States Constitution (1787), which prohibits any religious test as a qualification for public office, and following the 1689 Toleration Act, which provided limited toleration for Protestant Dissenters, increasingly influenced opinion in Britain, where complete religious toleration was achieved in the nineteenth century.

Further reading

Constitution of the United States (19 September 1787) at www.avalon.law.yale.edu/18th_century/declare.asp.

Frederick Copleston, *A History of Philosophy*, Vol. 5, Part I (Hobbes to Paley), New York: Image Books, 1964.

M. Cranston, *John Locke: A Biography*, London: Longmans, Green, 1957.

Declaration of Independence (4 July 1776) at www.avalon.law. yale.edu/18th_century/declare.asp.

Thomas Hobbes, *Leviathan*, ed. J. C. A. Gaskin, Oxford: Oxford University Press, 1998.

IEP Contributors, 'John Locke' (updated 2001), in J. Fieser and B. Dowden (eds), *Internet Encyclopedia of Philosophy*, at www.iep.utm.edu.

John Locke, *An Essay Concerning Human Understanding*, Amherst, NY: Prometheus Books, 1995.

John Locke, *A Letter Concerning Toleration*, trans. William Popple, at http://oregonstate.edu/instruct/ph1302/Texts/ locke/locke2/locke-t/locke/toleration.html

John Locke, *A Letter Concerning Toleration*, ed. James H. Tully, Indianapolis: Hackett Publishing Company, 1983.

John Locke, *Second Treatise of Government,* ed. C. B. Macpherson, Indianapolis/Cambridge: Hackett Publishing Company, 1980.

D. J. O'Connor, *John Locke*, Harmondsworth: Penguin, 1952.

W. Uzgalis, 'John Locke' (revised 2007), in E. N. Zalta (ed.), *Stanford Encyclopaedia of Philosophy*, at http://plato.stanford. edu.

9

Baruch de Spinoza
(1632–77)
Monism
God or nature

Context

What is the difference between God and nature? For Spinoza, whose philosophy is summed up in the phrase, *deus, sive natura*, there is none. A monist, he held that only one substance, God or nature, exists. This characterization of ultimate reality is not based on any empirical evidence. As one of the great seventeenth-century rationalist philosophers, Spinoza rejected experience as the source of knowledge, believing that reason is capable of grasping the fundamental truths about the universe and the essence of God. In his major work, *Ethics*, he expounds his metaphysical system, using Cartesian concepts to construct a strikingly original view of ultimate reality. The only substance (that which is in itself, and is conceived through itself and independently of any other conception), God, has two attributes (that which is perceived to constitute the essence of a substance) of which we are aware: thought and extension. Spinoza believes that God has infinite attributes, which express his eternal and infinite essentiality, but that the others are unknown to us.

Baruch de Spinoza (1632–77)

Since Aristotle, a substance had been defined as that which can exist by itself and which does not depend on anything else. For Descartes, the world contains two basic ones: mind and body. Spinoza rejects this Cartesian dualism. Reality is fundamentally monistic. Everything in the universe is a mode (the modifications of substance or that which exists in and is conceived through something other than itself) of the sole substance, God or nature. This substance exists necessarily, otherwise our concept of God would be one in which his essence does not involve his existence. As a necessary being, God is the self-caused cause of all that exists apart from himself, such that: everything is in God; depends upon him; and without him could not exist or be conceived. Further, God acts solely by the necessity of his own nature, so that everything that happens is predetermined by God, not through his free will, but as a result of his nature.

These are the concepts and language of the ontological argument, familiar from Anselm and Descartes. However, there are important differences between Spinoza's conception of God and that of the Judaeo-Christian tradition. Where they differ, Spinoza seems to resolve some of the problems surrounding the latter, but in a way that outraged Jews and Christians. According to the Judaeo-Christian concept, God is an infinite, transcendent and all-powerful being, who is also personal and loving. This God freely chose to create a universe that is wholly distinct from but dependent upon himself, apparently in order to provide an environment in which human beings, made in his own image, can come to know, love and ultimately enjoy a future life with him. But, is this a coherent concept of God? Is it intelligible to think in terms of a transcendent being 'choosing' to create the world? Does God need us, as much as we need him?

If so, is this consistent with the idea of an infinite and all-powerful being? Why does the world contain evil and suffering? Spinoza eliminates these difficulties by arguing that the universe is as it is, because there is no other way it could be. God did not 'choose' to create this or that world from a range of possibilities; it flows necessarily, and in a pre-determined way, from his nature. As an infinite being, there will be an infinite number of ways in which God's nature will (necessarily) manifest itself. It is not surprising that Spinoza was accused of both pantheism and atheism.

Spinoza explains that metaphysical errors arise from an anthropocentric view of reality. We find it impossible to think of things in nature not acting in the ways human beings do, with an end in view. We search for the final causes of things, because we assume that everything has a purpose and that nature itself exists in order to satisfy our needs. We convince ourselves that the universe was made, and is governed, by a ruler endowed with human freedom, who has designed everything for our convenience. Then, we are puzzled by the fact that, in addition to its many useful aspects, nature also contains such destructive forces as storms, earthquakes and diseases. We account for these as expressions of God's anger at human wrongdoing, while also falling back on the cliché that God's doings are beyond our understanding.

But, nature has no particular goal, and final causes are fictions we impose on the world. Worse, we diminish God's perfection, for, if God acts for an object, he must desire something that he lacks. Everything that exists is an expression of God, and was not made for our sake. But, having convinced ourselves that God created the world for us, we judge everything by the criterion of how it benefits us, regarding as best those aspects of it we find most beneficial. The explanations we attach to the world are the products of imagination. We should assess the perfection of things on the basis of their actual nature, not the extent to which they delight or offend us. Spinoza's monism and concept of God and nature are the key ideas discussed below.

Life

Baruch or Benedict Spinoza was born in Amsterdam, into a Jewish family, which had escaped the Spanish Inquisition by moving to Portugal and then the Netherlands. He studied Jewish theology (Rabbi Manasseh ben Israel was one of his teachers) and might have become a rabbi; but influenced by Descartes, his philosophical ideas proved unacceptable to the Jewish authorities. In 1656, he was expelled from the synagogue for his heresies, and subjected to censure and criticism he left Amsterdam. From about 1660, he lived in Rijnsberg, near Leyden, subsequently moving to Voorburg, near The Hague. There he lived frugally, earning his living as a lens-grinder, which severely damaged his health. He published his *The Principles of Descartes' Philosophy* in 1663.

In 1670, Spinoza published his *Theological–Political Treatise*. He rejected the view that the Bible is an exclusive source of knowledge about God. It is a means of conveying a moral message about loving our neighbours, so nothing in it can conflict with the results of philosophical speculation. He also advocated religious tolerance and the advantages of democratic government. The book was heavily criticized by the Reformed Church and was subsequently banned.

Spinoza's radical political views put his life at risk. He was associated with the lawyer and mathematician Jan de Witt, the Grand Pensionary of Holland, an upholder of republican values and an advocate of peace. De Witt was an opponent of the House of Orange (Orange–Nassau), which traditionally held the post of *stadtholder* and military leader of Holland. After the death of William II of Orange, in 1650, the *stadtholdership* was left vacant (the first *stadtholderless* period). However, the House of Orange was represented by his son, William III, the future King of England, who spent his life defending Protestantism and opposing the power of Louis XIV's France.

In 1672, Holland was attacked by France and England (Third Dutch War). Following a French invasion of the country, Jan de Witt and his brother Cornelius were killed by an angry mob, and the country turned to the young William III. He assumed the office of *stadtholder* and, by cutting the dykes, brought the French Army to a halt. Spinoza, who had been involved in a diplomatic mission to the French, was thought by many to be a spy, and was fortunate not to be killed himself. In his final years, he was visited (1676) by his fellow rationalist philosopher Leibniz, and concentrated on finishing his *Ethics*. However, he decided not to publish it, during his lifetime, because of the controversy it was bound to generate. Both the *Ethics* and his *Treatise on the Emendation of the Intellect* were published in 1677, after he died.

Key ideas

Monism

Why should there be only one substance, rather than many? Why should not mind, the essence of which is thinking, be one substance, and body, the essence of which is extension, another? Spinoza believes he can prove that there is only one from the definitions of such concepts as substance, attribute and mode. As substance is that which can only be conceived independently of any other conception, no two substances (if more than one existed) could have anything in common. If there were distinct substances, they would have to be distinguished by differences in their attributes or their modes. Differences in modes are irrelevant, as they are posterior, not prior, to substance. However, the attribute(s) constitutes the essence of a substance, so, if more than one substance existed, they would have to share the same attribute(s). But, this would make them identical with each other, and thus the same substance. Therefore, there cannot be several substances, but only one. While this seems to apply the principle of the identity of indiscernibles, it is only convincing if we think in terms of one attribute per substance (which is not, in fact, Spinoza's view). If substance is conceived as having more than one attribute, two substances could have (a) common and (a) different attribute(s), without being identical.

Spinoza believes he has established that there cannot be two substances in the universe. As there is then nothing else in the universe that could have produced the only substance that exists, it must be the cause of itself: its essence necessarily involves its existence. Further, this existence must be infinite, because, for it to exist only finitely, it would have to be limited by another substance of the same kind; but there is none. However, he does return to the question of the relationship between substance and attribute, so as to refute any suggestion that the existence of more than one attribute implies more than one substance. Though two attributes (such as thought and extension: the only ones we know about) can be conceived as distinct, they cannot be conceived as two different substances. Why not? Because it is the nature of substance that each of its attributes is conceived through substance itself, as all the attributes have always existed simultaneously in it; none of them could be produced by anything other than the substance; and each in its different way expresses the full reality of the substance. It is hard to regard this argument as anything more than a series of assertions.

But, Spinoza considers he has demonstrated that an absolutely infinite being, God, must not only necessarily exist, but must necessarily have infinite attributes, each of which manifests a particular eternal and infinite essence. And this necessarily produces the universe's infinite variety or plenitude. The more reality something has, the more attributes it possesses. From the necessity of the divine nature, there must follow an infinite number of things, in an infinite number of ways: all the things, in fact, which fall within the purview of an infinite intellect.

God or nature

Spinoza tells us that, as God is a necessary being, the modes of the divine nature follow from his nature necessarily, not contingently. This applies both to infinite modes of existence, such as the general scientific laws governing the universe, and such finite modes as human beings. Everything in the universe not only exists necessarily, but also necessarily operates in the way that it does, and so is subject to a rigid theological determinism. Of course, this formulation suggests a distinction between God and the universe or God and nature, which Spinoza rejects. God is the immanent cause of all things; and everything is God or nature, and these are just different aspects of the same fundamental substance or reality: whatever is, is in God.

But, Spinoza does indicate two different ways of viewing nature: *natura naturans* ('nature naturing') and *natura naturata* ('nature natured'). The first identifies the active and creative aspect of nature and encapsulates that aspect of God or nature which is considered to be a free cause. The second encapsulates the passive aspect of nature: the various modes of existence which flow from, or are produced by, the necessity of the nature of God. But Spinoza insists that the modes are not in any way separate from God. Without God they could neither exist nor be conceived, which makes it difficult to perceive any intelligible sense in which God can be regarded as a free cause. And, Spinoza explicitly rejects the idea. People think of God as a free cause, because they believe that he is free to produce, or not to produce, the things that flow from his nature. But this is like saying that God could bring it about that it would not follow from the nature of a triangle that its interior angles always equalled two right-angles.

For the order of nature to be different, God's nature would also have to be different. People who want to attribute an absolutely free will to God misunderstand the nature of reality. He could not have created things other than they are. This underlines the point that there is no teleological dimension to the universe. As the modes of existence flow necessarily from the divine nature, they have not been created to serve any plan or purpose. However, this does not detract from God or nature in any way. This ultimate reality just is, eternally and necessarily, and everything that exists does so in the highest perfection as expressions of God's most perfect nature.

Spinoza's metaphysics has major implications for traditional monotheists. As God and nature are the same, there can be no miracles. God cannot intervene to change events in the world; they all flow necessarily from his nature. Similarly, there is no point in intercessionary prayers. As far as human beings are concerned, we are modes of existence that combine the two attributes of God which have been identified: thought and extension. We have minds and bodies. But, these essences do not form a unity, or interact with each other, but operate in parallel (removing a problem that dogged Descartes). Further, we are as subject to determinism as anything else. It is a mistake to claim that human beings are above nature or that human misdeeds are aberrations which can be mastered. All our desires and the emotions that drive us, such as hatred, arise from the necessity of nature.

However, everything in the universe, including human beings, strives to preserve its own existence (*conatus*). We need to make full use of our reason, in order to gain as complete an understanding of the universe as possible. Errors arise from relying on empirical methods, which yield only confused and partial knowledge, leading to the belief that things in the universe happen contingently. Our reason enables us to understand that everything in the universe happens necessarily and thus to perceive them in their eternal or essential reality (*sub specie aeternitatis*). Exercising our reason is the source of our highest happiness, eventually enabling us to achieve intuitive knowledge of God. By perfecting the understanding, we can comprehend God's attributes and all that follows from the necessity of his nature.

Impact

- Spinoza's metaphysical system and monism inspired post-Kantian philosophers like G. W. F. Hegel and the doctrine of absolute idealism, which was popular in the nineteenth and early twentieth centuries.

- Even those who reject his speculative metaphysics should heed his warning about philosophical errors arising from an anthropocentric view of reality, particularly the belief that everything in nature must have a purpose, as nature exists to satisfy human needs.
- Spinoza seems to resolve some of the problems surrounding the Judaeo-Christian concept of God, but at a price that traditional monotheists are not prepared to pay.
- Spinoza's holistic view of the universe, as a vast and complex interdependent system, which can be regarded as God or Nature, is attractive to ecologists and environmentalists.

Further reading

J. Bennett, *A Study of Spinoza's Ethics*, Indianapolis: Hackett Publishing Company, 1984.

S. Blackburn, 'Spinoza, Benedictus de', in S. Blackburn, *Oxford Dictionary of Philosophy*, Oxford and New York: Oxford University Press, 1996.

E. Curley, *Spinoza's Metaphysics: An Essay in Interpretation*, Cambridge, MA: Harvard University Press, 1969.

D. Garrett (ed.), *The Cambridge Companion to Spinoza*, Cambridge: Cambridge University Press, 1996.

E. E. Kellett, 'Spinoza', in James Hastings (ed.), *Encyclopaedia of Religion and Ethics*, Vol. 11, Edinburgh: T & T Clark, 1930.

S. Nadler, 'Baruch Spinoza' (revised 2008), in *Stanford Encyclopaedia of Philosophy,* at http://plato.stanford.edu.

S. Nadler, *Spinoza: A Life*, Cambridge: Cambridge University Press, 2001.

Benedict de Spinoza, *Ethics*, trans. E. Curley (Introduction by Stuart Hampshire), new edition, London: Penguin, 2004.

Further reading

Benedict Spinoza, 'The Ethics', trans. R. H. M. Elwes, in *The Rationalists*, New York: Dolphin Books, 1960.

Benedict de Spinoza, *Theological–Political Treatise*, trans. M. Silverthorne and J. Israel, Cambridge: Cambridge University Press, 2007.

J. Waller, 'Spinoza's Metaphysics' (updated 2009), in J. Fieser and B. Dowden (eds), *Internet Encyclopedia of Philosophy*, at www.iep.utm.edu.

10

Gottfried Wilhelm Leibniz
(1646 – 1716)
The principle of sufficient reason and
other fundamental principles
of metaphysics
The best of all possible worlds and theodicy

Context

Who invented the differential calculus? People would probably say Newton, and be surprised to learn that Leibniz was
its co-inventor. Indeed, the question of who thought of it first
became a major bone of contention between the two. Un-
surprisingly, in 1713, a Royal Society committee, controlled
by Newton, which seems not to have taken evidence from
Leibniz, found in Newton's favour. However, any suggestion
that Newton must have discovered it, because of his scientific
pre-eminence, would be wide of the mark. Leibniz was a 'philosopher' in the seventeenth- and eighteenth-century sense:
a universal genius, whose major contributions cover the full
spectrum of knowledge, embracing mathematics, science and
engineering, as well as logic, metaphysics and theology; and
this despite the fact that he was not a university professor with
plenty of time for academic pursuits, but a busy civil servant,

who spent almost 50 years serving the Elector of Mainz and three Electors of Hanover. As a rationalist philosopher, he developed a breathtakingly original metaphysical system on the basis of a number of fundamental principles. These principles, including that of sufficient reason, and his concept of the best of all possible worlds, as set out in his *Discourse on Metaphysics, Monadology* and *Theodicy*, are the key ideas discussed below. However, these ideas form part of a complex whole, making them hard to explore in isolation; while achieving an overview of Leibniz's philosophy is made more difficult by the fact it is not set out, in full, in one or two major works.

Leibniz declares that human reasoning is based on two great principles: that of contradiction, which enables us to determine what is false; and that of sufficient reason, which enables us to recognize that no fact can exist, or statement be true, unless there is a sufficient reason why it should be as it is and not otherwise; though, in general, we do not know what these reasons are. He also holds that there are two kinds of truth: those of reasoning and those of fact. The first are necessary truths: their opposites are impossible, as they breach the principle of contradiction. The second, being matters of fact, are contingent: their opposite is possible. This suggests that the principle of sufficient reason applies to truths of reasoning, which are analytic and *a priori*, but not to factual ones, which are synthetic and *a posteriori*.

However, this is not Leibniz's view: the principle of sufficient reason does apply to factual truths, which have a factual, if not a logical, necessity. Further, though there may be an infinite sequence of things or events, extending through the universe of created beings, there nonetheless is (or must be) an ultimate and sufficient reason, outside the sequence of contingent events, which accounts for or 'explains' the whole series. This ultimate reason must be a necessary (as opposed to a contingent) being, in which all the events that will occur are present potentially: and this is God. Since this being is the reason for everything that occurs, has occurred and will occur, there is only one God, and he is, as Leibniz puts it, 'sufficient': that is, a complete explanation of all that happens. If this argument sounds familiar, it is because of its similarities to Aquinas' third way. According to the principle of sufficient reason, although the non-occurrence of events would not be self-contradictory, they could not be other than they are, because of the factual necessity that attaches to them. There is a sufficient reason(s) for every event; if we knew the reason, we would know why it occurred; if we knew why it occurred, we would see that it had to occur.

Thus far, Leibniz considers his argument for God's existence to be *a posteriori*: God must exist, because contingent beings exist, and a necessary being is the only ultimate and sufficient reason for their existence. However, Leibniz believes that God's existence can be proved *a priori*. God is a perfect being, whose essence includes existence, or in whom possibility is sufficient to produce actuality: as Descartes put it, he is the only being whose existence is inseparable from his essence. God must exist necessarily, as nothing is capable of preventing that which involves no limit, negation or contradiction. His power, knowledge and will are infinite, and he creates or changes things according to the principle of the greatest good.

Among the infinity of possible universes God could have created, subject only to the limitation of the law of contradiction, there must be a sufficient reason for his choice of the particular one we inhabit, rather than another. The sufficient reason is its degree of perfection, combining the greatest possible variety with the greatest possible order and leading to the greatest possible good. Thus, for Leibniz, despite appearances to the contrary, this world is the best of all possible worlds. Other principles that are distinctive of Leibniz's philosophy, such as the predicate-in-subject principle, the identity of indiscernibles and the monad, are discussed with the key ideas.

Life

Leibniz was born near Leipzig, towards the close of the Thirty Years War, the devastating religious conflict between Roman Catholics and Protestants. Despite the death of his father, a professor at the University of Leipzig, when he was only six, he showed prodigious intellectual gifts and entered the university in 1661. As well as ancient and scholastic philosophy, which deeply interested him, he was influenced by the work of such contemporary thinkers as Descartes, Hobbes and Galileo. After completing his doctorate at the University of Altdorf, Leibniz accepted employment with the Elector of Mainz, a German prince with the right to vote for the Holy Roman Emperor, who ruled Germany, an office traditionally held by the Austrian Hapsburg family. During this period, he wrote a book, the *Catholic Demonstrations*, which was an attempt to find common ground between Protestants and Roman Catholics.

In 1672 the Elector sent Leibniz to Paris to try to persuade Louis XIV to attack the Turks. The motive for this mission seems to have been to divert Louis from pursuing his expansionist policies in Europe, which included achieving dominance in Germany. Leibniz stayed in France for four years, getting to know such leading intellectuals as Nicholas Malebranche, a follower of Descartes, and the Dutch mathematician and scientist Christiaan Huygens. He also began work on the differential calculus, and visited England in 1673.

After his employer's death, Leibniz was appointed librarian to Duke Johann Friedrich of Brunswick, Elector of Hanover, and on his way there visited Spinoza in Holland, shortly before the latter's death. He was subsequently librarian and adviser to Johann's brother and successor, Ernst August, husband of Sophia, a grand-daughter of James I, and to their son, Georg Ludwig, who, in 1714, became King of England (George I), in succession to Queen Anne under the terms of the Act of Settlement (1701). This excluded Roman Catholics, in particular, the descendants of James II, from the throne of England. Unfortunately, Leibniz (by this time, Baron von Leibniz) could not accompany George to England, due to the acrimonious dispute with Sir Isaac Newton about the discovery of the calculus.

Although known primarily as a philosopher, Leibniz had wide intellectual interests. He did not sum up his ideas in a single book, so they have to be traced through his many writings, which include *Meditations on Knowledge, Truth and Ideas* (1684), *Discourse on Metaphysics* (1686), *On the Ultimate Origination of Things* (1697), *New Essays on Human Understanding* (1704), *Theodicy* (1710), *Monadology* (1714) and *Principles of Nature and Grace* (1714). He corresponded extensively with other thinkers, such as the French philosopher and theologian Antoine Arnauld, and the British clergyman and theologian Samuel Clarke.

Key ideas

The principle of sufficient reason and other fundamental principles of metaphysics

By the principle of sufficient reason, nothing occurs, and no fact can exist or statement be true, without a sufficient reason(s) for it to be as it is and not otherwise. Leibniz also holds that, in every true affirmative proposition, the content of any individual subject always includes all its predicates, such that, if one perfectly understands the concept of the subject, one would know all its predicates. This is the predicate-in-subject principle. Further, this tells us the nature of an individual substance: it is a complete concept, full knowledge of which would enable us to deduce all the predicates attributable to it in the past, present and future. As finite beings, we lack this insight, and must rely on empirical observation. But, with God's knowledge, we could see, for example, the reason for all the predicates attributable to Alexander the Great, and know, *a priori*, everything he would do during his lifetime.

Nothing that happens is really contingent, in the sense of its occurrence or non-occurrence not being certain. However, while insisting that whatever happens does so for a sufficient reason, and is certain, Leibniz does not eliminate the distinction between the certain and the necessary. Future contingencies are assured by God, who foresees them, but they are not necessary. For example, Julius Caesar will become dictator of Rome and overthrow the Roman republic; this action is contained in his subject and is certain to happen. But, this does not make it necessary. If the contrary occurred, it would not breach the law of contradiction and so would not be impossible in itself. Though God always chooses what is best, this does not prevent the less than perfect being possible in itself. There are sufficient reasons for contingent propositions being as they are, which is *a priori* proof of their truth and certainty, but this is not the demonstrative necessity of the propositions of maths or logic, which involve the principle of contradiction and whether their essences are possible or impossible in themselves, irrespective of the free will of God or of creatures.

This introduces another of Leibniz's fundamental principles: the identity of indiscernibles, or Leibniz's Law. As there is, for each individual substance, a complete concept from which all its properties can be deduced, two substances may not be identical, but differ numerically. Nature does not contain two beings that are exactly alike: either their properties are not identical or they are the same unique individual substance. Leibniz uses the term 'monad' to refer to each unique individual substance. These monads are the fundamental, unextended, pre-programmed, metaphysical components of reality. They are associated with, and somehow give form and unity to, bodies; in the case of human beings, the monads are their souls. As the concept of them includes every predicate which has, does or will apply to them, and the destruction of one would affect the universe as a whole, their existence can only begin or end simultaneously, and they are indestructible. Although they are self-contained, causing only their own thoughts, and do not affect each other (they are 'windowless'), with each one being, in a sense, a miniature universe that mirrors the universe as a whole, interaction does seem to occur in the universe: both between mind and body, and between bodies. However, this is achieved according to the principle of pre-existing harmony. The appearance of causal relationships is in fact produced by God who harmonizes everything; which also eliminates the problem of how mind and body interact.

The best of all possible worlds and theodicy

God's ideas include an infinite number of possible universes, so there must be a sufficient reason for his choice of
this one. And, this is its fitness or degree of perfection, from
which God is able to produce the greatest good. Within the
world, under God's direction, there is the greatest possible
order, variety and perfection (the principle of plenitude), and
these are the *a priori* reasons why things cannot be otherwise
than they are. And, while soul and body follow their own
laws, they work in unison because of the pre-established harmony between all substances, which God has established.
Thus, everything in the universe derives from God, who
orchestrates it.

However, given the universe's God-centred nature, why
is there evil and suffering? This problem poses a challenge
to any belief that the world was created from nothing by an
omnipotent, omniscient and all-loving God (the traditional
Judaeo-Christian concept of God), who could, presumably,
have created one containing none; and Leibniz's insistence
that it is the best possible one makes this challenge even more
acute. He does not try to evade the issue, accepting that, if God
is an absolutely perfect being, it follows that he must always
act in the most perfect way, both metaphysically and morally.
Of Plato's proposed alternatives in the *Euthyphro*: is something good because God wills it, or does God will it because
it is good? Leibniz dismisses the first option. God's works are
not good only for the purely formal reason that he has made
them. To maintain that things are good, not according to an
objective standard of goodness, but merely because God wills
them, would be to make them good merely by definition: there
would be no divine love or justice, only divine power.

Gottfried Wilhelm Leibniz (1646–1716)

If an infinite God chose to create this world, it must be the best possible one, despite its evil, inhumanity and hardship; to say it is not involves a contradiction. Leibniz makes a number of attempts to reconcile the evil and suffering in the world with the Judaeo-Christian concept of God, inventing the term 'theodicy' to describe them. He argues that our knowledge of the general harmony of the universe, and the hidden reasons for God's conduct, is very limited. Our finite minds cannot understand them or penetrate God's infinite purposes. He also argues that the best of all possible worlds does not mean no evil, only less than in any alternative, and that, although it is beyond our comprehension, the evil that exists in the world is necessary, in order for it to be the best of all possible worlds. A third argument is the Augustinian one of *privatio boni*: evil is the relative lack of goodness that is an inevitable feature of finite creatures.

Privatio boni seems to be theodicy by definition. Evil may be 'lack of good', but the suffering it causes is no less real or significant. Voltaire's sardonic response, in *Candide*, was to ask what, if this really is the best of all possible worlds, the others are like. In *Dialogues Concerning Natural Religion*, David Hume suggests a whole variety of ways in which limited human intelligence can restructure this supposedly best of all possible worlds, so as to cause less pain and suffering to its occupants.

Impact

- Leibniz's metaphysical system had a major impact on eighteenth-century philosophy, and, although he rejected it, particularly on Kant, who learned about it via Wolff and Knutzen.

- In the twentieth century, Leibniz's treatment of logical principles and contribution to the development of logic has influenced analytic philosophers and logicians, such as Bertrand Russell, and existentialist philosophers, such as Martin Heidegger.
- Leibniz's idea that ours is the best of all possible worlds, though much ridiculed, is an inevitable one for Christians and all believers in an all-powerful and all-loving creator God, because otherwise why would such a God have chosen to create this particular world?
- Leibniz's various forms of theodicy continue to be invoked by Christians, when trying to explain why God chose to create a world which contains evil and suffering.

Further reading

S. Blackburn, 'Leibniz, Gottfried Wilhelm', in S. Blackburn, *Oxford Dictionary of Philosophy*, Oxford and New York: Oxford University Press, 1996.

C. D. Broad, *Leibniz: An Introduction*, Cambridge: Cambridge University Press, 1975.

H. D. Burnham, 'Leibniz: Metaphysics' (updated 2005), in J. Fieser and B. Dowden (eds), *Internet Encyclopedia of Philosophy*, at www.iep.utm.edu.

N. Jolley, *Leibniz*, London and New York: Routledge, 2005.

G. W. Leibniz, 'Discourse on Metaphysics' and 'Monadology', trans. R. H. M. Elwes, in *The Rationalists*, New York: Dolphin Books, 1960.

G. W. Leibniz, *Discourse on Metaphysics and Other Essays*, trans. D. Garber and R. Ariew, Indianapolis/Cambridge: Hackett Publishing Company, 1992.

Gottfried Wilhelm Leibniz (1646–1716)

G. W. Leibniz, *Monadology*, trans. G. R. Montgomery, Mineola, NY: Dover Publications, 2005.

G. W. Leibniz, *Theodicy: Essays on the Goodness of God, the Freedom of Man and the Origin of Sin* (2005), trans. E. M. Huggard and ed. A. M. Farrer, at http://www.gutenberg.org/ebooks/17147.

B. C. Look, 'Gottfried Wilhelm Leibniz' (2007), in E. N. Zalta (ed.), *Stanford Encyclopaedia of Philosophy*, at http://plato.stanford.edu.

New World Encyclopedia contributors, 'Gottfried Leibniz', *New World Encyclopedia,* 29 August 2008, at www.newworld encyclopedia.org/entry/Gottfried_Leibniz?oldid=794772.

G. M. Ross, *Leibniz*, Oxford: Oxford University Press, 1984.

Bertrand Russell, *The Philosophy of Leibniz*, London and New York: Routledge, 1992.

11

George Berkeley
(1685–1753)
No such things as abstract ideas
Subjective idealism, the non-existence of
an external world and the existence of God

Context

Is Bishop George Berkeley really a philosopher in the British empirical tradition of John Locke and David Hume? The notion seems a strange one, partly because he is much less well known than his fellow empiricist philosophers, but also because his empiricism led him to a rather eccentric conception of the nature of ultimate reality.

So what exactly are his views? Berkeley was an empiricist, but a radical one. Yes, he is an empiricist, because he holds that what we know are ideas or sense-data in the Lockean sense. However, unlike Locke, Berkeley does not believe that the ideas we perceive are produced by objects external to ourselves, and which exist independently of us. In fact, he is a subjective idealist or immaterialist, maintaining that the objects we perceive, which we think have an independent existence, exist only in that we perceive them. For Berkeley, *esse est percipi*: to be is to be perceived. He opposes the view that material things exist, so his position is the complete opposite of what is known as materialism or physicalism: the doctrine that only material things exist.

Why does he hold a view that is so counter-intuitive and contrary to common sense? His views are a reaction to both the empiricism of Locke and the rationalism of Descartes. He rejects Locke's theory of perception, which holds that we do not perceive material objects directly, but representationally, via the ideas or sense-data, to which, somehow, the objects are believed to give rise. The problem with this theory is that it provides no satisfactory account of how material objects produce perceptions in us. Again, as we cannot get outside the ideas or sense-data we perceive, to the things they represent, we have no means of assessing the degree to which our ideas correspond to objects in the external world or of knowing things as they are in themselves. So, how, according to Locke's theory, can we check that our picture of the external world is accurate, or, for that matter, verify that the external world exists? What is the criterion? For, even empiricists have to admit the possibility of our experiencing ideas, which we believe arise from objects outside ourselves, but which have no external cause. However, the rationalist approach is equally unsatisfactory, as it cannot explain how, if mind and body are distinct substances, they can interact with each other.

Berkeley rejects the notion of an external world and material objects which exist independently of their being perceived, in favour of a philosophical theory which, in his view, by making God its ultimate guarantor, safeguards the continuity and coherence of human experience, conquers scepticism and defends Christian belief. For Berkeley, material objects are, in fact, aggregates of ideas or perceptions, which are dependent on the minds perceiving them. He argues that when we talk of a 'thing' or a 'being', we are in fact identifying two entirely distinct and heterogeneous entities, spirits and ideas, which have nothing in common with each other. While the former are active, indivisible substances, the latter are inert, fleeting dependent beings, which do not subsist by themselves, but are supported by, or exist in, the minds of spiritual substances.

As ideas are inert, they cannot produce other ideas, or be the source of the ideas we experience. So, does this mean that we produce the ideas we experience ourselves? If so, what evidence is there that anything exists apart from our own minds? What reason do we have for rejecting solipsism? But, Berkeley insists that we cannot be the cause of all the ideas we experience, because, although we can control the ideas we have in our minds during the process of reflection, we have no control over the production of the ones which come before our senses. However, that they must have a cause is demonstrated by the regular and predictable way in which they occur.

Therefore, they must be caused by some other spirit, and this is God. This means that there is no clash between the view that God causes and coordinates our ideas and the discoveries of science; scientific enquiry just discloses further evidence of regularity in the operations of nature, which are dependent on God. Further, as all ideas exist in the mind of God, this resolves the issue of whether the aggregates of perceptions, which we call external objects, continue to exist when not being perceived by human beings: they continue to be perceived by God.

The key ideas featured in this chapter are Berkeley's dismissal of Locke's theory of abstract ideas and his arguments for subjective idealism.

George Berkeley (1685–1753)

Life

Born in Dysert in County Kilkenny, George Berkeley was educated at Kilkenny College and entered Trinity College, Dublin, in 1700. He was elected to a fellowship in 1707 and then took orders in the Church of Ireland. At Trinity, he came under the influence of empiricist philosophy, as expounded by John Locke in his *An Essay Concerning Human Understanding*, and also the philosophical and scientific ideas of Hobbes, Descartes and Newton.

The 12 years Berkeley spent at Trinity were the most fruitful in terms of his achievements as a philosopher. He published his *Essay Towards a New Theory of Vision* in 1709, and this was followed by the *Treatise Concerning the Principles of Human Knowledge* (1710) and the *Dialogues Between Hylas and Philonous* (1713). These are Berkeley's major philosophical works, and they were all completed before he was 30.

After spending some time in London, where he got to know such leading literary figures as Joseph Addison, Jonathan Swift and Alexander Pope, Berkeley travelled in France and Italy and worked as a tutor, before being appointed Dean of Derry in 1724. During this period, he became concerned about the lack of organized religious activity in the American colonies, and he formed the plan of establishing a college in Bermuda to train Christian missionaries for America. After intensive efforts to create interest in the scheme, parliament voted him £20,000 for the purpose, and in 1728, he and his wife, Anne (Foster), sailed to Rhode Island, to wait for it to be paid.

However, the government of Sir Robert Walpole was notorious for its do-nothing policy of letting sleeping dogs lie. The grant was not forthcoming, and, as Berkeley was not at hand to do further lobbying for his project, he had to give it up, and return to England. During his four years in America, he wrote *Alciphron, or the Minute Philosopher*, in which he defended Christianity and Anglicanism against their critics, publishing the book shortly after his return home.

In 1734, he became Bishop of Cloyne, a very poor Irish see. He devoted most of the rest of his life to working in his diocese and helping to relieve its poverty. His final work, *Siris (A Chain of Philosophical Reflections and Enquiries Concerning the Virtues of Tar-Water and divers other subjects connected together and arising one from another)*, which appeared in 1744, dealt with the health benefits of drinking tar water, while also guiding its readers towards religious belief. In 1752, he moved to Oxford, in order to oversee the university career of one of his sons, but died early in the following year.

Key ideas

No such things as abstract ideas

We are familiar with particular things, such as the horse we see standing in a field, and we also have a general idea of horses as a class of animals, to which particular horses belong. But, how do we form these general ideas? One answer is the Platonic or rationalist one that we have an innate idea of the essence of a horse, or that the horses we see in the ordinary world are copies of the form or archetype of a horse in a transcendental world.

However, for Locke, all knowledge comes from experience. We form general ideas of things by a process of abstraction from our experience of particular instances. The difference between particular horses and our general idea of a horse is that the latter excludes what is specific to each individual horse, while retaining the common characteristics. We can proceed to further levels of abstraction. Some horses have characteristics, such as colours, in common with other objects, but not with other horses, so we form general ideas of those. We take our general ideas of a human being and a horse, and form another, more general idea of an animal, which includes human beings and many other living creatures. Eventually, we reach such universal ideas as substance, being and thing.

However, Berkeley vehemently rejects Locke's theory of abstract ideas. If all knowledge comes from the senses, how can we have knowledge of things beyond the senses? He contends that, although such qualities as shape or colour do not exist independently of each other, Lockean empiricists claim that the mind can isolate one from another and form an abstract idea of each.

Berkeley denies the possibility of our being able to form general ideas by abstraction from particulars. In his view, a term becomes general through use, not as a result of abstraction. A general term is the sign, not of an abstract idea, but of several particular ideas, which we then use to represent all other particular ideas of the same sort. He takes Locke's example of a triangle. Can we form an idea of a triangle, which is not of a specific kind, such as equilateral or scalene? Berkeley thinks not. When propositions about triangles are discussed, the general idea of a triangle involved is the idea of a specific type of triangle, which is used to stand for all triangles.

People think that, as general terms have a precise meaning, they must receive it from the abstract ideas to which they refer. Berkeley warns against our being misled by language. Abstract ideas are not necessary for ensuring consistency in the definition and use of terms. Further, referring to ideas is only one of language's many uses. Indeed, Berkeley maintains, we are less likely to be deceived by words if we understand that there are only particular ideas, and are not always searching for the abstract ideas to which we mistakenly believe general terms refer.

But, why is Berkeley so passionately committed to proving that abstract ideas do not exist? It is because of his particular version of empiricism, which rules out anything existing independently of our perceiving it. For Berkeley, to exist is to be perceived, so the only things that exist are those we perceive, or which exist in the mind of God. If there are abstract ideas, this suggests that there is a reality which we do not perceive, such as an external world and matter.

Subjective idealism, the non-existence of an external world and the existence of God

What exists? What is the nature of reality? These are questions which philosophers have addressed, and attempted to answer, over the centuries. Berkeley's answers are individualistic and surprising. He maintains that the objects of human knowledge are all ideas or perceptions: those imprinted on our senses, and the ones we perceive in reflection or which the memory or imagination form from those we have perceived. In addition to the succession of ideas, there is also something distinct from them, which perceives them, and performs such operations as willing, imagining and remembering them. This is the mind, soul or self.

He contends that, if we attend to the meaning of the word 'exist', as applied to sensible things, we know intuitively that the ideas imprinted on our senses cannot exist, except in a mind perceiving them. To Berkeley, what is said of the existence of unthinking things, apart from their being perceived, is unintelligible. Their *esse* is *percipi*, their being is to be perceived; and they do not exist outside the minds of the thinking beings that perceive them. The popular view that our perceptions correspond to objects existing independently of a perceiver arises from the erroneous doctrine of abstract ideas.

Such primary and secondary qualities of objects as extension, shape and motion are only ideas existing in the mind. They do not, as Locke argues, indicate the existence of an unthinking substratum of matter, or corporeal substance, which causes our perceptions. Further, Berkeley pertinently asks, even if external bodies exist, how could we know this or anything about them, when knowledge comes through our senses? We cannot go outside our senses to discover the connection between what are claimed to be independently existing objects and our ideas of them.

What about the argument that we can imagine, for example, trees, with nobody there to perceive them? All this shows, Berkeley insists, is our ability to imagine or form ideas in our minds. However, unlike those of reflection or memory, the succession of ideas which comes before our senses does not depend on our will. Therefore, they must have a cause, which produces and changes them. This must be a substance, but, as it is not a material one, it is incorporeal active substance or spirit: God. And, God's goodness is shown by the fact that, although he could cause us to experience ideas in a haphazard fashion, they follow a predictable pattern, according to laws of nature which he has laid down. If we observe the constant regularity and order of natural things, together with their magnificence and beauty, we will see clearly that they are God's handiwork.

How convincing is Berkeley's argument that everything that exists, exists in minds? It is completely contrary to the common sense view that there is an external world, which we learn about through our senses. Even those philosophers who hold that we are acquainted with sense-data, rather than objects themselves, accept that these are caused by things that exist independently of our minds.

Bertrand Russell agrees that Berkeley shows that it is not absurd to deny the existence of external objects, but thinks Berkeley confuses the thing apprehended with the act of apprehension, either of which might be termed an 'idea'. The mental act is certainly in the mind, but this is then transferred to the other sense of 'idea', the thing apprehended, leading to the conclusion that whatever can be apprehended must be in the mind. The ability to be acquainted with things other than itself is the mind's principal characteristic, and constitutes its power of knowing things. When the nature of knowledge is understood, Berkeley's grounds for holding that ideas, in the sense of the objects apprehended, must be mental, lack validity.

Impact

- Berkeley pinpoints the major problems of Locke's representative theory of perception, which does not offer: a satisfactory account of how material objects produce perceptions; criteria for assessing the degree to which our ideas correspond to objects in the external world; any means even of verifying that the external world exists, which can lead to scepticism.

- In his discussion and denial of abstract ideas, Berkeley argues cogently against what would now be called the referential theory of meaning: that the meaning of an expression is to be identified with that to which it refers; points out that referring to things is only one of language's uses; and warns of the dangers of being misled by language.

- Berkeley's subjective idealism adds a novel and unexpected dimension to the Christian belief that God is the sustainer of the world, by making God the ultimate guarantor of the continuity and coherence of human experience.
- Berkeley believed his ideas would highlight God's goodness, overcome scepticism and strengthen Christian belief, but, by carrying empiricism to extreme lengths, which defy common sense, it appears eccentric and incredible.

Further reading

H. Barker, 'Berkeley', in James Hastings (ed.), *Encyclopaedia of Religion and Ethics*, Vol. 2, Edinburgh: T & T Clark, 1982.

George Berkeley, *A New Theory of Vision and Other Writings* (Introduction by A. D. Lindsay), London: J. M. Dent & Sons, 1938.

George Berkeley, *Three Dialogues Between Hylas and Philonous*, ed. Robert M. Adams, Indianapolis/Cambridge: Hackett Publishing Company, 1979.

George Berkeley, *A Treatise Concerning the Principles of Human Knowledge*, ed. Kenneth P. Winkler, Indianapolis/Cambridge: Hackett Publishing Company, 1982.

F. C. Copleston, *A History of Philosophy*, Vol. 5, Part II (Berkeley to Hume), New York: Image Books, 1964.

Further reading

L. Downing, 'George Berkeley' (revised 2011), in E. N. Zalta (ed.), *Stanford Encyclopaedia of Philosophy*, at http://plato.stanford.edu.

D. E. Flage, 'George Berkeley' (updated 2005), in J. Fieser and B. Dowden (eds), *Internet Encyclopedia of Philosophy*, at www.iep.utm.edu.

A. C. Grayling, *Berkeley: The Central Arguments*, La Salle, IL: Open Court, 1986.

John Locke, *An Essay Concerning Human Understanding*, Amherst, NY: Prometheus Books, 1995.

Bertrand Russell, *The Problems of Philosophy*, reissued second edition, with Introduction by John Skorupski, Oxford and New York: Oxford University Press, 2001.

G. J. Warnock, *Berkeley*, Harmondsworth: Penguin, 1953.

12

Joseph Butler
(1692–1752)
The reasonableness of religious belief
The nature of human beings and the
authority of conscience

Context

What is the relationship between reason and revelation? Despite his Christianity, Locke insisted that, in matters of religion, we must not abandon reason: it must be the judge of revelation, and nothing contrary to it should be believed as a matter of faith. Others were prepared to go further, and, while retaining belief in God, rejected Christian dogmas altogether. In 1696, John Toland published his *Christianity Not Mysterious*, in which he maintained that true religion must be reasonable. Supernatural revelation may be a means of transmitting information, but cannot justify belief in propositions which conflict with our actual experience of the world. Like Matthew Tindal, in *Christianity as Old as the Creation*, Toland was putting forward an increasingly popular religious position in the seventeenth century: deism. While deists did not subscribe to a single set of ideas, they generally confined religious belief to propositions which (it was claimed) could be established by reason through natural theology. The outcome is a concept, not of the Christian God, but of an intelligent being, who created or designed the world, but who does not necessarily interfere in the natural order of the world, answer prayers, take account of human beings' conduct, or offer the hope of future life.

One of the most influential champions of religious orthodoxy against the deists was Bishop Joseph Butler. As his opponents were not denying God's existence, but only aspects of religious belief and Christian teaching based on revelation, his *Analogy of Religion* does not try to prove the truth of beliefs, such as those of life after death, but to establish that accepting them is not irrational, even though they are not objectively provable. Cleverly, Butler asks why scepticism fastens on to such religious beliefs, in particular, when this seems contrary to what any analogy with the natural world and the difficulties we have with it suggests. There is a lot we do not know about the natural world, while our knowledge of it is often based on what we regard as (most) probable; yet this lack of certainty does not lead the deists to doubt (all) their beliefs about it. Similarly, the fact that we doubt some of our religious beliefs does not justify our rejecting them, as it does not prove that they are false: while experience and a degree of pragmatism suggest reasons for accepting such teachings as those about life after death. He accepts that his arguments are not conclusive; the important point he wants to make is that people's standards of evidence differ between religious and purely empirical matters, with more rigorous requirements being applied to the former. He urges his readers to be guided by the balance of probability; as with other matters, religious beliefs should be judged on the basis of all the evidence taken together. Some of Butler's arguments from the *Analogy* are considered in the key ideas section.

In the 'Dissertation on the Nature of Virtue', Butler addresses ethical issues, which are also discussed below. He was particularly concerned about the dangers of Hobbes' views on morality. He denies that human nature is dominated by overriding self-interest, which makes us essentially egotistical, self-centred and selfish; its ethical components are self-love, benevolence and conscience. Against Hobbes, he argues that our nature, of which conscience is such an essential part, inclines us towards co-operation with, and benevolent treatment of, our fellow human beings, just as much as it does towards securing our own lives, health and property. Conscience is not an artificial construct, produced by socialization, nor just a metaphor for whatever moral principles we choose to guide our behaviour, but a natural God-given faculty that enables us to reflect on and make appropriate ethical judgements about our conduct. When conscience rules us, we act according to our (higher) nature; when it does not, we act against our nature.

Conscience and happiness are also closely related. Butler deprecates the view that virtue consists in exclusive pursuit of the aim of maximizing human happiness, without regard to the moral quality of the actions that produce happiness. We should pursue our own and others' happiness indirectly, through actions of which our consciences approve: true happiness comes from doing what is right. Again, conscience and self-love coincide: by doing what our conscience tells us, we do what is in our own best interests, because we fulfil our true nature as human beings. As a result, we will be happy.

Life

Born at Wantage, Berkshire, Joseph Butler's Presbyterian parents wanted him to become a Presbyterian minister, and he was educated at dissenting academies in Gloucester and Tewkesbury. However, increasingly drawn to the Church of England, with his parents' agreement, he entered Oriel College, Oxford, in 1715. After graduating, in 1718, he was appointed preacher at the Rolls Chapel, Chancery Lane, where the Chancery records (Rolls) were kept, holding the position until 1726. His *Fifteen Sermons Preached at the Rolls Chapel*, in which he expounds his ideas on ethics and moral philosophy, were published in 1726.

After being rector of Haughton-le-Skerne, near Darlington, he was appointed to the well-endowed benefice of Stanhope, in rural Durham. He became a prebendary (canon) of Rochester in 1733, and was appointed clerk of the closet (senior chaplain) to Queen Caroline, the wife of George II, in 1736. This was the year he published his *The Analogy of Religion, Natural and Revealed to the Constitution and Course of Nature*, to which was affixed the 'Dissertation on the Nature of Virtue'.

Butler became a favourite of Queen Caroline, who, before her death (1737), urged her husband to advance his career; and, in 1738, Butler became Bishop of Bristol. However, Butler was dissatisfied with his appointment to the most impoverished see in England; but, in 1740, he received the deanery of St Paul's, which he held concurrently with Bristol until 1750. During the eighteenth century, this kind of pluralism (clergy holding more than one parish or senior appointment at the same time) was widespread in the Church of England, and Butler, despite his reputation as a conscientious and hardworking clergyman, was no exception to the practice. Unlike some of his contemporaries, though, he was not rapacious or materialistic; he was concerned to relieve poverty; and he did not neglect his duties. Always a believer in a restrained and rational approach to religion, he disliked John Wesley's religious enthusiasm and tried to prevent him preaching in his diocese. Butler is reputed to have refused the see of Canterbury, when Archbishop John Potter died in 1747, but there is no clear evidence that it was offered to him. In 1750, he became Bishop of Durham, the Church of England's wealthiest see. This was Butler's last ecclesiastical position. Due to illness, he moved to Bath, where he died. He is buried in Bristol Cathedral.

Key ideas

The reasonableness of religious belief

In *The Analogy*, Butler regrets that Christianity is almost assumed to be fictitious. This strong presumption against the truth of Christian teachings is based on an analogy with nature and our knowledge of the empirical world. They cannot be proved by empirical means, so are considered to be false. But, the fact that something is beyond the scope of our faculties, and cannot be proved or completely understood, does not make it untrue. And, we apply this principle to the empirical world, where our inability to comprehend aspects of how it operates does not lead to total scepticism: the standard we apply is that of probability, not certainty.

Butler makes an important distinction between probability and certainty. We develop our knowledge of the world through observation of events. For example, we observe one event following another and infer a causal relationship between them. Observation of numerous daily occurrences of the same series of events produces a conviction that they will always follow the same pattern. However, this is not the demonstrative certainty of mathematical or logical propositions: their non-occurrence would not breach the law of contradiction. Probability is about what is more likely to occur, so is a matter of degree. The more often we observe an event, the more probable we think it is that it will re-occur; and eventually this becomes a conviction. Butler accepts that knowledge based on probability is not entirely unsatisfactory; but, whereas nothing would be merely probable to a being of infinite intelligence, like God, it is the most that finite human beings can hope for. Indeed, probability is the very guide of our lives.

With difficult questions, such as those arising in religion, certainty is usually unattainable, given the inadequate nature of the evidence. Decisions must be reached on the basis of probability, even though doubt will remain. Further, while some religious truths, such as God's existence, can be discovered through experience, there are others, such as whether there is life after death, which only revelation can answer. Analogy with nature shows that we must use whatever means are appropriate for obtaining knowledge. As there are religious questions which experience cannot answer, either we turn to revelation, or accept that we cannot answer them. Again, it is as prudent to believe what we think will lead to our happiness, as it is to believe what we certainly know to be true. Thus, our approach to religious questions, and to the status of revelation, should be guided by probability and prudence.

Take the question of life after death. We are born into the present world as helpless infants and grow into mature adults. Thus, in relation to the human species, it seems to be a general law of nature that we go through stages of existence and understanding which differ greatly from each other.

Indeed, is it possible to conceive of stages of life more different than those of being in the womb/infancy and adulthood? Therefore, the proposition that, after death, we will enter a state of life as different from our present one as adulthood is from infancy, fits in with the analogy from nature. Butler rejects what appears to be the powerful counter-argument that physical death clearly involves the termination of human and other life. Our limited knowledge does not extend to what death is in itself, but is confined to such effects as the disintegration of flesh, skin and bones: the analogy with nature does not warrant the conclusion that life itself is extinguished.

With miracles, is the presumption against them so strong as to make them incredible? They appear to have the purpose of giving us information which goes beyond that which we derive from nature, lending credibility to the view that they are part of God's scheme of things. As for their improbability, we must not think in terms of ordinary natural events, but such extraordinary phenomena as tempests and earthquakes. What would the presumption be against these, were we only familiar with the ordinary course of nature? We should approach the idea of divine revelation in the same spirit. If God chooses to instruct us through revelation, we are unlikely to be in a position to judge how he would do so. And, why should we expect revelation to be any less problematic than natural events? We find that, in some respects, nature operates by general laws, and conclude that it always does. But our general laws account for only a limited number of natural events: there are many irregularities that we do not understand. Thus, the analogy with nature makes it very likely that, if revelation does occur, it will contain things that differ sharply from our expectations. All we can do is to use our reason to judge its meaning and morality, and the evidence for it.

The nature of human beings and the authority of conscience

What is our true nature as human beings? According to Butler, we need to understand our human constitution. Then, we can work out our purpose as human beings, just as we can that of a watch, by studying its components. But first, we need to know how these components fit together. Just as a machine needs a mechanism, which regulates the operation of its components, so do human beings. We have the God-given faculty of conscience, which exercises control over our passions and appetites. And, because we have this moral faculty, our nature is as clearly adapted to virtue as a watch is to the measurement of time. A watch that cannot measure time is an artefact failing to fulfil its purpose; and so is a human being who does not behave morally. Indeed, for Butler, conscience imposes on human beings an obligation to behave morally, which precedes even Christian revelation.

But, does not self-interest drive us to put our own interests above those of others? This is to misunderstand the true nature of self-interest, which coincides perfectly with virtue. Only moral conduct, leading to social approval, a satisfied conscience and a future reward in heaven, is genuinely self-interested. Also, as we all have a conscience, we can reach consensus about what constitutes moral conduct. Of course, unlike machines, we can choose to behave in ways which defy our true nature; but, unlike animals, we are not forced to follow our strongest passion. Conscience enables us to be autonomous, moral agents, choosing actions which accord with its dictates. Through reflection, we can bring our actions before the faculty of conscience, and we will necessarily be drawn towards moral behaviour; only when we behave rationally and morally, and are thus true to our God-given nature, are we fully human.

But, as we possess a conscience, why do we often behave badly? Because, in a particular situation, what conscience tells us may not be our strongest impulse. A particular passion may override it, leading to actions that conscience condemns. Nonetheless, conscience's authority, if not always its power, is absolute. When we fail to be guided by it, and yield to our passions, our constitution is controlled by motivations which flout our obligations as rational, moral creatures. Just as a country's constitution may be violated and set aside by forces that prevail over its authority, so the human constitution may be violated by overriding passions.

Society and human beings can only achieve their goals when they act under proper direction. When we resist our conscience, we create a disharmony, which shakes the foundations of our human nature, and prevents its proper functioning. When we recognize its authority and affirm our real nature as rational, moral beings, we conquer the lower elements of our nature, which we share with animals; attain the highest level of humanity; and fulfil our obligations to God and to our true nature as moral beings, capable of achieving happiness and the fullest expression of human life.

Impact

- Butler's case for regarding religious and Christian beliefs, such as life after death, as reasonable though not provable, were particularly influential in the nineteenth century, when his admirers included W. E. Gladstone and J. H. Newman.

- Today, those who already believe/are close to believing in God are more likely to find his arguments for specifically Christian teachings and revelation persuasive than, for example, those, such as agnostics, who are unwilling to believe anything that cannot be proved empirically.

- Butler provides a positive characterization of human nature, which is an attractive counterblast to Hobbesian pessimism and determinism.

- Even if we reject Butler's analysis of conscience, it has proved a useful way of highlighting our ability to reflect on our actions, to overcome our passions, and to behave in ways that show respect for the welfare and happiness of others.

Further reading

J. H. Bernard, 'Butler', in James Hastings (ed.), *Encyclopaedia of Religion and Ethics*, Vol. 2, Edinburgh: T & T Clark, 1930.

Joseph Butler, *Five Sermons* (with 'A Dissertation Upon the Nature of Virtue'), ed. A. S. L. Darwall, Indianapolis: Hackett Publishing Company, 1983 (selected from *Fifteen Sermons Preached at the Rolls Chapel*).

Joseph Butler, *The Analogy of Religion*, ed. W. E. Gladstone, London and New York: Oxford University Press, 1907.

Joseph Butler, *The Works of Joseph Butler: Containing The Analogy of Religion and Sixteen Celebrated Sermons*, Chestnut Hill, MA: Adamant Media Corporation, 2000.

F. C. Copleston, *A History of Philosophy*, Vol. 5, Part I (Hobbes to Paley), New York: Image Books, 1964.

Joseph Butler (1692–1752)

C. Cunliffe (ed.), *Joseph Butler's Moral and Religious Thought*, Oxford and New York: Oxford University Press, 1992.

E. C. Mossner, *Bishop Butler and the Age of Reason*, New York: Macmillan, 1936.

D. E. White, 'Joseph Butler' (updated 2009), in J. Fieser and B. Dowden (eds), *Internet Encyclopedia of Philosophy*, at www.iep.utm.edu.

13

David Hume
(1711–76)
Basing knowledge on experience and the limits of human knowledge
The logical gap between 'is' and 'ought'

Context

Why was David Hume, regarded by many as Britain's greatest philosopher, more celebrated in his own lifetime as a historian? Hume provides some answers in his entertaining and commendably concise autobiography, written shortly before his death. A keen student of philosophy from his earliest years, his first book, the *Treatise of Human Nature*, fell still-born from the press. However, being blessed with what he calls a cheerful and sanguine disposition, he refused to be deterred from writing works of philosophy, despite their luke-warm or hostile reception. Keen to express his literary talents, he also decided to write a history of England, but, as he chose to favour the Tory, rather than the Whig, side of issues, this also embroiled him in controversy. But, the historical works ultimately proved very successful, and Hume became a lion-ized and wealthy author.

Hume addresses a range of philosophical questions. What do we know? How do we know what we know? What are the limits of human knowledge? On what basis do we claim to have knowledge? Does knowledge involve certainty? Does knowledge come from reason or experience? His conclusions are uncompromisingly and radically empiricist. Like Locke, he maintains that knowledge comes from experience, and his discussion of this issue and the limits of human knowledge, in his *Enquiry Concerning Human Understanding*, is one of the key ideas discussed below.

Hume believes that, as we cannot go outside our experience, there are definite boundaries as to what we can know and questions we will never be able to answer. For example, time and again experience shows us causal connections between events. However, our conviction that those we have witnessed will continue to occur arises from our being accustomed to them; it is not due to the ability of our reason to demonstrate that a particular effect must follow, of necessity, from a particular cause. As our concepts come from experience, we cannot use them to obtain knowledge that goes beyond experience. Thus, a measure of scepticism is a valuable aid to philosophical enquiry: but not the extreme scepticism adopted by Descartes in his *Meditations*, which involves doubting everything, and which is valueless and unsustainable. Hume's is moderate scepticism, which highlights the limitations of human understanding, curbs dogmatism, and makes people more receptive to the views of others. Therefore, his conclusions are also very different from those of Descartes, who uses reason to search for something absolutely certain that will provide a secure basis for knowledge, and believes that he has found it.

Unlike Kant, Hume takes a soft determinist position on the issue of human freedom, holding that any reconciliation of freedom and necessity is a purely verbal question. Human actions are undeniably connected with motives, and one follows the other. Human freedom, or free will, simply means that individuals are free to act, or not to act, according to the determination of their will, as opposed to their being subject to external coercion; but there can be no such thing as human freedom when it is opposed to causal necessity.

Hume addresses issues of moral philosophy and philosophy of religion, as well as epistemology. He does not think that reason can be the basis of morality, or provide the motive for behaving morally. But his view differs from Butler's, in that he does not regard conscience-guided self-interest as the key to moral conduct. He believes that human beings have a natural sympathy for, or benevolence towards, others, which is the basis of morality. Other human beings closely resemble us, so we feel that their persons, interests, pains and pleasures are significant. We also see that benevolence and sympathy promote happiness and well-being, and so approve of them. The other key idea, from *A Treatise of Human Nature*, is Hume's discussion of the important metaethical question of how we justify a move from statements of facts to those of value: from those about what is the case to what we ought to do about it.

In relation to religious claims, Hume is sceptical, and concerned about the effects of superstition and possible excesses of popular religion. On miracles, he argues, in the *Enquiry*, that, as the evidence for them is based on human testimony, it is less compelling than the evidence of our own senses. When people claim to have seen a miracle, experience itself should make us doubt it. Hume addresses the arguments for God's existence in both the *Enquiry* and the *Dialogues Concerning Natural Religion*. On the popular design argument, which tries to establish God's existence and/or nature on the basis of an analogy between a human artefact and the universe, Hume points out that the similarity between objects of human design and the universe is not so striking that we are entitled to infer similar causes. Further, when we see a house, we know an architect has designed it, but we have no experience of the design of worlds. Any conclusions we draw about the cause of the latter goes beyond our experience.

Life

David Hume was born in Edinburgh. After his father's death, when he was very young, he was brought up by his mother, Katherine, on the family's small estate at Ninewells, near Berwick. As he showed precocious intellectual ability, he went to Edinburgh University before he was 12. However, though keenly interested in a wide range of subjects, including philosophy, history and literature, he showed no inclination for law, which his family wanted him to take up as a career.

After working for a sugar merchant in Bristol, Hume went to live in La Flèche in Anjou, where Descartes had attended the Jesuit college. He stayed there until 1737, reading the works of such authors as Pierre Bayle and Nicholas Malebranche, and working on the draft of the *Treatise of Human Nature*. Back in England, he prepared the book for publication in three parts ('Of the Understanding', 'Of the Passions' and 'Of Morals') in 1739 and 1740. However, its reception was disappointing, while even the removal of some more controversial parts, such as that on miracles, out of deference to Bishop Butler, did not prevent the book's empirical and sceptical approach giving him the reputation of an atheist. He became an object of suspicion to the religious and cultural leaders of eighteenth-century Scotland, which may have been a factor in his not being appointed professor of philosophy at Edinburgh University, in 1745, or of Logic at Glasgow University, a few years later. Hume worked as a tutor, and was then secretary to Lieutenant-General James St Clair, which involved him in a military expedition against France during the War of the Austrian Succession, and diplomatic trips to the Continent.

Hume published further works of philosophy, including *An Enquiry Concerning Human Understanding* (1748) and *An Enquiry Concerning the Principles of Morals* (1751), which presented many of the *Treatise*'s central ideas in more readable form. But he turned increasingly to history, including his multi-volume *History of England* from Julius Caesar's invasion to the Glorious Revolution of 1688 (published 1754–62), which brought him fame and financial independence. As Librarian to the Faculty of Advocates in Edinburgh, from 1752, he was able to use its resources for his historical researches.

Still dogged by controversy, he decided not to include his essay 'Of Suicide', which treats the issue sympathetically, in his *Four Dissertations* (1757). His *Essays Moral, Political and Literary*, which include his essays on economics and trade, appeared the following year. In 1763, he became secretary to the Marquess of Hertford, the British ambassador to France, and then secretary to the British Embassy in Paris, where he was fêted by the intellectual elite, such as Denis Diderot and other *philosophes* (contemporary French philosophers).From 1767 to 1769, he served as Under-Secretary of State to Lord Hertford's brother, Henry Seymour Conway, in the Marquess of Rockingham's government.

Ever generous, Hume befriended Jean-Jacques Rousseau, but the latter was unstable and became hostile to Hume, who put his side of events in *A Concise and Genuine Account of the Dispute between Mr Hume and Mr Rousseau*. Back in Scotland after 1769, he devoted his remaining years to preparing new editions of his works, and completing his *Dialogues Concerning Natural Religion*, which was published posthumously in 1779.

Key ideas

Basing knowledge on experience and the limits of human knowledge

Where does our knowledge come from? Hume identifies two types of mental perceptions: immediate impressions or sensations, such as seeing and feeling, and thoughts or ideas; and as the latter come from the former, everything we know is based on an impression or sensation. This may not appear to be the case: we seem to have ideas, such as that of a virtuous horse, to which no impressions correspond. But (Hume argues) we are deceived by our imagination's ability to create combinations of ideas. If we break the combinations down into simple ideas, we will identify corresponding impressions. The virtuous horse just brings together the ideas of virtue and a familiar animal. Even the idea of an infinitely wise and good God comes from thinking about our own powers and then imagining them as unlimited.

But, how can we present our thoughts or ideas to the memory or imagination in a regular fashion? Hume's answer is the mind's capacity to organize them according to three principles of association: resemblance, contiguity in place or time, and cause and effect. All our mental operations depend upon these principles.

Hume divides all forms of human enquiry into two groups: those concerning relations of ideas, and matters of fact. The first group, consisting of *a priori* propositions, relates to mathematics, logic and verbal definitions, where truth can be established by thought alone and use of the law of contradiction. For example, denying that two plus two makes four, or that a house is a building, is self-contradictory. But, this is not the case with matters of fact. Denying that the sun will rise tomorrow involves no contradiction. Knowledge of matters of fact is based on observation and experience and the relation of cause and effect. Our experience of the constant conjunction of particular objects means we know, for example, that fire produces heat and light, and that we can infer one from the other.

Hume explores the implications of experience as our source of knowledge. As far as causation is concerned, we tend to think of particular causes and effects as being necessarily connected. However, this is not, as the rationalists argue, absolutely certain knowledge, deriving from a direct intellectual intuition of these causal relationships, but is an unshakable expectation, based on regular observation of one event invariably being followed by another. However, we tend to overlook this point with things we have been familiar with from birth. We may think we have always known the effects of one billiard ball striking another, but in theory, any outcome is possible: the first ball could return in a straight line. It is only through experience that we know that the impact of the first ball transmits motion to the second.

As we only form the idea of what we regard as necessarily connected events through experience, by habitually observing cause and effect, it is impossible to define a cause satisfactorily. It is no more than one object being followed by another, where all the objects similar to the first are followed by objects similar to the second. And, as we acquire our knowledge of cause and effect (such as it is) through experience, we cannot extend it beyond experience. Contrary to the claims of rationalists and metaphysicians, we cannot determine the ultimate cause of any natural process. So, if we try to attribute events to the will of God, we merely engage in pointless speculation.

The logical gap between 'is' and 'ought'

Moral evaluation invariably involves the facts of a particular situation. But, what justifies the move from a statement of those facts, of what is the case, to a moral judgement about what we ought to do about them? For some moral philosophers, the answer is straightforward. Certain facts dictate particular moral judgements and actions. If people are suffering, we ought to help them, because we ought to maximize general happiness. Indeed, some moral philosophers would argue that, unless it concerns meeting human needs, and improving the human predicament, a response would not even qualify as a moral one.

In a tantalizingly elusive way, David Hume draws attention to the issue of the relationship between facts and evaluation, between 'is' and 'ought', without telling us clearly what it is. He notes that, in every moral system he has ever studied, the author first discusses facts (or alleged facts), from the existence of God to observations about human beings and human affairs, all of which are expressed in propositions that contain only an 'is' or an 'is not'. He is then surprised to discover that these factual propositions have given way to statements that contain only an 'ought' or an 'ought not'. This change happens imperceptibly, but it is obviously a very important one.

Hume says that he cannot conceive how an 'ought' proposition can be deduced from an 'is' one. As there is an obvious logical gap between the two kinds of proposition, the writers should give reasons to justify their apparently illegitimate move from one type of proposition to the other. However, they invariably fail to do so. Hume adds, enigmatically, that observing, and, presumably, challenging, this move would undermine vulgar (ordinary) systems of morality; it is certainly a warning against superficial or badly thought-out moral systems.

The traditional interpretation is that Hume is being ironic. When he says that he does not understand how the move from what is the case to what we ought to do can be made, and wants an explanation, he is actually saying that it cannot be made. He is suggesting that such a move, as from 'x is suffering' to 'we ought to help x', is logically flawed, as no evaluation (what we ought to do) follows from any factual statement. He is making the point that we cannot move from a minor premise ('x is starving') to a conclusion ('we ought to give x food'), except by way of a major premise, which, here, would be, 'we ought always to give food to those who are starving'.

But, although putting in a major premise creates a syllogism, and satisfies the demands of logic, is this what Hume is getting at? The substantial question is: does a particular situation, or people being in a particular situation, as when they are suffering, require (logically) that we should act, and act in a particular way?

Impact

- Hume provides an extremely influential statement of empiricist epistemology: that all knowledge comes from observation and experience; that we organize our thoughts through three principles of association – resemblance, contiguity in space and time, and cause and effect; and that all our mental operations depend on them.

- Accepting Hume's radically empiricist view, that knowledge of cause and effect comes from experience, and is limited to it, means that we cannot determine the ultimate cause of any natural process or legitimately attribute any event to God as its cause.
- Hume's identification of the 'is/ought gap' has had a major impact on moral philosophy and metaethical debate and still attracts conflicting interpretations from moral philosophers and ethicists.
- The apparent logical 'gap' between statements of fact and statements of what we ought to do (evaluation) highlights the question of what the precise relationship between the two types of statement is and underlines the importance of taking account of it when constructing moral arguments.

Further reading

A. J. Ayer, *Hume, A Very Short Introduction*, Oxford and New York: Oxford University Press, 2000.

F. C. Copleston, *A History of Philosophy*, Vol. 5, Part II (Berkeley to Hume), New York: Image Books, 1964.

J. Fieser, 'Hume: Metaphysical and Epistemological Theories' (updated 2004), in J. Fieser and B. Dowden (eds), *Internet Encyclopedia of Philosophy*, at www.iep.utm.edu.

W. D. Hudson (ed.), *The Is/Ought Question*, London: Macmillan, 1969.

David Hume, *A Treatise of Human Nature*, Mineola, NY: Dover Publications, 2003.

David Hume, *An Enquiry Concerning Human Understanding*, ed. T. L. Beauchamp, Oxford and New York: Oxford University Press, 1999.

David Hume, *Dialogues Concerning Natural Religion*, ed. R. H. Popkin, second edition, Indianapolis/Cambridge: Hackett Publishing Company, 1998.

David Hume, *My Own Life* (1776: ed. J. Lynch) http://ethnicity. rutgers.edu/~jlynch/Texts/humelife.html.

D. Mills Daniel, *Briefly: Hume's An Enquiry Concerning Human Understanding*, London: SCM Press, 2007.

W. E. Morris, 'David Hume' (revised 2009), in E. N. Zalta (ed.), *Stanford Encyclopaedia of Philosophy*, at http://plato. stanford.edu.

E. C. Mossner, *The Life of David Hume*, second edition, Oxford and New York: Oxford University Press, 1980.

14

Jean-Jacques Rousseau
(1712–78)
The social contract and the general will
Interpreting the idea of the general will

Context

Should our opinion of a philosopher influence our assessment of his ideas? Probably not: but even those who agree with his ideas will find little to applaud in Rousseau's character or conduct. Unlike John Locke, Thomas Paine or John Stuart Mill, there is nothing admirable or exemplary about the way he led his life. He was quarrelsome, paranoid, as shown in his treatment of David Hume, who was trying to help him, he switched between Protestantism and Roman Catholicism for reasons seemingly unrelated to religious conviction, and was relentlessly self-pitying. Yes, he had an unhappy childhood, but sympathy for him is inevitably tempered by his own behaviour as a parent. Handing over to an orphanage the five children he had with his mistress, Thérèse le Vasseur, cannot have contributed to their happiness, or even any degree of life expectancy.

A product of the age of Enlightenment, and an associate of Diderot and Voltaire, Rousseau's ideas were largely at odds with Enlightenment thinking. So far from celebrating reason and the benefits of civilization, his first major philosophical work, the *Discourse on the Sciences and Arts*, takes the opposite view. In his entry for a competition, run by the Academy of Dijon, about whether the revival of the arts and sciences had improved morality, Rousseau argues that they produce ambition and vanity, and cause a decline in moral standards. In his *Discourse on the Origin of Inequality*, he offers a very different account of what human beings are like in the state of nature from that of Thomas Hobbes in *Leviathan*. He puts forward the concept of the noble savage and ideas about nature and feelings which helped to inspire the romantic movement. Human beings are naturally good, and selfishness and inequality the products of civilization. The human instinct for self-preservation, which Rousseau calls 'self love', does not necessarily lead to aggression towards others, because we also have a natural instinct of pity, which makes us want to alleviate suffering.

So why do we have inequality and the other evils which afflict human relationships? Unlike animals, human beings possess reason. We are conscious of our freedom and ability to make choices, so we want to leave the state of nature and create societies on the basis of mutual obligations. We can see the advantages, but fail to appreciate the risks. According to Rousseau, the first person who encloses a piece of ground, claims it as his, and then discovers that other people are willing to accept this expropriation, establishes civil society. However, this sort of society is generally worse than the state of nature. It institutionalizes selfishness, greed and oppression, and destroys our natural compassion. In contrast to the harmless, self-preserving instinct of self-love, Rousseau calls the destructive competitiveness and the drive for recognition by, and superiority over, others, which is widespread in such a society, 'love of self'.

Jean-Jacques Rousseau (1712–78)

By forming the wrong kind of society, human beings have enslaved themselves. Our laws and political institutions protect privilege, empower the rich, subjugate the poor, and banish liberty. In his *The Social Contract*, Rousseau explores a different sort of society from the one inhabited by the majority, based on a legitimate social contract, which secures equality and freedom, and develops his concept of the general will, which he introduced in his *Discourse on Political Economy*; and these are the key ideas discussed below.

In *Émile: or, On Education*, Rousseau outlines ideas which have since been popular with child-centred educationalists. Émile's education is not designed to teach him a formal, academic curriculum, but to foster his natural inclination towards goodness and to produce a well-integrated moral being who will not be subject to the destructive impulses of love of self. However, male and female education will not follow exactly the same pattern, as Rousseau believes that men and women have specific, gender-determined roles in society. Like *The Social Contract*, the book was banned in France, because of its endorsement of natural religion at the expense of traditional Christian teaching. In *Reveries of the Solitary Walker*, Rousseau reflects on his life, the positive contribution his ideas have made and the lack of appreciation for them. The autobiographical *The Confessions* provides a frank account of Rousseau's life, including such ignominious episodes as the way he disposed of his children.

Life

The son of a watchmaker, Isaac Rousseau, Jean-Jacques Rousseau was born in Geneva, a Protestant city associated

146

with John Calvin, one of the leaders of the Reformation. His unhappy childhood probably embittered him. His mother died shortly after his birth and he was brought up by an aunt. When his father was forced to flee from Geneva for fighting a duel, Rousseau was apprenticed to an engraver in 1725. He hated it and decided to leave Geneva in 1728. He had been introduced to a Roman Catholic noblewoman, Louise-Eleanore de la Tour du Pil, Baronne de Warens, who specialized in persuading Protestants to convert. Through her influence, Rousseau went to Turin, where he was received into the Roman Catholic Church. In 1731, he returned to the Baronne, trained as a music copier and teacher and made up for gaps in his education by extensive reading. He and the Baronne became lovers, but in 1742 he moved on to Paris to seek his fortune.

In 1743, he was appointed secretary to the Comte de Montaigne, the French ambassador to Venice, but, temperamentally quarrelsome, and feeling that he was being treated as a mere servant, he fell out with his employer. Back in Paris, in 1744, he met the philosopher and playwright Voltaire, and became a friend and associate of the philosopher Denis Diderot, the editor of the *Encyclopédie*, which brought together articles containing innovative and anti-clerical ideas on a range of philosophical, scientific and other subjects. Rousseau became a contributor, and also began to build a reputation as a composer.

In 1749, Rousseau won a prize offered by the Academy of Dijon for an essay on whether the revival of the arts and sciences had done more to corrupt or purify morals. Controversially, Rousseau took the former view, winning the prize, and becoming an instant celebrity. He also formed a relationship with a servant-girl, Thérèse le Vasseur. They had five children together, all of whom were sent to an orphanage.

In 1753, he entered the Dijon competition again. His essay, 'A Discourse Upon the Origin and Foundation of the Inequality Among Mankind', argued that the problems of the human situation arise from human beings living in an over-sophisticated and luxurious society, where their benevolent instincts are repressed, and they are deprived of the happiness and innocence of the state of nature. Although it did not win, it was published in 1758.

Between 1756 and 1762, Rousseau lived in Montmorency, producing his novel *La Nouvelle Heloise* (1761), *Émile: or, On Education* (1762) and *The Social Contract* (1762). By this time, the hostility his writings had aroused in France forced him to move back to Geneva, where he re-converted to Protestantism. However, his books were denounced and banned there too, and in 1763, he gave up his Genevan citizenship. He spent the rest of his life travelling around Europe, including England, which he visited in 1766 with David Hume, who tried to befriend him. However, increasingly paranoid and unreasonable, Rousseau quarrelled with Hume and, despite fears of arrest, returned to France. He died in Ermenonville, where he was a guest of the Marquis de Girardin. Other books, such as *Considerations on the Government of Poland*, *The Confessions* and *Reveries of the Solitary Walker*, were published after his death.

Key ideas

The social contract and the general will

Rousseau says that human beings are born free but are everywhere in chains. Why is this so? Because of the kind of societies we have created. Human beings reach a point where the disadvantages of life in the state of nature out-weigh its benefits. Even the strongest individual cannot always defend him- or herself, so there need to be laws regulating conduct, to prevent people harming each other. An association, a civil society, needs to be formed. But, for Rousseau, the challenge is not just finding a form of asso-ciation that will protect each member's person and goods. It must also allow each member to obey only himself and remain as free as in the state of nature. The social contract, which binds all members of society to obey its laws, should preserve liberty while ensuring security. However, people have overlooked the pitfalls, and existing society delivers the opposite of what was intended. Based on arbitrary power and the rule of the strongest, it imposes a situation of slavery and wretchedness on most of its members.

Can there be a society which will unite its members and harness their collective power, in order to protect each individ-ual's person and property, but which will retain the freedom of the state of nature? In his *The Social Contract*, Rousseau propounds a solution to this fundamental problem. When the social contract is formed, each individual submits his person to the community. A collective body is thus created, and a par-ticular state comes into being. As individuals, its members are citizens, in so far as they share in the sovereign power of the state, but they are also subjects, in so far as they put themselves under the state's laws. Thus, in Rousseau's con-ception of the social contract, the act of association consists of a reciprocal commitment between society and the individual. Each person in fact makes a contract with himself and is thus doubly committed: as a member of the sovereign body in rela-tion to the individuals that comprise society and as a member of the state in relation to the sovereign power.

As the state's sovereign power derives from and consists of the individuals who compose it, it cannot have any interest contrary to theirs, while the sovereign power does not need to give guarantees to its individual subjects, because it is impossible for it to wish to hurt all of its members or any particular member. Problems only arise when an individual (or individuals) has a private will that is contrary to the general will he shares as a citizen. As individuals, they may try to enjoy the rights of a citizen without performing the duties of a subject. To prevent the social contract being an empty formula, it is implicit in the commitment each individual makes that whoever refuses to obey its general will shall be constrained to do so by the whole of society. This is what Rousseau describes as being forced to be free.

By participating in society, the individual sacrifices some of the advantages of the state of nature, but gains far more than he loses. His rights to life and property are respected by other members of the state, and protected by its collective force against outsiders. So far from destroying natural rights, the social contract substitutes moral and lawful equality for the inequalities that nature imposes, so that although they are unequal in strength and intelligence, members of society become equal as a result of it.

Interpreting the idea of the general will

For Rousseau, to renounce one's freedom is to renounce one's humanity, and freedom is only possible in a state where the general will of all its members is directed towards achieving the end for which it was established: the common good. Thus, the term 'general will' encapsulates Rousseau's conception of the state and its sovereign power and also both how this power should be exercised and how it will in fact be exercised. This is perhaps where confusion arises. No society or state, however perfectly conceived, will invariably serve its members' common interests; but Rousseau's account of the general will glides between how the state ought to operate and how it does operate, without marking this crucial distinction.

Further, there are important respects in which Rousseau's conception of the state and the general will is at variance with the values of modern, democratic, pluralistic society. He explains that it is the conflict between private interests which makes the creation of civil society necessary. Once it exists, and a social bond unites its members, private interests must be given up, and society governed on the basis of common interests. Of course, the members of any society have to sacrifice some of their private interests for it to exist or function at all, but, in Western democracies, they still pursue them within a framework of laws and mutual obligations. Rousseau does not see it this way. In the society he envisages, the general will, serving the common interest, should eliminate private wills serving private interests. Thus, the individual becomes subsumed in the state and is free only to the extent he or she is an equal participant in the general will. This is a very different view of individual freedom, individual rights and the relationship between the state and the individual from those of Locke and John Stuart Mill.

Indeed, Rousseau is emphatic about the need to curb the private will. The general will always promotes the public good and equality, but those of individuals or groups do not. Society cannot permit organizations capable of becoming alternative sources of authority or objects of allegiance. If groups or sectional associations are formed, the will of each of them will become general in relation to its own members, but private in relation to the state. In an often quoted passage, Rousseau contrasts what he calls the will of all with the general will. The latter's concern is solely with the common interest, but the will of all pursues private interests, being no more than the sum of individual desires. Members of society share an overriding common interest, which can only be served through their general will, and, however numerous and pressing their individual desires and private interests may be, they must sacrifice them to it.

Rousseau maintains that, since the general will can only be exercised by all the members of a society, there are implications for the way it is to be governed. He seems to be saying that there must be direct democracy; a delegated system, such as representative democracy, is unacceptable. He also insists that the social contract gives society absolute power over its members. Are there any limits? Only that they may do as they please with such goods and freedom as are left to them after they have fulfilled their obligations to society. Rousseau does envisage a degree of religious liberty. There will be a civil religion, to reinforce social unity, but the state will tolerate the individual beliefs of those who are themselves tolerant; but not of atheists, whose refusal to subscribe to the state religion makes them unreliable citizens.

Impact

- Rousseau's view that human beings are naturally inclined to goodness and compassion had an enormous impact on the romantic movement and on those who believe that people should be guided by their emotions, rather than their reason.

- He identifies, and seeks to resolve, the key question of how to reconcile the role of the state as the protector of life and property with individual freedom, although his solution is unacceptable to libertarians.
- His concept of the general will encapsulates the view that society is formed, and exists, to promote the common good of all its members, even though this role may conflict with the interests of individual members or groups within it.
- His conception of society does not accord with the nature of a modern, democratic, pluralist society, and, whatever his intention, appears to have elements of totalitarianism.

Further reading

C. Bertram, 'Jean-Jacques Rousseau' (2010), in E. N. Zalta (ed.), *Stanford Encyclopaedia of Philosophy*, at http://plato.stanford.edu.

A. Cobban, *Rousseau and the Modern State*, second edition, London: Allen & Unwin, 1964.

L. Damrosch, *Jean-Jacques Rousseau, Restless Genius*, New York: Houghton Mifflin Harcourt, 2007.

J. J. Delaney, 'Jean-Jacques Rousseau' (updated 2005), in J. Fieser and B. Dowden (eds), *Internet Encyclopedia of Philosophy*, at www.iep.utm.edu.

Jean-Jacques Rousseau, *Émile*, Teddington: The Echo Library, 2007.

Jean-Jacques Rousseau, *Reveries of the Solitary Walker*, trans. P. France, London: Penguin, 1979.

Jean-Jacques Rousseau, *The Basic Political Writings* ('Discourse on the Sciences and Arts', 'Discourse on Inequality', 'Discourse on Political Economy', 'On the Social Contract'), trans. and ed. D. A. Cress, Indianapolis/Cambridge: Hackett Publishing Company, 1987.

Jean-Jacques Rousseau, *The Confessions*, trans. J. M. Cohen, London: Penguin, 2005.

Jean-Jacques Rousseau, *The Social Contract*, ed. M. Cranston, Harmondsworth: Penguin, 1968.

D. Thomson, 'Rousseau and the General Will', in D. Thomson (ed.), *Political Ideas*, Harmondsworth: Penguin, 1966.

15

Immanuel Kant
(1724–1804)
Deontological ethics and the categorical imperative of morality
Moral freedom and responsibility

Context

Is Kant a rationalist or an empiricist? To the empiricist, experience is the only or main source of knowledge. For the rationalist, we only discover truth through reason. Both cannot be right. Rationalists must explain the role of the senses in gaining knowledge; empiricists have to account for our general categories of thought, such as space, time, substance and causation, which enable us to organize the information we receive through our senses. Do these also come from experience? Locke's answer is that we arrive at them through a process of abstraction from experience. Kant's is very different: although knowledge begins with experience, it does not all come from it.

In his *Critique of Pure Reason*, Kant maintains that there are strict limits to our theoretical knowledge of the world. This is because we structure our sense experience, by imposing upon it what he calls the *a priori* intuitions of time and space.

Sense experience is then thought about by means of the *a priori* categories of the understanding, such as causality, reality and necessity. Thus, so far from originating in experience, as empiricists believe, the *a priori* intuitions and categories originate in human beings themselves and determine how we experience the world. Therefore, no legitimate inference can be made from them to what the world is like in itself. But, Kant also rejects the rationalist view that human beings have a faculty of intellectual intuition, which gives us direct knowledge of ultimate reality.

Kant's position is that the theoretical reason cannot go beyond the limits of human experience and prove the existence of suprasensible beings, such as God. Nor can there be direct intuition of such beings. Thus, speculative metaphysics, which tries to go beyond experience and establish the nature of ultimate reality, cannot succeed. Only a limited kind of metaphysics, which describes or analyses how we experience the world and the concepts we use, in order to be able to do so, is possible. In the *Critique of Pure Reason*, Kant also provides a detailed refutation of the traditional arguments for God's existence: the ontological, cosmological and design arguments. In fact, as he explains in the *Critique of Practical Reason*, we have to depend on the practical reason, which is reason directed towards moral issues, for what we can know of God and suprasensible reality. However, he warns that we must not try to erect metaphysical theories about God and ultimate reality on the basis of knowledge that we possess solely for moral purposes.

But, what is the link between God and morality? Kant argues that there are certain things that the practical reason needs to postulate or assume, in order to make complete sense of morality. These postulates of the practical reason are freedom, immortality of the soul and God. In his *Groundwork of the Metaphysics of Moral*, he maintains that the principles of the moral law, which unconditionally bind all rational beings, including human beings, are not to be found in human nature, or in any part of our ordinary experience, but are discovered *a priori*, through our reason. In order to have wills which are our own, and to be able to adopt maxims or rules of conduct, which comply with the categorical imperative of the moral law, and to be responsible for our actions, we must be free. Kant's concepts of the categorical imperative and moral freedom and responsibility are the two key ideas discussed in this chapter.

We can see why freedom is so important to morality, but why do we need God and immortality? It seems particularly strange, given Kant's stress on the independence of morality and the importance of excluding any extraneous elements from moral decision-making. He insists that we must not allow our wills to be determined by considerations other than the fitness of our rules of conduct to serve as universal moral laws for all rational beings, the obvious sources of spurious moral principles being such empirical factors as human desires and inclinations. However, they would also arise if moral principles are taken from an all-perfect divine will. Kant's point is that the autonomy of morality means that actions are not right just because they satisfy certain human desires, maximize happiness or, even, because they reflect God's will.

But, although the supreme good for all rational beings is to obey the moral law for its own sake, and so be worthy of happiness, our concept of the highest good also includes the notion of the complete good, where we receive happiness in proportion to our moral virtue. Therefore Kant argues that the practical reason needs to postulate God, as the means of ensuring receipt of the happiness we deserve; and also immortality, to give us the opportunity to become worthy of happiness, through developing wills, which do not need to be commanded, in order to obey the moral law. For purposes of morality, therefore, reason, in its practical use, can provide what reason in its theoretical or speculative use cannot: some knowledge of God and suprasensible reality.

Life

Immanuel Kant, regarded by many as the greatest philosopher of the modern era, was born in Königsberg, East Prussia. Although not from a wealthy background, Kant was able to attend the town's Collegium Fredericianum, and he enrolled at the University of Königsberg in 1740, where his interests included science and astronomy, as well as philosophy. After graduating, he worked as a tutor for a number of years, before returning to Königsberg as a *Privatdozent* (lecturer) at the university in 1755. After turning down a professorship at the University of Jena, he became professor of logic and metaphysics at Königsberg in 1770.

Even if we regard pursuit of philosophical enquiry as involving much study-bound reflection, Kant's life was particularly uneventful. In many ways, it was exactly what we would expect that of a professional philosopher to be. Apart from his teaching responsibilities at the university, where his lectures covered such subjects as physics, geography and anthropology, he gave himself almost entirely to study, thought and writing. In order to use his time efficiently, he rose before five o'clock in the morning, and followed a strict daily routine, allocating fixed periods of time to each activity. However, despite the pressures on time, imposed by his work and his enormous literary output in the latter part of his life, he was not reclusive, and, although he did not travel outside Germany, he enjoyed the company of others and conversation.

His philosophical development divides into two periods: the pre-critical period, which lasted more or less until his appointment as professor at Königsberg; and his critical period, during which he wrote the books that have made him famous. Until the early 1770s, Kant seems to have accepted the philosophical system of Christian Wolff, the principal exponent of Leibniz's philosophy, which he had been taught by Martin Knutzen, a professor at Königsberg when Kant was a student. However, particularly through the influence of Hume, he underwent what he describes as a Copernican revolution, coming to believe that human beings will always experience objects in a particular way, because of the way that the human mind is constructed.

Due to his unorthodox views, some of Kant's philosophical and theological ideas also proved controversial when they were published. In 1794, the government of the religiously conservative King Frederick William II of Prussia, in response to his *Religion Within the Boundaries of Mere Reason*, which questioned aspects of biblical teaching, Christian theology and church organization, instructed him not to write about religion. Kant felt bound to comply with this order until Frederick William's death in 1797. Kant was also an opponent of war and militarism and an advocate of peaceful methods of resolving international issues.

Kant's books include *Critique of Pure Reason* (1781; second edition, 1787), *Prolegomena to any Future Metaphysic* (1783), *Groundwork of the Metaphysics of Morals* (1785), *Critique of Practical Reason* (1788), *Critique of Judgement* (1790), *Religion Within the Boundaries of Mere Reason* (1793), *On Perpetual Peace* (1795) and *Metaphysics of Morals* (1797).

Immanuel Kant (1724–1804)

Key ideas

Deontological ethics and the categorical imperative of morality

What makes actions right? For some moral philosophers, it is their consequences, such as the pleasure or happiness they produce. For deontologists, like Kant, however, rightness relates to the action itself and to our obligation to perform it. We have a duty to perform actions, such as keeping promises or not harming others, because of their intrinsic rightness.

Why do they think consequentialism fails? First, there is the impossibility of calculating all the consequences of actions into the future. Also, many actions, such as persecuting minority groups, may make many people happy but are still wrong. Kant also points out that happiness, which many consequentialists regard as the only thing desirable as an end, is an indeterminate concept that means different things to different people and depends on empirical elements that cannot be guaranteed.

How does Kant's deontological system work? Only rational beings possess a will and the ability to act according to moral principles (what Kant calls the moral law) which come from the reason. Intention is important. To act morally, we must apply moral principles for their own sake and not for other motives, such as personal advantage. As inclinations and interests may clash with the moral law, we often have to overcome them, in order to do the right thing. For this reason, and because we are imperfect human beings whose wills are influenced by other factors, the moral law has to take the form of commands or imperatives, which we ought to perform.

Kant explains the difference between hypothetical and moral imperatives. The former are conditional, indicating an action necessary for achieving an optional end. But, moral imperatives are unconditional or categorical, commanding actions that are necessary in themselves, for no rational being can opt out of morality. Kant gives various formulations of the categorical imperative of morality. The first is to act only in accordance with a moral precept that we can will as a universal law for all rational beings. But, could this formulation allow adoption of outrageously immoral rules of conduct? Taken by itself, perhaps, but it is an important test of moral principles. If they cannot function as universal moral laws, applicable to all rational beings, they should be rejected.

Kant observes that the will is determined by an end. But, most of our ends have only relative worth, in relation to particular desires, so cannot be the source of universal moral principles and categorical imperatives. An end in itself, which has absolute worth, is needed. This yields another formulation of the categorical imperative: that the only things with absolute worth are human and all rational beings. This is a convincing basis of morality. Even if we are consequentialists, why should we worry about others' happiness, unless we value other human beings?

Kant goes much further. Human beings have absolute worth, and every maxim we adopt should lead only to actions that always treat humanity, whether ourselves or others, as ends in themselves, and never simply as means to achieving our own ends. Kant provides a compelling image of how we should discharge our moral responsibilities with his idea of all rational beings regarding themselves as members of a kingdom of ends, acting as if they are adopting maxims which are to serve as universal laws for all rational beings, and treating themselves and others as ends not means.

Immanuel Kant (1724–1804)

Moral freedom and responsibility

Kant maintains that, to function as moral beings, that is, to have wills which are their own, and to be able to adopt as their rules of conduct the universal categorical imperatives of the moral law, human beings must be free. But, how can human beings be free when subject to the causality of laws of nature? Kant accepts that we cannot prove our freedom. However, he accounts for it by invoking his important distinction between the world of sense: things as they appear to us, because of the kind of beings we are, of which our senses give us knowledge and within which our actions are determined by desires and inclinations; and the world of understanding or the intelligible world: things as they are in themselves, to which, because we possess reason, human beings belong.

Therefore, there are two standpoints from which to view our relationship with the moral law. As part of the world of sense, we are subject to laws of nature, but as part of the world of understanding, we freely subject ourselves to moral laws, which come from the reason and which are independent of nature. It is because we are part of the world of sense and our actions are determined by desires and inclinations, that moral laws have to be expressed as imperatives.

Kant does not play down the difficulties of his analysis. The claim that we are free seems to contradict the natural necessity of laws of nature. While freedom is a mere idea of reason, laws of nature are an objective reality. But, we cannot give up the idea of freedom, which is essential if there is going to be moral responsibility. We just have to accept that, although we cannot explain it, there actually is no contradiction between holding that beings, subject to the laws of nature, are also independent of them and capable of freely obeying moral laws given by the reason.

Therefore, Kant is an unequivocal upholder of freewill, completely dismissing the determinist view that human beings, as rational beings, cannot freely choose how to act. This includes rejection of the soft determinism of Hobbes, Locke and Hume: that we are free, if we are not subject to external coercion and are able to act in accordance with our inclinations. This is an equivocation; it waters freedom down, and makes it meaningless. For Kant, freedom means our being able to overcome these inclinations, so that we have a genuine choice as to whether to perform or not perform an action. Only if we have this kind of freedom, can we be held responsible for our actions.

Kant's claim may be unprovable, as he admits, but it does accord with our experience. We know that we are subject to inclinations, which sometimes impel us to behave in ways that are wrong and which harm others. But, we are also aware of being able to reason and obey the moral laws, which will enable us to overcome those inclinations. The extent to which we obey the moral laws of reason, or succumb to our inclinations, could be regarded as the measure of how far we are fully rational members of the world of understanding.

Impact

- Kant's argument that happiness is an indeterminate concept, which cannot serve as a satisfactory basis for formulating moral principles or rules, remains a serious objection to utilitarianism.
- The first formulation of the categorical imperative provides an important test of moral principles: those which cannot function as universal moral laws, which apply to all rational beings, should be rejected.

- It is hard to see any point in having moral principles or trying to behave morally, unless we accept the second formulation of the categorical imperative: that human beings have absolute worth and must always be treated as ends, never simply as means.
- Kant gives cogent expression to the freewillist view that, unless we are free, and capable of overcoming our inclinations, we cannot be held responsible for our actions, and exposes the equivocal nature of soft determinism.

Further reading

Immanuel Kant, *Critique of Practical Reason*, trans. W. S. Pluhar, Indianapolis/Cambridge: Hackett, 2002.

Immanuel Kant, *Critique of Pure Reason*, ed. V. Politis, London: Everyman, 1993.

Immanuel Kant, *Groundwork of the Metaphysics of Morals*, ed. M. Gregor, Cambridge: Cambridge University Press, 1997.

Immanuel Kant, *Religion with the Boundaries of Mere Reason*, eds A. Wood and G. Di Giovanni, Cambridge: Cambridge University Press, 1998.

F. C. Copleston, *A History of Philosophy*, Vol. 6, Part I (The French Enlightenment to Kant) and Part II (Kant), New York: Image Books, 1964.

R. Johnson, 'Kant's Moral Philosophy' (revised 2008), in E. N. Zalta (ed.), *Stanford Encyclopaedia of Philosophy*, at http://plato.stanford.edu.

M. McCormick, *Immanuel Kant: Metaphysics* (updated 2005), in J. Fieser and B. Dowden (eds), *Internet Encyclopedia of Philosophy*, at www.iep.utm.edu.

D. Mills Daniel, *Briefly: Kant's Critique of Practical Reason (The Concept of the Highest Good and the Postulates of the Practical Reason)*, London: SCM Press, 2009.

D. Mills Daniel, *Briefly: Kant's Groundwork of the Metaphysics of Morals*, London: SCM Press, 2006.

D. Mills Daniel, *Briefly: Kant's Religion with the Boundaries of Mere Reason*, London: SCM Press, 2007.

H. J. Paton, *The Categorical Imperative*, Philadelphia: University of Pennsylvania Press, 1971.

M. Rohlf, 'Immanuel Kant' (2010), in E. N. Zalta (ed.), *Stanford Encyclopaedia of Philosophy*, at http://plato.stanford.edu.

16

Thomas Paine
(1737–1809)
The past cannot bind the present
Democracy, representative government
and human rights

Context

Is Tom Paine a philosopher? A propagandist, radical, campaigner for freedom, equality, justice and peace, yes: but a philosopher? It is not the first category into which one would put him. But philosophy is about ideas, and Paine put forward some very important ideas about human rights, the nature of government and society and how they should be organized, which have had a fundamental impact on thinking about these issues. We should also not think of philosophers as people who theorize in isolation from the hurly-burly of life. Paine played a major role in the American Revolution and War of Independence and was actively involved in the French Revolution; and much of what he wrote was intended as propaganda or responses to his critics. However, this does not devalue his ideas as serious contributions to political thought, any more than it does those of John Locke.

Paine had been involved in political campaigning, for his fellow excise officers, before he left for Philadelphia in 1774, but it was in America, as relations between the colonies and Britain degenerated into armed conflict, that he achieved fame as a propagandist for the American cause. In his pamphlet *Common Sense*, he maintains the impossibility of any reconciliation with Britain. In ousting James II, in 1689, and inviting William and Mary to become its monarchs, the English nation had ended absolute monarchy, but, in the third quarter of the eighteenth century, the English Constitution remained unacceptably flawed.

Based on a hereditary, undemocratic system, it allowed the king and the nobility, though unaccountable to the people, to wield great power, through the royal exercise of patronage, used to obtain support in the House of Commons and the House of Lords. The Commons, though elected, was not democratic. Only those who met certain property qualifications were able to vote for its members. And, voting in open hustings, instead of by secret ballot, encouraged bribery and manipulation of the electorate. There were also rotten boroughs, with no or very few voters, and pocket boroughs, where the landowner decided who would be the MP.

Paine subjects the principle of heredity in government, the most extreme expression of which is the doctrine of the Divine Right of Kings, to withering attack. Even if God chose a particular person to rule, at a particular point in history, this would not entitle his successors to govern after him: God would need to choose again on each monarch's death. Hereditary monarchy also clashed with social contract theory: one generation agreeing that a particular person should govern cannot bind future generations. Paine points to the results of monarchical government in England: wars and the impoverishment of the people. America should do things differently, and entrust sovereignty to the people, who alone are entitled to exercise it. Only independence can unite Americans of different origins and views, and their mission should be to oppose tyranny and to embrace freedom, which is under threat everywhere.

In his celebrated book *Rights of Man*, Paine defends the French Revolution against its critics, particularly Edmund Burke, developing his case against established forms of government and the hereditary principle, and contending passionately for democracy, equality and human rights; and these key ideas are discussed below. Elsewhere in the book, Paine, on the utilitarian grounds of maximizing general happiness, argues for policies now taken for granted in a democratic welfare state: lower taxes for the poor, free education for their children, old-age pensions and schemes to provide employment. In *Agrarian Justice*, he addresses the injustices of land ownership and the social obligations of those who own a disproportionate share of a nation's wealth.

How is Paine viewed today? Given his courageous advocacy of democracy, social justice and human rights, and his contribution to the American and French Revolutions, he shoul be widely honoured. But, opinions of him vary. To the former Labour leader and President of the Thomas Paine Society, Michael Foot, he was 'the greatest exile' ever forced to leave Britain, but for President Theodore Roosevelt, he was a 'filthy little atheist'. Indeed, in the United States, whose debt to Paine is so great, his major role in achieving American independence does not seem to be fully appreciated. One reason may be that Paine's ideas on the meaning of democracy and equality remain too radical for American tastes. The other concerns Paine's religious views. Though no atheist, he was, like other leaders of the American Revolution, such as George Washington and Thomas Jefferson, a deist. However, he was an outspoken and uncompromising one, who, in *The Age of Reason*, rejects such Christian dogmas as the redemption as derogatory of God and unedifying to human beings. For Paine, God is simply the first cause of the universe, and religious duty consists of believing in one God, showing mercy to one's fellow creatures, and trying to make them happy.

Life

Born in Thetford, Norfolk, and educated at Thetford Grammar School, Paine was then apprenticed to his father, a staymaker. After unsuccessful attempts to run away to sea, he served on a privateer at the start of the Seven Years War between Britain and France. In 1759, he established a staymaking business in Sandwich, Kent, and married his first wife, Mary Lambert. However, when the enterprise failed and his wife died, Paine became an exciseman in Lincolnshire. Dismissed for incompetence, he took up teaching, before returning to the excise service in 1768. Based in Lewes for the next six years, he joined the town council, married a widow, Elizabeth Ollive, and ran a shop with her. But, a growing interest in politics led him to take up the issue of excise officers' low pay. After going to London to make the excisemen's case and lobby MPs, he was dismissed for unauthorized absence from duty.

With a second business failure, bankruptcy and separation from his wife, Paine's life reached a crisis. In 1774, he left for America with a letter of recommendation from Benjamin Franklin, Pennsylvania's representative in Britain, and joined the *Pennsylvania Magazine* in Philadelphia. Arriving when friction between Britain and the colonies, over taxation and other issues, was flaring into armed conflict, Paine embraced the cause of independence wholeheartedly. His 1776 pamphlet *Common Sense*, arguing the case for independence, had an immense impact, probably helping to bring about the Declaration of Independence. He went on waging a propaganda campaign against Britain through his magazine *Crisis*.

Paine was secretary to the Congressional Committee on Foreign Affairs (1777–9), and, as clerk to the Pennsylvania Assembly, may have drafted the preamble to its 1780 Act abolishing slavery. In 1781, he went to France, to seek support for America. France's intervention contributed to the British Navy's loss of control of the seas and to Britain's ultimate defeat. The state of New York recognized Paine's contribution to American independence by giving him a farm in New Rochelle, where he devoted himself to scientific research: into an iron bridge and a smokeless candle.

In 1787, Paine went to France and Britain, and published his *Prospects on the Rubicon*, urging peaceful relations between the two countries. After the outbreak of the French Revolution, in 1789, he was invited to go to France, and became a member of the French Convention. Parts I and II of his *Rights of Man* appeared in 1791 and 1792. However, he was now in trouble on both sides of the Channel. Declared an outlaw in Britain for his revolutionary ideas, he clashed with the extremists in France, by opposing Louis XVI's execution, in 1793. Narrowly avoiding execution, he was only released from prison, in 1794, following intervention by the US representative in France and future President, James Monroe.

Paine completed *The Age of Reason* in 1795. He also wrote *The Decline and Fall of the English System of Finance* (1796), a *Letter to George Washington* (1797), in which he complained about the US President's indifference to his plight as a prisoner in France, and *Agrarian Justice* (1797). In 1802, the Treaty of Amiens brought a brief peace between France and Britain, and he returned to the United States. But, his criticisms of Christianity in *The Age of Reason* led to hostility towards him in America. In his remaining years, he took to drink and led a rather solitary and impoverished existence at New Rochelle and in New York, where he died.

Key ideas

The past cannot bind the present

In November 1789, the philosopher and dissenting minister Dr Richard Price preached to the Society for Commemorating the Revolution in Great Britain, to mark the anniversary of the Glorious Revolution of 1688. This same year had seen the fall of the Bastille, and in his sermon, 'A Discourse on the Love of Our Country', Price discussed true patriotism, which is not trying to ensure dominion over other nations, but promoting truth, virtue and liberty. He warned against the attitude of adulation that people adopt towards governments, thus inviting despotism. Civil governments are their people's servants; their authority that of the community which gives it to them. The lesson of the Glorious Revolution was that, in overthrowing James II and replacing him with William and Mary, the country had been saved from tyranny. The people of England had gained three fundamental rights: liberty of conscience in religious matters; the right to resist power when abused by those exercising it; and that of choosing their own government, removing it for misconduct, and devising their own form of government. This last right did not belong to individuals, but to the whole nation. Price urged on his listeners awareness that the Glorious Revolution had not left the constitution in a perfect state. A genuinely representative government had not yet been achieved, so there was only the appearance, not the reality, of liberty.

In his *Reflections on the Revolution in France* (1790), Edmund Burke challenged Price's interpretation. James II had been rightly deprived of his crown for misconduct, but he denied that monarchs receive their right to rule from the people. The act for settling the crown on William and Mary had removed the nation's right to make any further changes: the Lords and Commons had declared, in the name of all the people, that they and their posterity submitted themselves to William and Mary and their heirs for ever. Thus, even if the right to elect kings belonged to the nation before the Revolution, it had been permanently renounced in 1689.

Paine dismissed Burke's arguments in *Rights of Man*. The claim that Parliament, by its declaration at the time of the Glorious Revolution, had bound the nation to accept and obey the monarch to the end of time was ridiculous. No legislature or group of people, in any country, at any time, had the right to make decisions for future generations, and thus to determine a nation's form of government down the centuries. Any such attempts are null and void. The parliament of 1688 had no right to bind future generations, or even to control the present one.

Trying to govern beyond the grave was the most absurd of all tyrannies. One human being has no rights over another, nor is one generation entitled to decide what succeeding generations will do. When a human being, or a whole generation, ceases to be, so does its powers and views. It has no share in the concerns of this world, and lacks any authority to decide who will govern a nation, or how it will be governed. A nation has the right to do whatever it chooses. What count are the wishes and rights of the living. Their freedom cannot be controlled or willed away by the dead. Yet, this was what Burke wanted. The parliament of 1688 might as well have legislated that its members should live for ever, as to try to make their authority do so.

Democracy, representative government and human rights

In *Rights of Man*, Paine also champions political equality and democracy. Government, the management of a nation's affairs, cannot be the property of any one man or family. However, in Britain and elsewhere, the nation's rights have been usurped by force and turned into an inheritance. But, this does not change what is right. Every citizen has a share in sovereignty, which belongs to the whole nation; so no individual or group is entitled to any authority not expressly derived from it. The nation is always entitled to abolish any form of government and set up a different one that it believes will better suit its interests and promote its well-being.

Further, Paine argues that history shows that intellectual abilities are not distributed according to social class. Unless states are governed in a way that reflects this fact of nature, they will be badly ruled, because they do not allow some of their most able people a part in running their affairs. Direct democracy, where each citizen votes on every issue, is the basis for establishing an acceptable form of government. However, it is incapable of extension, due to the inconvenience of its form. By grafting the representative system onto democracy, a form of government is produced that is capable of embracing and bringing together the whole nation and of satisfying its various interests. Representative government is calculated to produce the best laws, because it draws on the wisdom of the whole nation and is able to make its government the nation's common centre.

Paine also calls for recognition of natural or basic human rights, which each individual has by virtue of his or her existence as a human being, and which were clearly stated in the French National Assembly's *Declaration of the Rights of Man and of Citizens*: that human beings are born, and always continue to be, free and equal in respect of their rights. The purpose of creating a society is to preserve these natural and inalienable human rights, which are liberty, property, security and the right to resist oppression. Within society, individuals are entitled to pursue their own comfort and happiness, provided they do not harm the rights of others.

Paine contends that these natural human rights, which express the essential equality and inherent dignity of each individual human being, are the foundation of such civil rights as the right to vote and to participate in government, which all human beings are morally entitled to exercise, but which, both then and now, societies or states deny to their members. He would have strongly approved of the fact that his view of human rights, equality and dignity is enshrined in the Universal Declaration of Human Rights (1948), which, in its Preamble, affirms that freedom, justice and peace are based on fundamental human rights, the dignity and worth of the individual human being, and the equal rights of men and women; and, in Article 1, declares that all human beings are born free and equal in dignity and rights, and, as they are endowed with reason and conscience, should act towards one another in a spirit of brotherhood.

Impact

- Paine's life and work demonstrate that thinkers can also participate successfully in implementing their philosophical and political ideas.
- He made out a convincing case against having any hereditary element in government, as it is likely to be an obstacle to political and social reform.
- He issued an effective warning against allowing the form of government in the present to be determined by tradition or the decisions of previous generations.
- His consistent advocacy of individual freedom, representative democracy, human equality, social justice and human rights have inspired political and social reformers since his day, contributed to parliamentary reform, and find expression in the Universal Declaration of Human Rights.

Further reading

A. J. Ayer, *Thomas Paine*, London: Faber and Faber, 1989.

H. N. Brailsford, *Shelley, Godwin and Their Circle,* London: Oxford University Press, 1913.

Edmund Burke, *Reflections on the French Revolution and Other Essays* (Introduction by A. J. Grieve), London: J. M. Dent & Sons, 1910.

Michael Foot, *Debts of Honour*, London: Picador, 1981.

Bruce Kuklick (ed.), *Paine: Political Writings* (revised edition), Cambridge: Cambridge University Press, 2000.

New World Encyclopedia contributors, 'Thomas Paine', *New World Encyclopedia,* 3 April 2008, at www.newworldencyclo pedia.org/entry/Thomas_Paine?oldid=687242.

Thomas Paine (1737–1809)

Thomas Paine, *Rights of Man*, ed. Henry Collins, Harmondsworth: Penguin, 1971.

Thomas Paine, *Rights of Man*, Mineola, NY: Dover, 1999.

Thomas Paine Society UK at www.thomaspainesocietyuk.org.uk.

Richard Price, *A Discourse on the Love of our Country* (1789), at www.constitution.org/price/price_8.htm.

17

Jeremy Bentham
(1748–1832)
Utilitarian ethics: the maximization
of happiness
The rights of animals

Context

What was Jeremy Bentham's contribution to the far-reaching social progress and political reform that took place in nineteenth-century Britain? According to Bentham's most famous disciple, John Stuart Mill, he was largely responsible for the spirit of scrutiny and enquiry which led to it. By being the great questioner of the status quo, who subjected existing legal, political and social institutions to relentless examination and criticism, refusing to regard any as sacrosanct, he had helped to bring about major and fruitful reforms. His way of thinking and writings had fostered a climate of opinion that accepted nothing on the basis of authority. Opinions and attitudes that had been regarded as unchallengeable were forced to defend themselves, and found wanting. Bentham's empirical approach demanded that opinions be based on evidence, while he insisted that judgements be based on reason, not an appeal to tradition.

Jeremy Bentham (1748–1832)

In relation to the law, Bentham was scathingly critical of such widely held doctrines as natural law, natural rights and the idea of a social contract, dismissing them as erroneous and serious obstacles to reform. He advocated legal positivism, which, contrary to the views of Aquinas and others, holds that laws are not based on objective values, deriving from the nature of the world or the will of God, but are simply commands of the sovereign power, which can be the state or monarch. They are laws because they are enacted and enforced by the individual or body with the authority and power to do so. What are Bentham's arguments? Rights, he maintains, derive from laws, which are enacted by governments. Therefore, they presuppose governments, so cannot precede them. Unlike so-called natural rights, which are vague and capable of being interpreted in different ways, rights under law are specific. He also regards natural law doctrines as potentially subversive of law and government. As they purport to predate them, and to derive from the individual's status as a human being, or his or her being made in the image of God, they can be used to challenge existing laws, leading to social disorder and anarchy.

Bentham understands freedom negatively. Human beings are free, if they are not subject to external constraint and able to choose how they act. As Bentham rejects the idea of a social contract as the basis of civil society, laws and political institutions cannot be judged against life in a state of nature, which precedes the creation of social and political organizations. However, as laws restrict individual liberty, they are an evil: albeit a necessary one, if there is to be social order, rather than anarchy.

Bentham believes that nature has placed human beings under the control of the fundamental motivations of pleasure and pain. As we naturally always seek those things that give us pleasure, and avoid those that cause us pain, pleasure and pain do, as a matter of fact, provide our standards of good or bad, right or wrong. Therefore, we should accept the utilitarian view that pleasure is the only thing that is good in itself and determine our actions according to the utilitarian standard: that right actions are those which maximize pleasure or minimize pain. Bentham argues that collective human experience provides a kind of proof of utilitarianism: most people, on most occasions, do apply the utilitarian standard to their actions and use it to judge those of others. His version of utilitarianism, and the issues it raises, is one of the key ideas discussed below. The other is his application of utilitarianism to the issue of animal rights.

While there are legitimate philosophical criticisms of the ethical theories of consequentialism and utilitarianism, Bentham's role as an advocate and inspirer of much needed reforms must be acknowledged. However well late eighteenth- and early nineteenth-century Britain compared with the repressive autocracies across the English Channel, its political and legal systems were unrepresentative, inefficient and corrupt. A small minority monopolized power, while the vast majority had no say in how the country was run; little chance of securing justice in the courts of law; and few opportunities for economic and social advancement. By the end of the nineteenth century, Britain was a very different place, which had a lot to do with Bentham and utilitarianism.

By providing a helpful criterion for testing laws and political institutions, and insisting that they operated in a way that promoted the greatest happiness of the greatest number, Benthamite utilitarianism helped to eliminate abuses and injustice. Again, suggesting that one person's happiness matters just as much as another's, irrespective of their position in the social hierarchy, encouraged fairness and equality, and pointed towards democracy as the only completely acceptable form of government.

Life

Jeremy Bentham, the founder of utilitarianism, was the son of Jeremiah Bentham, clerk to the Scriveners' Company. Born in London, he attended Westminster School from 1755 and then went up to The Queen's College, Oxford, in 1760. After reading law at Lincoln's Inn, he was called to the bar in 1768. However, he did not practise as a barrister, and his private means enabled him to concentrate instead on research and writing and on developing his own thinking on key issues. Between 1785 and 1788, he was in Russia, visiting his brother, Samuel, the engineer and naval architect.

In 1776, he published his *Fragment on Government*, criticizing Sir William Blackstone's *Commentaries on the Laws of England* (1765–9), which defends the anomalies and absurdities of English common law. During the 1780s, he also published *Defence of Usury* (1787) and *An Introduction to the Principles of Morals* (1789).

The utilitarian ideal of promoting the greatest happiness of the greatest number was not a new one, but Bentham may have attached the term 'utilitarian(ism)' to it, or encouraged use of the term in this context. In his writings, he sought to establish the utilitarian principle of the greatest happiness for all those whose interest is involved as the all-important criterion in ethics, law and government, and was a vigorous campaigner for legal, penal and social reform. On the Continent, his books were translated into French by his Swiss disciple Etienne Dumont and exerted a considerable influence.

A friend and associate of the philosopher and historian James Mill, Bentham took a keen interest in the education of Mill's son, John Stuart Mill. In 1824, with Mill's help, Bentham started the *Westminster Review*, to promote radical and utilitarian ideas. A supporter of the expansion of educational opportunities, he inspired the founders of University College, London, which opened in 1826, and from which the University of London developed. He put forward detailed proposals for a new kind of prison, the Panopticon ('all-seeing'), the design of which would enable warders to observe prisoners, without the latter knowing that they were being watched. The failure of governments to implement this plan, or to apply the greatest happiness principle generally, led him to favour democracy.

During his lifetime, Bentham's publications also included *Catechism of Parliamentary Reform* (1809) and *Church-of-Englandism* (1818). After his death, a multi-volume edition of his writings was published by his literary executor, the linguist and writer Sir John Bowring, editor of the *Westminster Review* and a future MP and governor of Hong Kong. When Jeremy Bentham died, in 1832, his skeleton was preserved, according to instructions in his will, and is now kept in a wooden cabinet at University College, London.

Key ideas

Utilitarian ethics: the maximization of happiness

For consequentialist philosophers, the basis of morality lies in the value of the consequences of actions. For utilitarians, like Bentham, this means those that produce pleasure or happiness. We should determine the rightness or wrongness of actions by how far they maximize pleasure and/or diminish pain. The effects of potential actions, especially those of legislators and governments, need to be tested against the principle of utility, that element in an action which produces pleasure or happiness for the party affected.

In his *An Introduction to the Principles of Morals and Legislation*, Bentham accepts that, as the first principle of morality, and the criterion against which actions must be tested, the principle of utility cannot itself be proved. However, he argues that nature has placed human beings under the control of the fundamental motivations of pleasure and pain. As we naturally always seek those things which give us pleasure, and avoid those that cause us pain, we should accept them as our standards of right or wrong. Further, collective human experience provides proof of a kind. Most people, on most occasions, do apply the utilitarian standard.

Bentham believes that individuals and governments should have the happiness of others or their citizens, that is, general happiness, as their sole object. This can only be achieved by acting, legislating and governing in conformity with the principle of utility. When considering an action, individuals and governments should test it against the principle of utility, by carrying out a felicific or hedonic calculus (calculation of happiness). They must weigh the pleasures they think an action will produce against possible pains and only perform it if convinced it will produce a balance of pleasure over pain. Governments should use rewards and punishments to promote the happiness of society and ensure that individual members do not pursue their own at the expense of that of others. But, can we calculate all, or even most, of the consequences of our actions into the future, as Bentham seems to suggest?

Many would say not. This is a reason for utilitarians to accept established moral rules and laws, such as those that prohibit murder and theft. Experience has shown that applying them generally produces more pleasure than pain, even if it does not in a particular situation.

Bentham's statement of utilitarianism raises other issues. He talks about pleasure, which is a transitory (and possibly measurable) sensation, but seems to equate it with happiness. But, human happiness is not a transitory experience, nor does it seem to be determined solely, or even mainly, by pleasure or pain. It seems to arise, in part, from coping successfully with life's sometimes painful challenges. Again, it is perfectly intelligible to say that the right thing to do is not the one that produces most (immediate) pleasure.

Further, Bentham fails to define pleasure. Are there higher pleasures, such as intellectual pursuits, and lower ones, such as eating and drinking? And, where is the moral imperative for our choosing to perform actions which promote others' pleasure and happiness, rather than focusing exclusively on those which promote our own, but produce less overall? Giving other people's interests at least equal weight with our own must mean recognizing them as intrinsically valuable beings, whose happiness should matter to us.

The rights of animals

Ethics is anthropocentric. It is almost exclusively concerned with human beings and their welfare. But, should it be? We share our world with other living beings: animals. Though not rational or self-conscious, they are sentient or conscious and clearly capable of experiencing pain and suffering. Ethics has not ignored them completely. In most developed Western countries, there is a consensus that animals should not be cruelly treated.

However, they are not given the same moral status as human beings. Their value is seen as instrumental, not intrinsic. They are spared cruel treatment, only to the extent that it fits in with human needs. Many are kept in factory farms and then slaughtered, to provide us with cheap food. They are subjected to painful experiments, to ensure the safety of our medicines. Is this ethical speciesism (limiting full moral status to human beings) justified?

Animals, as sentient beings, are capable of experiencing pain. Therefore, utilitarians can argue that, even if we feel entitled to make use of them and in fact do so, we should always seek to minimize their pain. In *An Introduction to the Principles of Morals and Legislation*, Jeremy Bentham points out that, although animals are capable of happiness, human indifference and neglect of their interests has degraded them to the level of mere things. However, he does not maintain that it is wrong to slaughter animals for food, or to kill those that threaten us. We do so to feed and protect ourselves, and the animals themselves are none the worse for it. The death they suffer at our hands is often speedier and less painful than the one they would undergo, if nature were left to take its course.

Bentham draws a parallel between treatment of slaves in the past, due to their being regarded as inferior human beings, and our treatment of animals. He looks forward to a time when the number of legs a living being has or the hairiness of its skin is not seen as an adequate reason for denying it moral status. He thinks that a fully grown horse or dog is, in fact, more rational than an infant of up to a month old. But, it is not because animals can talk or reason that they merit moral status. Though conscious, they are not self-conscious and so are not equivalent to human beings.

So what entitles animals to moral status? It is their capacity to suffer. We can slaughter them for food, because, unlike human beings, they do not have a long-protracted anticipation of future misery. They will not be aware, as the prospective victims of cannibals would, of what awaits them. However, they must be killed humanely, to minimize their suffering.

Impact

- Bentham's insistence that governments and legislators should promote general happiness, in a pre-democratic society, where the majority's interests and well-being were largely neglected, was taken up by social and political reformers in the nineteenth century and contributed to the establishment of a democratic system of government.
- Whatever its shortcomings as a principle to guide individual ethical decisions, the greatest happiness of the greatest number is an effective standard for identifying and removing political, legal and social abuses, inequalities and injustices.
- Bentham locates the basis of the moral status of animals in their capacity to feel pain and to suffer.
- His views on animal rights called into question the sharp dividing-line, on the scale of moral status, separating the human species from others, and have inspired animal welfare campaigns and legislation.

Further reading

Jeremy Bentham, *A Fragment on Government*, ed. R. Harrison, Cambridge: Cambridge University Press, 1988.

Jeremy Bentham (1748–1832)

Jeremy Bentham, *An Introduction to the Principles of Morals and Legislation*, Mineola, NY: Dover Publications, 2007.

Jeremy Bentham, *Selected Writings on Utilitarianism*, ed. R. Harrison, Ware: Wordsworth, 2000.

J. Driver, 'The History of Utilitarianism' (2009), in E. N. Zalta (ed.), *Stanford Encyclopaedia of Philosophy*, at http://plato.stanford.edu.

R. Harrison, *Bentham*, London: Routledge and Kegan Paul, 1983.

J. S. Mill, *Utilitarianism*, ed. G. Sher, second edition, Indianapolis/Cambridge: Hackett Publishing Company, 2001.

D. Mills Daniel, *Briefly: Bentham's An Introduction to the Principles of Morals and Legislation*, London: SCM Press, 2009.

T. Regan, *The Case for Animal Rights*, Berkeley/Los Angeles: University of California Press, 1983.

P. Singer, *Practical Ethics*, second edition, Cambridge: Cambridge University Press, 1993.

W. Sweet, 'Jeremy Bentham' (updated 2008), in J. Fieser and B. Dowden (eds), *Internet Encyclopedia of Philosophy*, at www.iep.utm.edu.

M. Warnock, *Utilitarianism*, London: Fontana, 1970.

18

John Stuart Mill
(1806–73)
The principle of liberty/harm principle
and the role of the individual in society
Utilitarian ethics: quantity versus
quality of pleasure and the use of
secondary principles

Context

Whose name is synonymous with the British empiricist tradition and liberal (and also Liberal) principles in the nineteenth
century? It is that of the utilitarian philosopher and champion
of individual freedom, John Stuart Mill. Influenced by Locke,
Hume and Bentham, Mill's work in logic, epistemology and
moral and political philosophy has had a tremendous impact on nineteenth-century and subsequent thought. In his
System of Logic, he propounds a thoroughgoing empiricism.
Knowledge does not come from rational intuition, but from
experience, the criterion by which even the rules of logic and
mathematics must be tested. But how, without accepting the
rationalist view that there are truths known independently
of experience, can empiricists account for logical and mathematical truths, which seem necessary and certain? They can

either deny that they are necessary and certain, or accept that they lack factual content. Controversially, Mill adopts the first alternative and argues that logical and mathematical truths are inductive generalizations, based on very many supporting instances, which differ from scientific hypotheses, not in kind, but in degree of probability.

Mill rules out the absolutely certain basis for knowledge, sought by rationalist philosophers like Descartes. Induction is the key to knowledge. Though verified by experience time and time again, empirical generalizations can never be logically certain. They could be proved wrong in the future. But, Mill rejects Berkeley's subjective idealism. Material objects exist independently of us as the permanent possibilities of sensation. Further, in the *Examination of Sir William Hamilton's Philosophy*, he rejects Kant's view that what we experience are *phenomena*, things as they appear to us, which should be distinguished from *noumena*, things as they are in themselves, to which we have no access. Our concept of cause is not *a priori*, but is learned from experience, by observing the regularities of the world.

In his *Utilitarianism*, Mill offers a proof of the principle of utility by analogy with visibility. Their being seen is the only proof that things are visible, so the only proof that something is desirable is that we actually desire it. Individually, we desire happiness, while general happiness is that of the aggregate of all persons. Therefore, happiness is what human conduct aims at, and the principle of utility is the sole criterion of morality. G. E. Moore criticizes this proof as involving a naturalistic fallacy. He argues that 'desirable' does not mean what we are able to desire, in the way that 'visible' means what we are able to see. It refers to what it is good for us to desire. However, this difference makes it impossible to argue that our only test of what we should desire is what we actually desire. But, Mill does not seem to be attempting a strict proof that happiness is desirable as an end. Indeed, he acknowledges that it is impossible to do so. Rather, he is inviting us to observe what people actually value, and happiness is obviously one of these things.

Mill's version of utilitarianism, which is one of the key ideas discussed below, differs from Bentham's and his father's. His concern is not solely with quantity of pleasure. He believes there are grades of pleasure, and that those associated with the mind, such as literary and artistic pursuits, are more valuable than purely physical ones, such as eating and drinking.

One of Mill's priorities was the defence of individual liberty, also discussed in this chapter. In his view, political change and social progress are only possible if there is individual freedom, enabling gifted and innovative individuals to show the rest of society the way forward. He regrets people's lack of interest in the free development of individuality, when individual freedom underpins the diversity of views and culture which fosters social progress. Severely critical of democratic systems of government, he argues that uncritical acceptance of the majority view can lead to oppression of minorities who do not conform to majority opinion. In economics, Mill espouses the free trade ideas of Adam Smith and David Ricardo, and opposes state education, fearing that governments would use it as a means of indoctrination.

In *The Subjection of Women*, Mill condemns women's subordinate position in nineteenth-century society, and argues for their equality and political rights. He describes married women's situation and their husbands' unfettered control over them as a form of bondage. The only legal slaves in Britain are the mistresses of every house. While admiring aspects of Christian ethical teaching, such as Jesus' golden rule, Mill considers that, though the natural order of the world may suggest a benevolent creator or designer, the problem of evil rules out an omnipotent and omniscient God.

Life

The son of James and Harriet Mill, John Stuart Mill was born in London. His father, the Scottish utilitarian philosopher and author of *A History of India* (1818), eventually became chief examiner of the East India Company, which governed India, and responsible for all the Company's correspondence with its administrators in India. James Mill's interest in economics, and authorship of *Elements of Political Economy* (1821), led to friendship with utilitarianism's founder, Jeremy Bentham, who took a keen interest in his son's education.

Mill's education by his father was unusually ambitious, and designed to equip him to be a leading exponent of utilitarian ideas. He started Greek at three, Latin at eight, and logic and political economy at 12. Denied friends of his own age, he did not take part in sport, and was also expected to pass on what he had learned to his brothers and sisters. This intense programme may have contributed to the severe depression he suffered at about 20. The discovery of poetry, particularly Wordsworth's, gave him a different perspective on pleasure and happiness from that given by Bentham and his father, and made him think in terms of their quality.

After studying law, Mill joined the East India Company, in 1823, becoming chief examiner in 1856, in succession to the satirical novelist Thomas Love Peacock, who had taken over the post from Mill's father. He worked for the Company until the British government assumed responsibility for India, in 1858, following the Indian Mutiny, which exposed weaknesses in Company administration. Mill opposed the move and subsequently retired on a pension.

In 1830, Mill fell in love with a married woman, Harriet Taylor, wife of John Taylor. Although Mill's family did not approve of the relationship, they finally married in 1851, following Taylor's death. Both Mill and his wife suffered from illness and travelled extensively to improve their health. Harriet Mill died in Avignon, in 1858; Mill returned to France, for part of each year, for the rest of his life.

During this time, Mill was developing and writing about his views on philosophical and political issues, and working out his own version of utilitarianism. He started the *London Review* in the mid 1830s, merging it with *Westminster Review*, to create the *London and Westminster Review*, which supported parliamentary reform. It was subsequently sold to the publisher John Chapman and, as the *Westminster Review*, survived until just before the First World War.

Mill's *System of Logic* appeared in 1843, followed by *Principles of Political Economy* (1848) and his essay *On Liberty* (1859), which he dedicated to his wife, whom he described as the inspirer and co-author of all that is best in his writings. Mill's other works include *Utilitarianism* (1861), *Considerations on Representative Government* (1861), *Examination of Sir William Hamilton's Philosophy* (1865) and *The Subjection of Women* (1869).

Elected Liberal MP for Westminster in 1865, Mill campaigned for women's rights, proposing the enfranchisement of women and proportional representation during the debates on the bill that became the (Second) Reform Act, 1867. He was severely critical of the tough measures taken by the governor of Jamaica,

E. J. Eyre, to deal with a native rising. Defeated in the general election of 1868, he retired to France with his step-daughter Helen, dying in Avignon in 1873. Helen Taylor published his *Autobiography* and *Three Essays in Religion* after his death.

Key ideas

The principle of liberty/harm principle and the role of the individual in society

As mid nineteenth-century society moved hesitantly towards a more democratic system of government, Mill did not think it would be a panacea for all political ills. Even in democratic societies, individuals and minorities, though not subject to political persecution, as in totalitarian states, are often oppressed by the tyranny of public opinion, which tries to coerce them into accepting the majority view.

In *On Liberty*, Mill enunciates his principle of liberty, to demarcate the boundary between society's legitimate interference with individual freedom and the state's unacceptable intrusions into it. For Mill, the only purpose for which a civilized community can rightfully coerce any of its members, against their will, is to prevent harm to others. Actions that affect only the individual's good, whether physical or moral, and which do not harm others, do not justify curtailing individual liberty. In areas that concern only him- or herself, the individual's independence is, of right, absolute. But, is the principle of liberty as easy to apply as Mill suggests? The problem is that many activities do not fall neatly on one or other side of the dividing line. Smoking, for example, does most harm to the smoker, but also affects others, and may impose the costs of healthcare on society as a whole.

For Mill, individual liberty and the right to express our views freely are important, not only for the individual, but also for society, which gains from them. In a free society, human opinions and conduct are generally rational and sensible, precisely because they can be corrected through discussion and experience. Truth is usually arrived at through the interaction of opposite points of view. A suppressed opinion may turn out to be true, and, even if the majority view is right, unless challenged, it will be held as a mere dogma. Further, Mill believes that there is nothing wrong with expressing our views robustly. People with strong views often put them forward with a passion that opponents find objectionable, but this is the nature of public debate.

Mill also urges people to express their individuality in the way they lead their lives. Again, society is the gainer. Mid nineteenth-century English, European and American society was increasingly subject to the tyranny of mass public opinion, as reflected in mass circulation newspapers, which discouraged individuality and originality, and impoverished human life. People are too willing to let society decide how they should live, rather than choosing for themselves.

Democratic governments tend to pander to their mass electorates, in order to cling to power, creating a society in which individuals are lost in the crowd. However, political and social progress require diversity of opinions and lifestyles that clash with and challenge each other, giving people a real choice. Therefore, Mill urges cultivation of individuality, because society needs eccentrics who are prepared to stand out from the crowd and flout mass opinion. Their value lies less in their being right than in their refusal to conform, which sets an example others can follow.

To enrich human society, and to ensure human progress, we need to express our opinions, and contribute to the melting-pot of different ideas that challenge accepted views, and from which truth emerges. By leading or encouraging others to lead distinctively individual ways of life, we help to ensure a range of lifestyles that confront the conventional pattern and offer people a choice as to how to lead their own.

Utilitarian ethics: quantity versus quality of pleasure and the use of secondary principles

Like Bentham, Mill argues, in *Utilitarianism*, for a utilitarian theory of ethics. Pleasure and absence of pain are the only things desirable as ends, and actions are right to the extent that they promote pleasure and happiness, and wrong to the extent that they cause pain. However, Mill is not solely concerned with quantity of pleasure and determining the rightness or wrongness of actions through attempts to calculate the amounts of pleasure or pain that different possible courses of action may produce. He believes that there are grades or levels of pleasure, and that intellectual pleasures, like literary and artistic pursuits, are more valuable than physical ones, such as eating and drinking. As Mill famously expresses it, it is better to be a human being dissatisfied than a pig satisfied, and better to be Socrates dissatisfied than a fool satisfied.

But, given an equal quantity of pleasure, why should we regard intellectual pleasures as superior to purely physical ones? Mill argues that the former's greater value is established by the fact that those who are familiar with both types of pleasure, and therefore qualified to judge, consider them more worthwhile. Those who have experienced, and enjoyed, intellectual pleasures may be more aware of life's imperfections than those who have not, but would not change places with them. Thus, Mill's version of utilitarianism is not open to the charge of being crudely hedonistic. Intellectual pleasures are rated above non-intellectual ones, while he emphasizes utilitarianism's unselfishness. Utilitarians should be as concerned about others' pleasures and happiness, the general happiness, as their own.

Mill does not ask us to try to work out the effects of all possible courses of action on the general happiness before we act. He appreciates the difficulties of making such calculations, and they are unnecessary. He does not believe that acceptance of a basic moral principle, like utilitarianism, is inconsistent with the use of secondary ones, which are compatible with it. Established secondary principles, such as those forbidding murder or theft, can be applied, because experience has shown that, in general, they promote happiness. The fundamental principle of utility need only be invoked when secondary principles conflict with each other.

Mill's argument for a hierarchy of pleasures, which recognizes qualitative as well as quantitative distinctions among them, does seem convincing. And, those who have experienced both intellectual and non-intellectual pleasures do appear to value the former more highly. However, it departs from pure utilitarianism. If pleasures are graded, and actions assessed by criteria other than the quantity of pleasure they produce, pleasure cannot be the only thing desirable as an end. Mill's account of happiness seems to have less in common with the maximization of pleasure than with Aristotle's *eudaimonia*.

There are problems, too, with using secondary moral principles. It may be sensible, but may mean performing actions that will not create most happiness in a particular situation. Again, although happiness is certainly one of the things that people desire, it does not seem to be the only thing we desire as an end. Mill also fails to explain why people ought to be as concerned for others' happiness as for their own. He says that concern for others' happiness harmonizes with the obligations we naturally feel towards others. But, this is no more than an expression of hope or an empirical assertion which may not be true.

Impact

- Mill's principle of liberty/harm principle lays down the boundary between society's legitimate interference with individual freedom and unacceptable intrusions into it, in a way that has never been more relevant than in today's era of the overmighty state.
- He continues to remind us of the dangers and weaknesses of a democratic system of government and the need to safeguard the rights of individuals and minorities.
- He appreciated the need to modify the principle of utility and to recognize that all pleasures are not of equal value.
- He shows how secondary principles can be incorporated into a system of utilitarian ethics.

Further reading

Jeremy Bentham, *An Introduction to the Principles of Morals and Legislation*, Mineola, NY: Dover Publications, 2007.

N. Capaldi, *John Stuart Mill: A Biography*, Cambridge: Cambridge University Press, 2004.

C. Heydt, 'John Stuart Mill' (updated 2006), in J. Fieser and B. Dowden (eds), *Internet Encyclopedia of Philosophy*, at www.iep.utm.edu.

J. S. Mill, *Autobiography*, ed. J. M. Robson, London: Penguin, 1989.

J. S. Mill, *On Liberty and Other Essays*, ed. J. Gray, Oxford and New York: Oxford University Press, 1998.

J. S. Mill, *Utilitarianism*, ed. G. Sher, second edition, Indianapolis/Cambridge: Hackett Publishing Company, 2001.

D. Mills Daniel, *Briefly: Mill's On Liberty*, London: SCM Press, 2006.

D. Mills Daniel, *Briefly: Mill's Utilitarianism*, London: SCM Press, 2006.

W. Thomas, *John Stuart Mill*, Oxford: Oxford University Press, 1985.

M. Warnock, *Utilitarianism*, London: Fontana, 1970.

F. Wilson, 'John Stuart Mill' (revised 2007), in E. N. Zalta (ed.), *Stanford Encyclopaedia of Philosophy*, at http://plato.stanford.edu.

19

Søren Kierkegaard
(1813–55)
Faith and the individual's relationship
with God
Putting God above morality

Context

What exactly is existentialism? Many people have heard of it, but are not sure what it is. Studying Kierkegaard is a good way to find out, because he is its founder. However, as represented by such diverse thinkers as Kierkegaard himself, Jean-Paul Sartre, Martin Heidegger and Rudolf Bultmann, existentialism cannot be easily defined or tied down to a coherent set of philosophical ideas. It is best viewed as an approach to life and how to lead it. What existentialist thinkers have in common is an emphasis on the individual and the individual's need to choose his or her values and way of life for him- or herself, against the background of a universe that appears to lack a clear, rational purpose; and on the individual human being's ability to make such choices, which may appear absurd ones to both him- or herself and others.

In Kierkegaard's case, his choice is for God. But, this is to make his position seem simpler than it is. Due to the range of his perspectives on religious and other issues, Kierkegaard writes his books under such pseudonyms as 'Johannes Climacus' and

'Johannes de silentio', in order to dissociate himself from the views they contain. He can then criticize them and take up opposing views, if he wishes. This causes difficulties for readers, as it is by no means clear precisely which views he actually holds.

Kierkegaard characterizes Christianity as involving a constantly reaffirmed commitment to a God, who cannot be objectively known and whose existence cannot be proved scientifically. Belief in God is a matter of faith, which requires the suspension of reason, because it is contrary to it. Christian faith is absurd, not only because it defies reason, but also because of its content. Not only does it teach that God is infinite, all-powerful and all-knowing, but also that God became incarnate in the person of Jesus at a particular point in history. However, Kierkegaard insists that it is only through faith that the individual can realize his or her authentic self. This imposes a huge responsibility on the individual, who must make an existential choice for or against God. This choice will determine the individual's future, not just in this life but for eternity. Further, the individual cannot hand over the life-choice he or she makes, as the followers of the German philosopher G. W. F. Hegel do, to a philosophical system and universal ethical precepts, or, as in the case of the Roman Catholics, to a priestly hierarchy.

Faith is not a vague hope about what may happen in the next life. It relates to this life and to the belief that, for and through God, anything, however absurd, is possible. The question then arises as to whether anyone is capable of making the existentialist choice for God and thus plunging confidently into the absurd. Faith is not easy, and, in *Fear and Trembling*, Abraham is acknowledged as the exemplar of faith, because he adheres to his faith in God, despite being severely tested, to the apparently absurd length of being told by God to sacrifice his son, Isaac, and consenting to do so. People can look at the example of Abraham, and see if they are equal to such a challenge of faith. Faith and the individual's relationship with God is one of the key ideas discussed in this chapter.

If Abraham is right, the paradox of faith, that the single individual is higher than universal ethical precepts, must be accepted. For Kierkegaard, this involves, and justifies, a teleological suspension of the ethical: the second idea discussed below. This is the situation of generally accepted ethical rules being suspended for the higher purpose of serving God, as Abraham did. But, the question as to whether what God commands is good or right is an intelligible one, asked even by religious believers, who sometimes question what are taken to be God's commands. Logically, it is an open question whether what God commands is good or right: it would not be self-contradictory to hold that a divine decree is ethically unacceptable. In his *Euthyphro*, Plato explores the issue of whether something is good or right because God (or the gods) wills it, or whether God wills it because it is right. Through the discussion between Socrates and the self-righteous religious bigot Euthyphro, he demonstrates that goodness and rightness cannot be equated with, or defined in terms of, being willed by God; and that ethical standards are distinct from, and independent of, God.

Kierkegaard was a noted polemicist against Hegel's philosophy and established religion, as represented by the Danish People's Church, which came under the influence of Hegelianism, and against the corrupting effects of social change and democratic systems of government on the individual.

Life

Søren Abaye Kierkegaard was born in Copenhagen. His father, Michael Pedersen Kierkegaard, a self-made businessman, who had retired early in order to pursue his interests in philosophy and theology, was by then 57. However, although successful and wealthy, he was tormented by fear and guilt. As a child, beset by poverty and loneliness, he had once cursed the name of God. He also felt guilty about the fact that he had made one of his servants, Anne Lund, pregnant while his first wife was expecting a baby. After the latter's death, Anne became his second wife and the mother of his seven children. Michael was haunted by the belief that, as a punishment, his children would die young. In fact, only two of his children, Søren and his brother Peter, who became a bishop, survived beyond the age of 34.

At school, Kierkegaard showed intellectual promise, despite being teased for his smallness and on account of his father's insistence that his clothes were not discarded until completely worn out. His father wanted him to become a pastor in the Danish State Church, and he entered the University of Copenhagen in 1830 to study theology. But, Kierkegaard decided that he did not wish to do so, and, while he and his father had previously got on fairly well, relations between them deteriorated. However, they were reconciled before Michael's death in 1838. Anne had died in 1834, and Kierkegaard was left with sufficient wealth to lead a life of research and writing.

In the late 1830s, Kierkegaard met and fell in love with the 16-year-old Regine Olsen. He pursued her, and she finally agreed to marry him. But, once they were engaged, he decided, for reasons that are unclear, that marrying Regine would be a mistake. He then behaved so badly towards her that, the following year, she ended their engagement. However, he seems to have gone on loving her for the rest of his life.

After receiving his doctorate, in 1841, Kierkegaard opted for the life of an independent scholar and writer, publishing such books as *Either/Or* (1843), *Fear and Trembling* (1843),

Philosophical Fragments (1844), *Practice in Christianity* (1850) and *For Self-Examination: Judge for Yourself* (1851). His focus on the implications of religious belief and a relationship with God for the individual led him to reject the prevailing Hegelian philosophy of the period, while his preoccupation with the individual, individual choice and despair mean that he is regarded as the first existentialist thinker and writer.

Kierkegaard's views, and his vigorous expression of them, led to lengthy disputes with the Danish State Church, which he condemned for its hypocrisy, lack of religious vitality and accommodation to bourgeois values. He pursued his criticisms in various publications, including his own periodical, *The Instant*. However, although his aim was to draw attention to the shortcomings of Christianity and Protestantism, as practised in nineteenth-century Denmark, it was widely misinterpreted as personal attacks on the late Bishop J. P. Mynster, a family friend, and Bishop Hans Larsen Martenson, one of Kierkegaard's university teachers. In 1855, Kierkegaard collapsed in the street, dying a month later, after refusing to receive the sacrament from a clergyman of the State Church. At his funeral, his brother apologized for his behaviour.

Key ideas

Faith and the individual's relationship with God

What does it mean to have faith in God? What are its implications for how we should lead our lives and make our ethical decisions? In *Fear and Trembling*, Kierkegaard explores the nature of faith in God by focusing on Abraham, who is an exemplar of faith. At God's command, he leaves his own country, to become a foreigner in the Promised Land. God tells him he will be the forefather of many generations, and he goes on believing it, despite the fact that, realistically, he and his wife, Sarah, are far too old to have children. And then, when the long hoped-for son finally arrives, God tests him again and orders him to sacrifice Isaac. But Abraham's faith is equal to the test. When God demands it, no sacrifice, even of a son, is too great.

So, what, Kierkegaard asks, is faith such as that of Abraham? It is not a vague hope about what may happen in the next life, but relates to this life, and to the conviction that, for and through God, anything, however absurd, is possible. This is why Abraham responds cheerfully and trustingly to God's extraordinary command, which shatters all accepted ethical principles, and overturns the responsibilities of father to son. Unlike Abraham, anyone lacking such total faith would be plunged into despair.

But, what about Abraham's conduct? The sacrifice he is prepared to make is not just of his own comfort, or even of himself. It involves laying down the life of someone else, his only son. So is Abraham's willingness to do so, in obedience to God's command, admirable or outrageous? People say they admire Abraham's faith, and what he offered to do because of it. But, Kierkegaard asks, what if somebody today shows the same degree of faith, and tries to copy him?

Ethically, Abraham agrees to murder his son. Would not the same clergy, who commend Abraham as an example, condemn a modern Abraham and want to put him in an asylum for the insane or execute him? Society would also discourage such a man in case foolish people try to copy him. The nature of modern society means that faith and its consequences, particularly its implications for accepted ethical standards, are acceptable only if locked safely away in the past. So, should

God's commands take precedence over morality? Kierkegaard considers whether, if there is a conflict between God's command and an accepted moral principle, the individual of faith should obey God's command, or abide by the universal ethical precept. He poses this dilemma in the context of the moral philosophies of Kant and Hegel.

Kant argues that moral laws, which must be obeyed for their own sake, and not for any other motive, or because of their consequences, and which human beings discover *a priori*, in their reason, apply universally and directly to all human beings as rational beings. Rational beings should never act, except according to maxims that they could also will should become universal laws. Hegel argues that moral laws are expressed in national life, laws and customs. Instead of discovering moral laws in his own reason, the individual should comply with his nation's universally accepted ethical precepts and let them determine his ethical life.

Putting God above morality

However, for Kierkegaard, Hegel's ethical approach, in particular, means that universal morality becomes the end of everything outside itself, thus eliminating individual moral decision-making, which it regards as a form of moral evil. And, where does this leave the man of faith, like Abraham, who is prepared to breach a fundamental principle of accepted morality in order to obey God's command? Kierkegaard argues that either he is wrong and should be condemned, or he is right, and a paradox of faith must be accepted: that the single individual is capable of an absolute relation with God and is higher than universal ethical precepts. These can then be set aside, or teleologically suspended (as Kierkegaard expresses it), to serve the higher purpose of obeying God.

But, what if the man of faith is wrong? In that case, he is simply a murderer. This underlines the terrifying responsibility the man of faith assumes, when he makes the choice for God and to obey God, and, in consequence, defies society and its universal ethical precepts. One who subordinates his individuality to the state or society runs no risks, but the man of faith must bear the full burden of responsibility for his teleological suspension of the ethical. He must be prepared to face society's condemnation.

There is an alternative: to subsume the duty to God in universal ethical duties, so that duty to God just becomes behaving ethically. But, for Kierkegaard, this would make Hegel right and mean that individual moral choice must be given up, in favour of obeying universally accepted ethical precepts. God would then simply vanish into morality, and any other way of serving him would become unacceptable, preventing Abraham's being held up as an exemplar of faith.

However, as there is an individual relationship with, and an absolute duty to, God, the individual is higher than morality, while his relation to God determines his relation to morality, not the other way round. And, as in the Abraham story, if duty to God, and obeying his commands, is absolute, and that is the choice the individual has made, it is ethical precepts which become relative.

However, this duty to God cannot be accommodated within society's universally accepted ethical code, according to which Abraham is a murderer. Kierkegaard notes the pressure that society places on the individual to follow its ethical precepts. It wants its members to renounce individual decision-making, fearing the consequences. It would also be much easier for God-obedient individuals, such as Abraham, if they could be like everybody else and abide by society's ethical code. For, as what he is doing is between himself and God, he stands outside society's accepted ethical code and cannot explain his actions to those whose lives are wholly governed by it.

Impact

- The first (Christian) existentialist writer, Kierkegaard stresses the importance of the individual, individual freedom and individual choice, and highlights the ethical dilemma that may confront religious believers: whether to give priority to their relationship with God and the absolute duty to obey God's commands, or to conform with society's generally accepted ethical principles.
- Kierkegaard always believed his writings would be widely studied after his death, and his focus on individual responsibility, life-forming and life-changing individual choices and their consequences has had a major impact on the thinking of both theistic and non-theistic philosophers and theologians, including Paul Tillich, Martin Buber and Jean-Paul Sartre.
- Kierkegaard seems to accept that there is no objective criterion for distinguishing the genuinely religious person from the religious fanatic; that society is bound to be suspicious of individuals who maintain that its ethical code can be teleologically suspended; and that, from fear of the damage such people may do, including their impact on the

impressionable or impetuous, it may decide to discourage or restrain them.

- For many moderate religious people, Kierkegaard's ideas are perverse, extreme and unacceptable, because: if God is all-loving, as Christianity teaches, he would never issue commands that breach fundamental ethical principles or involve harming others; Plato and Kant are right that ethical standards are independent even of the will of God, so actions that breach those standards would still be wrong, whatever God may decree; and that, as Locke insists, reason must always be the test of faith.

Further reading

J. B. Garff and B. H. Kirmmse (trans.), *Søren Kierkegaard: A Biography*, Princeton, NJ: Princeton University Press, 2007.

D. J. Gouwens, *Kierkegaard as Religious Thinker*, Cambridge: Cambridge University Press, 1996.

A. Hannay and G. D. Marino (eds), *The Cambridge Companion to Kierkegaard*, Cambridge: Cambridge University Press, 1998.

Søren Kierkegaard, *Either/Or: A Fragment of Life*, trans. A. Hannay, London: Penguin, 1992.

Søren Kierkegaard, *Fear and Trembling*, eds C. S. Evans and S. Walsh, Cambridge: Cambridge University Press, 2006.

Søren Kierkegaard, *Papers and Journals*, trans. A. Hannay, London: Penguin, 1996.

W. McDonald, 'Søren Kierkegaard' (updated 2005), in J. Fieser and B. Dowden (eds), *Internet Encyclopedia of Philosophy*, at www.iep.utm.edu.

Søren Kierkegaard (1813–55)

W. McDonald, 'Søren Kierkegaard' (revised 2009), in E. N. Zalta (ed.), *Stanford Encyclopaedia of Philosophy*, at http://plato.stanford.edu.

D. Mills Daniel, *Kierkegaard's Fear and Trembling*, London: SCM Press, 2007.

Plato, *Defence of Socrates, Euthyphro, Crito*, trans. and ed. D. Gallop, Oxford and New York: Oxford University Press, 1999.

J. Watkin, *Kierkegaard*, London: Geoffrey Chapman, 1997.

20

Friedrich Nietzsche
(1844–1900)
Master and slave moralities
The new philosophers

Context

What should we make of Nietzsche? Why does he command so much attention: more than some other philosophers, whose ideas are of greater value, and perhaps more than he deserves? It may be that his very outrageousness attracts devotees. What he writes seems perverse and dangerous and to cross the line (as Nietzsche himself did) between reason and unreason, between sanity and insanity. Of course, he does offer some startling insights. By the use of aphorism, paradox and irony he deconstructs aspects of human life to try to enable his readers to appreciate what he believes lies at the heart of authentic human existence: individuals who are free and honest with themselves. However, he does not pursue a consistent line. Just as we think we are beginning to understand his arguments, he goes off in another direction and we lose our way. And, this seems to be Nietzsche's intention. He wants us in a state of confusion and doubt, which may make us more receptive to his ideas.

One of Nietzsche's themes is that human beings try to simplify everything, thus debasing human existence. Our lack of imagination and preference for things to be straightforward reveals itself in the comfortable fictions with which we attempt to dissolve life's complexities. However, our preference for the easy route means we can understand and explain nothing. We seize on science, because its empirical methods seem to allow us to believe in anything we can see or touch. But, science is only one approach to interpreting the world. It is the same with all our concepts, such as cause and effect, free will, determinism and reason. We have invented them for purposes of description and communication. However, we nurture the illusion that they penetrate to the core of ultimate reality.

Another point Nietzsche likes to make is that human beings are prone to scepticism and dogmatism, which diminish the human spirit. Scepticism encourages a non-committal attitude to life and drains away our vitality; religious dogmatism negates the human spirit, by branding natural passions and our desire for independence as sinful, while preaching sterile asceticism. Nietzsche criticizes both Buddhism and Christianity for their animosity towards the human spirit, characterizing Christian doctrine as a perversion of the human will. Within Christianity, the unworldly saint is extolled as the exemplar of the Christian life, which Christians should emulate. But, we must repudiate his or her example: by using his will to resist natural human desires and condemning them as sinful, he provides a shocking and obsessive display of religious neurosis. Not only is Christianity's stress on sin unhealthy, it teaches the holiness of suffering and the superiority of those who suffer over the noble and naturally powerful. Christianity perverts the human will to power by making it seek power in its own contradiction: lack of power.

Further, by choosing to designate as 'sinful' or 'evil' aggressive behaviour and exploitation of the weak and powerless, we undermine the naturally powerful, who should be society's masters. Foolishly, we commend suffering and call those who suffer 'good', when the truly good, the powerful and noble, rightly resent suffering and weakness and deplore pity. Thus, we exalt and protect the feeble and dependent, society's natural slaves. We need to renounce such upside-down values, recognizing that pity and altruistic behaviour lack moral worth. Our lives must celebrate the absurdities and inequalities of existence, not try to blunt the raw edges by applying superficially appealing, but fundamentally misconceived, notions of 'good' and 'evil' to it. Nietzsche's view of ethics, expressed in his concept of master and slave moralities, is one of the key ideas discussed below.

What should we do? Nietzsche's answer is to call for a new generation of leaders who will combine outstanding intellectual abilities with exceptional qualities of leadership. These are the 'new philosophers' (the second key idea explored below). They will lead human beings beyond the timid norms of received social and religious morality and our threadbare notions of 'good' and 'evil'.

Nietzsche dismisses the work of other philosophers. Plato has had the same malign effect as Christianity. By focusing on transcendental goodness and an eternal, unchanging, spiritual world, he has fostered contempt for mere physical existence. Schopenhauer's philosophy, influenced by Buddhism, is rejected as pessimistic and life-denying, while Kant and Hegel have merely prepared the ground for the new philosophers.

Given their content, the charge that Nietzsche's ideas helped to promote German nationalism, militarism and anti-semitism and inspired the Nazis seems fair; the German government printed copies of *Thus Spake Zarathustra* during the First World War to encourage the war effort. However, it could be argued that Aryanism and Nazism would have flourished without Nietzsche; that his paradoxical style makes it possible to find quotations to support almost any view; and that it was Nietzsche's sister, not Nietzsche, who fawned over Hitler.

Life

Friedrich Wilhelm Nietzsche was born in Röcken bei Lützen, near Leipzig, Germany, the son of Karl Ludwig, a Lutheran minister. After his father's death in 1849, his mother Franziska moved the family to Naumburg an der Saale. From 1858, he attended Schulpforta, a well-regarded boarding school, entering Bonn University in 1864 to study philology and theology. The following year, impressed by the lectures of the classicist and philologist Friedrich Wilhelm Ritschl, he followed him to Leipzig University. There, he dropped theology, maintaining his interest in philology and classics. He also developed an enthusiasm for the music of Richard Wagner.

In the same year, Nietzsche read Schopenhauer's *The World as Will and Idea* and was deeply influenced by the latter's atheism and pessimistic view of the world and life. Later, however, he came to see both Wagner and Schopenhauer as philosophical rivals and opponents. While doing his year's compulsory military service, Nietzsche sustained a serious chest injury, which had a lasting effect on his health.

In 1869, after graduating from Leipzig, Nietzsche was appointed as lecturer in classical philology at the University of Basle in Switzerland, becoming a full professor in 1870. During this time, his friendship with Wagner, who had a house in Switzerland, developed. During the short Franco–Prussian War, which saw the defeat of Louis Napoleon's France and the creation of the German Empire, presided over by King Wilhelm I of Prussia, who became the first *Kaiser* (emperor), Nietzsche was a medical attendant for three months. This war service, during which he looked after the wounded, caused further damage to his physical and mental health.

His first book, *The Birth of Tragedy out of the Spirit of Music*, was published in 1872 and received some negative attention. In 1879, with his health deteriorating, Nietzsche resigned from the University of Basle and became a peripatetic scholar and writer, dividing his time between short residences in various European cities and his mother's home at Naumburg. He proposed marriage to a young Russian student, Lou von Salome, with whom he seems to have been infatuated, but she refused him.

In 1889, while residing in Turin, Nietzsche suffered a complete mental collapse, supposedly after witnessing a horse being beaten, and entered an asylum. After his discharge, in 1890, he was cared for by his mother until her death in 1897, and then by his sister, Elisabeth Forster-Nietzsche, who had returned from Paraguay, where she and her husband had tried to create an anti-semitic German colony. She moved Nietzsche and his manuscripts to Weimar, where Nietzsche died. His books include *Human, All Too Human: A Book for Free Spirits* (1878); *Thus Spake Zarathustra: A Book for Everyone and No One* (1883–5); *Beyond Good and Evil: Prelude to a Philosophy of the Future* (1886); *On the Genealogy of Morals: A Polemic* (1887) and *Twilight of the Idols, or How to Philosophise with a Hammer* (1889).

After his death, his sister sought to promote his philosophical ideas, and developed the house in Weimar into a place of pilgrimage for disciples of Nietzsche and his writings. During the 1920s, she became a fervent admirer and supporter of Adolf Hitler and Nazism, making a present of Nietzsche's walking-stick to Hitler when he visited the house shortly before her death in 1935.

Key ideas

Master and slave moralities

Nietzsche challenges conventional morality, seeking to counteract what he regards as the malign consequences of Christian ethical teaching. He seeks to provoke traditional moralists by putting forward an individualistic and perverse theory of morality. It is aristocratic, hierarchical societies that reject human equality, attach different values to different kinds of people and practise slavery, which have always elevated the human race. What possible justification can he have for such a view?

He maintains that intellectual and cultural progress require a real distance between social classes, with the ruling class looking down at those it considers its underlings. Not injuring, abusing or exploiting other people may make for good manners between individuals, but should be reserved for other members of the ruling class. Trying to make them society's basic principles denies life, the essence of which is exploitation and oppression of the weak. To pursue their will to power, and to dominate their society, members of a healthy aristocracy do to others what they refrain from doing to each other. Exploitation is not a characteristic of a decadent or imperfect, primitive society, but part of the fundamental nature of living things. It arises from the true will to power, which is simply the will to life.

Thus, Nietzsche identifies two basic types of morality: master and slave moralities. The first defines 'good' in terms of proud, exalted states of the soul, regarding the difference between 'good' and 'bad' as that between 'noble' and 'despicable'. Representatives of this kind of morality despise the cowardly, self-disparaging and craven. They do not need others' approval. They see themselves as creating values. The aristocrat may help the unfortunate, but from excess of power, not pity. He relishes his own power, particularly that over himself, and respects all that is severe and harsh. Such people take pride in themselves. They disdain empathetic feelings, and are far removed from a moral code based on pity or altruistic behaviour. The aspect of the master morality, most at odds with current views, is that duties extend only to peers, and that masters are entitled to treat those beneath them as they wish, in a way that transcends any concept of good and evil. Noble morality is characterized by the ability and duty to be grateful or vengeful, within a circle of equals, and a need for enemies, as outlets for envy and combativeness.

Slave morality reflects the value judgements of the oppressed, suffering and weary. They gain nothing from the virtues of the powerful, and so stress such moral qualities as pity, kindness and helpfulness, which improve their own lot or help them to bear oppression. According to slave morality, those who arouse fear by being powerful or dangerous are evil: for, in slave morality, the good person is harmless and good-natured. It equates good with stupid, and emphasizes longing for freedom, while reverence and devotion characterize the aristocratic mentality. Nietzsche maintains that the fundamental tendency of contemporary, democratic societies, which embody the morality of the slave or the herd, is to make ourselves small.

Friedrich Nietzsche (1844–1900)

Human progress will not be achieved by creating a society characterized by unlimited human love and democratic justice for all, but by returning to a more brutal but passionate aristocratic hierarchy. The distinction between good and evil is an invention of slave morality, which invokes Christian teaching to reverse the natural order. The masterful people have no time for the distinction between good and evil. For them, the only important difference is between that which is good (themselves) and that which is bad (those lower than themselves).

The new philosophers

In keeping with his distinction between master and slave morality, and unreserved admiration for the former, Nietzsche longs for a new breed of philosophers whose role it will be to champion and promote master morality and to challenge the false values of democratic society. Courageous, independent and self-reliant, they will have no patience with Christian teaching, which always sides with the victims of master morality and tries to defend them against their oppressors. Christianity, which teaches the sacrifice of freedom and pride, is suited only to the attitudes and aspirations of the slave. The new philosophers will also reject the values of parliamentary democracy, a system of government devised by and for the downtrodden and suffering.

Nor (unlike Nietzsche himself, of course) will they just be thinkers and writers. They will not be mere academic philosophers, like Kant and Hegel, who have merely described the value-judgements of the past intelligibly. Although the new philosophers may build on their labours, they will be men of action, leaders and lawmakers, who will not only lay down a new set of moral values for society, but will exemplify it in the way they lead their own lives. As creators of values, based on the will to power, they will impose their new values on others.

As men of tomorrow, the new philosophers will be at odds with contemporary society, as it moves towards democracy, and they will expose its hypocrisy, smugness and falsehood. They will denounce weakness of the will and advocate strength and the will to power. In a society that honours only the herd animal, and clamours for equal rights, which inhibit the development of the individual, they will proclaim the importance of the individual's being different and of being able to live independently. They will affirm the truth that the greatest person is the one who does not recognize the difference between good and evil, right and wrong, and is undeterred in his or her pursuit of the will to power, by this distinction.

The new philosophers will recognize that concepts like democratic justice are false judgements, imposed onto the world, which make it easier for the weakest among us to survive. They will question whether such values as good and evil really are opposites, or even exist. Part of the problem with past thinkers has been their taking morality as a given. Nietzsche wants us to enter a new realm of dangerous insights, with the apparently positive values of religion and morality turned on their heads.

From Nietzsche's point of view, the exponents of master morality must be ever active, to ensure its victory. They must challenge the corrosive, egalitarian values of democracy. Of course, those who oppose the master morality in principle or who feel that they will be losers rather than winners, if it prevails, also have the strongest possible reason to prevent its succeeding.

Impact

- Nietzsche's books and ideas have influenced subsequent thinkers, including Albert Camus, Jacques Derrida, Michel Foucault, Martin Heidegger, Jean-Paul Sartre and Oswald Spengler, although, as he does not put forward a coherent set of ideas, people tend to choose those which appeal to them.
- However, he does consistently laud power and domination by the powerful, and to deride democracy, equality, social justice, compassion and Christianity.
- It is easy to see why, in the inter-war period, with his sister's encouragement, Nietzsche's ideas were taken up by the Nazis, and they continue to be admired by extremist right-wing and racist groups.
- Nietzsche's writings challenge us to review and reaffirm, and to be able to articulate, the ethical values upon which Western, democratic society is based.

Further reading

K. Ansell-Pearson, *How to Read Nietzsche*, London: Granta, 2005.

A. Hoover, *Friedrich Nietzsche: His Life and Thought*, Westport, CT: Praeger, 1994.

L. Lampert, *Nietzsche's Task: An Interpretation of Beyond Good and Evil*, New Haven, CT: Yale University Press, 2001.

D. Mills Daniel and Dafydd E. Mills Daniel, *Briefly: Nietzsche's Beyond Good and Evil*, London: SCM Press, 2007.

Friedrich Nietzsche, *Beyond Good and Evil*, trans. M. Faber, Oxford and New York: Oxford University Press, 1998.

Further reading

Friedrich Nietzsche, *Human, All Too Human*, trans. M. Faber and S. Lehmann, London: Penguin, 1994.

Friedrich Nietzsche, *The Genealogy of Morals*, trans. H. Samuel and ed. T. N. R. Rogers, New York: Dover Publications, 2003.

Friedrich Nietzsche, *Thus Spake Zarathustra*, Ware: Wordsworth, 1997.

Friedrich Nietzsche, *Twilight of the Idols with The Anti-Christ and Ecce Homo* (Introduction by R. Furness), Ware: Wordsworth, 1997.

T. T. Roberts, *Contesting Spirit: Nietzsche, Affirmation, Religion*, Princeton, NJ: Princeton University Press, 1998.

R. Wicks, 'Friedrich Nietzsche' (revised 2011), in E. N. Zalta (ed.), *Stanford Encyclopaedia of Philosophy*, at http://plato.stanford.edu.

D. Wilkerson, 'Friedrich Nietzsche' (2009) in J. Fieser and B. Dowden (eds), *Internet Encyclopedia of Philosophy*, at www.iep.utm.edu.

21

Bertrand Russell
(1872–1970)
The value of philosophy
Knowledge by acquaintance and
description, the inductive principle and
the theory of definite descriptions

Context

Why does Bertrand Russell attach so much importance to studying philosophy? By exploring the grounds of human beliefs and
fundamental questions about the universe and the meaning
of life, and pursuing knowledge for its own sake, he believes
that it brings to society a sense of justice and universal love, the
counterparts of the desire for truth. Russell's view of the value
of philosophy is one of the key ideas discussed below. In the
British empiricist tradition, Russell, like his friend G. E. Moore,
rejected absolute idealism, which maintains that ultimate reality
is a wholly rational and harmonious system, which is identified
with one absolute mind or spirit. Although initially attracted to it,
Russell decided that it was an example of philosophical system-
building exceeding the limits of philosophical knowledge.

Through *Principia Mathematica*, Russell played a key role
in the development of modern logic. Together with Gottlob

Frege, he subscribed to logicism, the view that mathematical truths are truths of logic, which are capable of being deduced from fundamental logical propositions. As they are analytic, the truths of mathematics are the same in all possible worlds, so mathematics must be logically necessary. He developed his theory of types to address the paradox (Russell's paradox) that he identified in mathematical set theory. While some classes or sets are members of themselves, others are not. For example, the class of all classes is itself a class, but the class of oranges is not itself an orange. But is the class of all classes which are not members of themselves, a member of itself? If it is a member of itself, it is not a member, and vice-versa. Russell's theory proposes a hierarchy of sets, with those at a lower level being ineligible for inclusion in those higher up.

Russell thinks that the meaning of language is to be found in that to which it refers or names. According to this referential theory of meaning, or logical atomism, language is analysable into elementary propositions, which are collections of names. These basic atoms of language denote objects, the basic elements of reality. And, logical atomism fits in with one of our everyday uses of language: to refer to things. But, by trying to reduce meaning to one function of language, this theory fails to give an account of the diverse way in which it is used. Many words, like conjunctions and prepositions, do not name anything. Also, when we enquire about the meaning of an expression, we are not asking what it refers to, but how it is about what it relates to, which involves a range of factors, such as who says it and to whom, the circumstances in which it is said, and so on.

Russell's consideration of epistemological issues resulted in his important distinction between knowledge by acquaintance and knowledge by description. The first occurs when we are directly aware of things, as of the sense-data which make up a table's appearance; they are what we actually experience, as opposed to things as they are in themselves: the physical objects we believe give rise to the sense-data. Knowledge by description derives from truths about something, which are related to things with which we are acquainted. We are not directly acquainted with a table as a physical object, but our knowledge of it as a physical object is linked to our acquaintance with the sense-data that make up its appearance. The second part of the key ideas section deals with this distinction, the inductive principle and Russell's theory of definite descriptions, which tackles the problem, related to the referential theory of meaning, of how we can use terms meaningfully, if there is nothing to which they refer.

In moral philosophy, Russell's metaethical stance is close to Moore's. An ethical intuitionist, he regards good as an indefinable, non-natural quality, which can only be known through intuition. His attitude to religion is sceptical and critical. In debate with the Roman Catholic philosopher Father Frederick Copleston, he counters the Thomist argument from contingency with the riposte that the universe is just there, and there is no reason for or purpose in seeking an explanation of it. He does not accept that Jesus as depicted in the Gospels is a supremely good man. His teaching in the Sermon on the Mount leads people to overlook his threats of eternal punishment for sinners. As a religion, Christianity has been too ready to persecute dissenters, while the Roman Catholic Church, by condemning contraception, helps to impose a life of misery on millions of human beings who need never have existed.

Life

Bertrand Arthur William Russell, the great-grandson of the sixth Duke of Bedford and grandson of the first Earl Russell (Lord John Russell), the Whig/Liberal politician and prime minister, was born in Trellech, South Wales. John Stuart Mill, who died a year later, was his lay godfather. Both his parents died when he was very young and he was brought up by his paternal grandparents, his grandmother, Lady Frances Russell, being a powerful influence on him, although he rejected her devout religious views. After reading mathematics and moral sciences (philosophy) at Trinity College, Cambridge, Russell was elected a prize fellow of Trinity in 1895 and appointed a lecturer in 1910. His interest in the philosophy of mathematics led him to focus on logic, which, with A. N. Whitehead, he decided to refashion. The outcome was *Principia Mathematica*, published in three volumes between 1910 and 1913.

From an early stage, Russell's interests extended beyond academic philosophy. In 1907, he stood for parliament as a candidate for the National Union of Women's Suffrage Societies. Believing that the First World War was not justified, he campaigned for peace and against conscription. As a result, he was dismissed from his lectureship at Trinity and was imprisoned for six months.

Between the wars, Russell visited Russia, China and the United States, and ran a progressive school in Sussex with his second wife, Dora. He became third Earl Russell, following his elder brother Frank's death, in 1931, but inherited no wealth with the title, as his brother had been bankrupt. As he had given away most of his own capital, he earned a living by lecturing, writing newspaper articles and, in addition to philosophy, books on such subjects as science, education, politics and marriage.

Bertrand Russell (1872–1970)

In the late 1930s, Russell went to the United States to take up visiting professorships, but a campaign against him, on the grounds of agnosticism and the allegation that his books promoted sexual immorality, prevented his appointment as professor at City College, New York in 1940. However, he taught at Harvard and Bryn Mawr College, Pennsylvania, and in 1944, following election to a fellowship at Trinity, returned to Cambridge.

After the war, Russell devoted much of his time to political activity. Committed to democracy, he was exercised by the problem of reconciling individual liberty with stable and efficient government. Though seeing socialism as a means of promoting social justice, he wanted to diminish the power of the state. Opposed to nationalism and war, he grew increasingly concerned about the possibility of another world war and became a leading member of the Campaign for Nuclear Disarmament. The sale of his archives to McMaster University, in Canada, enabled him to establish the Bertrand Russell Peace Foundation, in 1964. In 1967, he set up an International War Crimes Tribunal, with Jean-Paul Sartre, to investigate US war crimes in Vietnam.

Russell received the Order of Merit in 1949 and the Nobel Prize in Literature in 1950. Married four times, to Alys Pearsall Smith, Dora Black, Patricia Spence and Edith Finch, he also had celebrated affairs with Lady Ottoline Morrell, and Lady Constance Malleson (the actress Colette O'Niel). As well as *Principia Mathematica* and *The Problems of Philosophy*, Russell's books include *The Principles of Mathematics* (1902), *Our Knowledge of the External World* (1914), *Mysticism and Logic* (1917), *Why I Am Not a Christian* (1927), *An Enquiry Into Meaning and Truth* (1940), *History of Western Philosophy* (1945) and *Human Knowledge: Its Scope and Limits* (1948).

Key ideas

The value of philosophy

In *The Problems of Philosophy*, Russell gives a moving and mystical account of the benefits of philosophical study, which he sees as a lifetime's vocation. People may think philosophy involves hair-splitting controversies about matters which cannot be resolved, but this arises from misconceptions about its role. Its value, for those not studying it, is indirect, through its effect on the lives of those who do. People readily appreciate the importance of satisfying material needs, but not those of their minds. However, a worthwhile society requires more than material well-being. Philosophy aims to give unity to the sciences, and to extend knowledge, by critically examining the grounds of human beliefs. It also addresses fundamental questions about the nature of the universe and the meaning of life, which the human intellect will never be able to answer, unless its powers change completely. None of philosophy's existing answers seem definitive or true; but its task is to go on considering these questions.

Indeed, philosophy's value does not lie in its being able to answer such questions, but, paradoxically, in the doubts and uncertainty it creates by trying to do so. People tend not to question anything and to reject the unfamiliar. Philosophy shows that even everyday things give rise to problems, and by reducing certainty it eradicates dogmatism and promotes a sense of wonder. Perhaps, its chief value is in the greatness of the objects it contemplates. Philosophical enquiry enriches the individual by promoting the quest for knowledge for its own sake, while the philosophic life is calm and free, impelling us to widen our horizons and to engage with the world around us.

One thing philosophy should teach us is that we must not try to make the universe fit what we find in ourselves. There is a tendency to believe that everything is either human-made, a property of the mind, or unknowable and therefore of no account. But, such an attitude can only imprison the intellect. The free intellect will view things as God would, calmly, dispassionately and solely with a desire for knowledge. A mind, used to philosophical contemplation's freedom and impartiality, will then be able to carry them over into the world of action and emotion, where desire for truth has its counterparts in justice and universal love. This contemplation creates citizens of the world, freeing humanity from enslavement to narrow hopes and fears. So, we should study philosophy for the questions themselves, which enlarge our idea of what is possible, while through the universe's greatness, our minds will become great and capable of that union with the universe, which is their highest good.

Knowledge by acquaintance and description, the inductive principle and the theory of definite descriptions

What do we know? How do we know it? Does our knowledge have a secure basis? Russell distinguishes between knowledge by acquaintance, direct awareness of things, and knowledge by description, knowledge of truths about things. What are we acquainted with? Sense-data, relating to both particular things and universals, such as 'whiteness', are the obvious examples. Beyond sense-data, we are acquainted with memory, our source of knowledge about the past, and there is also introspection: we are aware of being aware of things. But, we are not acquainted with physical objects, or others' minds.

We know these by description. Our knowledge of them derives from truths about them, which are related to things with which we are acquainted. We are not directly acquainted with a table as a physical object, but our knowledge of it, as one, is connected to our acquaintance with the sense-data that make up its appearance.

On the basis of our acquaintance with the sense-data, we can formulate a description of the table, which applies to only that one object. Knowledge of truths, as well as of things, is based on acquaintance and is ultimately reducible to knowledge about what is known by acquaintance. Description makes it possible to go beyond private experience, giving us knowledge of things that we have not experienced.

Russell explains that our acquaintance with sense-data enables us to infer the existence of physical objects and an external world, which goes some way towards answering the question about how we are able to move beyond our own private experiences. But, to know more about matter and physical objects, other people or the past before the start of our individual memories, we need general laws and principles, so that we can draw the relevant inferences.

To predict future events, we rely on the principle of induction. However, our use of it presupposes the accuracy of our stores of sense-data, as applied to the external world. On the basis of past experience, we know that the occurrence of one sort of event is and will continue to be a sign of the occurrence of another event. Without such knowledge, we could not extend our knowledge beyond the extremely limited sphere of our immediate private experiences. But, despite its crucial importance, we cannot find an absolute justification for inductive reasoning. Our belief that the sun will rise tomorrow is based on the fact that it rose this morning and yesterday and the day before that. If things occur often enough, we regard the probability that they will occur again as tantamount to certainty. But, we never reach an ultimate justification of this belief. We always allude to previous experiences, which are themselves based on previous experiences.

Yet, this circularity of reasoning does not force us to abandon inductive processes. Even if experience cannot verify the inductive principle, it cannot disprove it either. Indeed, it would make life rather difficult if it could, as general scientific principles, like every event having a cause, as well as everyday beliefs, depend on it. We must be pragmatic, and just accept that our knowledge has limits.

Russell's theory of descriptions concerns his distinction between proper names, such as 'John', and definite descriptions, such as 'the youngest man in the room' or 'the present king of France'. The problem is that definite descriptions like this may not refer to anything; there may be nothing to which the description refers. The sentence 'John is tall' only seems to have the same logical structure as the definite description 'the youngest man in the room is tall'. While resembling a referring expression, the definite description is in fact more like sentences containing quantifiers, for example, 'some men are bald'.

Russell's recognition of the different logical forms underlying proper names and definite descriptions helps to resolve the logical problems. The meaningfulness of such a description as 'the present king of France' can be retained without the need for there to be an entity to which it refers. Russell's theory also shows how negative existential statements, such as 'the round square does not exist', can be meaningful, even though they have no actual reference. This also prevents ambiguities of language enticing philosophers into metaphysical notions: there does not need to be a special, metaphysical sense or dimension where a round square exists.

Impact

- Russell shows how philosophy benefits both the individual and society, and inspires others to study it by the example he gives.
- His distinction between knowledge by acquaintance and knowledge by description was a major contribution to the theory of knowledge.
- He explains that our inability to provide an absolute justification for the principle of induction does not detract from its importance: we must just accept the limitations of our knowledge.
- His recognition of the different logical forms underlying definite descriptions and proper names helped to resolve a range of logical problems.

Further reading

A. J. Ayer, *Russell*, London: Fontana, 1972.

A. J. Ayer, *Russell and Moore: The Analytical Heritage*, London: Macmillan, 1973.

R. Carey, 'Russell's Metaphysics' (revised 2008), in J. Fieser and B. Dowden (eds), *Internet Encyclopedia of Philosophy*, at www.iep.utm.edu.

A. D. Irvine, 'Bertrand Russell' (revised 2010), in E. N. Zalta (ed.), *Stanford Encyclopaedia of Philosophy*, at http://plato.stanford.edu.

D. Mills Daniel and M. Daniel, *Briefly: Russell's The Problems of Philosophy*, London: SCM Press, 2007.

Bertrand Russell and F. C. Copleston, 'A Debate on the Existence of God', in J. H. Hick (ed.), *The Existence of God*, New York and London: The Macmillan Company, 1972.

Bertrand Russell, *Logic and Knowledge*, Nottingham: Spokesman Books, 2007.

Bertrand Russell, 'On Denoting', *Mind*, New Series, Vol. 14, No. 56 (Oct. 1905), pp. 479–93, at http://www.jstor.org.

Bertrand Russell, *The Problems of Philosophy*, reissued second edition, with Introduction by John Skorupski, Oxford and New York: Oxford University Press, 2001.

G. Warnock, *English Philosophy since 1900*, Oxford: Oxford University Press, 1969.

22

G. E. Moore
(1873–1958)
The defence of common sense and proof
of the external world
The naturalistic fallacy and the open
question argument

Context

Why become a philosopher? Those who believe that it is due to people's surprise at finding themselves in a world they cannot explain, or a desire to wrestle with life's fundamental questions, may find it difficult to understand why George Edward Moore became one. When he went up to Cambridge to read classics, he seems to have had no intention of doing so. While many philosophers have engaged in wild metaphysical speculation and propounded elaborate philosophical systems, Moore represents the common sense point of view. He did not find the world puzzling or in need of explanation. What he found puzzling, and which drew him to philosophy, were the strange things some philosophers said about the world, for which they seemed to have no rational or empirical basis.

With Russell, he rejected absolute idealism, the dominant philosophical doctrine in the late nineteenth century. He found the views of the absolute idealists, such as F. H. Bradley and J. M. E. McTaggart, difficult to understand. Why did they put forward such outlandish theories? Could they really mean what they said? Moore challenges them to explain themselves. For example, in a 1903 *Mind* article, 'The Refutation of Idealism', he subjects monism, one aspect of absolute idealism, to rigorous scrutiny. It is the doctrine that, contrary to what appears to be the case, which is that the world consists of many different, unrelated things, ultimate reality is unified and consists of one fundamental substance, which is to be identified with an absolute mind or spirit.

Subtly, Moore highlights this doctrine's absurdity. Its exact meaning may be hard to determine, but it appears to assert that the universe is spiritual, and therefore wholly different from what the majority takes it to be, and has many unexpected properties. Chairs, tables and mountains, for example, are generally thought to be very different from human beings. However, unless the idealists use grossly misleading language, and if they are declaring that the whole universe is spiritual, then chairs, tables and mountains are more like us than we think. The idealists seem to be saying that they are, in some sense, neither lifeless nor unconscious. Indeed, to claim that reality is spiritual is to say that the whole universe has those very qualities that we regard as making human beings superior to the things we classify as inanimate.

As C. D. Broad points out in his obituary of Moore, he had absolutely no belief in the possibility of constructive or speculative metaphysics, being quick to pinpoint the inevitable confusions of such systems. His philosophical interests were wholly analytical and critical; and Broad judged that no philosopher had matched Moore's ability to analyse fundamental philosophical problems, expose fallacies and ambiguities, and identify alternative possibilities. His analytical approach to philosophy, as a means of clarifying, and trying to resolve, its problems, had a profound influence on the direction philosophy took in the twentieth century.

In the first key idea discussed below, Moore applies his analytical powers to defending common sense and proving the existence of the external world. He wonders why some philosophers question the common sense view that objects exist in the world independently of our minds. He focuses on the extraordinary nature of their views and the difficulty of finding grounds for preferring them to the common sense alternative, and offers a simple proof of the existence of external objects. But, though Moore does not doubt the existence of an external world, he accepts that analysing the propositions that express such truths, and explaining their meaning, is less straightforward; and his attempts to do so tend to be unsatisfactory. This may be due to his assumption that such analysis must involve breaking propositions down into their simplest components.

Moore was a major contributor to twentieth-century moral philosophy. In *Principia Ethica*, he observes that, when we describe a person as 'good' or 'bad' or an action as 'right' or 'wrong', we make an ethical judgement. But, moral philosophy has suffered from confusion, as philosophers try to answer ethical questions without being clear what the questions are. As a result, they commit metaethical errors in relation to the meaning and use of moral terms like 'good' and 'right'. To help prevent such errors, Moore develops the key ideas of the naturalistic fallacy and the open-question argument, also discussed below. But, Moore's analysis of ethical terms leads him to the rather odd conclusion that 'good' cannot be defined, because, like 'yellow', it is a simple and indefinable quality. So, while he makes important metaethical points, his own position is that of ethical non-naturalism and intuition-ism: goodness is a non-natural property that a particular thing possesses, which can only be apprehended by intuition. This position makes identifying what is good a highly individual process, reducing moral debate to an exchange of different intuitions.

Life

George Edward Moore was born in London, the son of Dr Daniel Moore and his wife Henrietta (Sturge), and brother of the poet and illustrator Thomas Sturge Moore, whose writings include *The Vinedresser and Other Poems* (1899). Between 1882 and 1892, Moore attended Dulwich College and then read first classics and then moral sciences (philosophy) at Trinity College, Cambridge, where he got to know Bertrand Russell, who shared his attitude towards absolute idealism.

After graduating in 1896, Moore submitted a dissertation on Kant's moral philosophy, and was elected to a six-year prize fellowship at Trinity, in 1898. This enabled him to develop his philosophical thinking, to write articles (his dissertation was published in *Mind*) and to lecture in London. Moore's first book, the influential *Principia Ethica*, based on some of his lectures, was published in 1903. After his fellowship ended, limited private means enabled Moore to continue studying philosophy until his appointment as a university lecturer in moral philosophy at Cambridge in 1911.

Moore was elected to a fellowship at Trinity in 1925, the year in which he was appointed professor of philosophy at Cambridge, a post he held until retirement in 1939. He also exerted a powerful influence on the world of philosophy out-side Cambridge as the editor of the philosophical journal *Mind* for over 25 years. He was a visiting professor at universities in the United States from 1940 to 1944.

Moore was a friend of and major influence on Bertrand Russell and Ludwig Wittgenstein (his successor as professor), while his writings, particularly the emphasis in *Principia Ethica* on appreciation of beauty and friendship, were an inspiration to such Bloomsbury Group members as John Maynard Keynes, Lytton Strachey and Virginia Woolf. In addition to articles and *Principia Ethica*, Moore published *Ethics* in 1912, *Philosophical Studies* in 1922 and *Some Main Problems of Philosophy* in 1953. He was awarded the Order of Merit (OM) in 1951.

He married Dorothy Ely, a Newnham graduate, in 1916. They had two sons, the poet Nicholas Moore and the music teacher and composer Timothy Moore. One of the twentieth century's greatest academic philosophers and teachers, Moore was also respected as a man of straightforward character, who enjoyed such simple pleasures as walking, gardening and talk-ing to friends. According to C. D. Broad, what made Moore so exceptional was that he combined the virtues of the ordinary, unpretentious Englishman, who is often muddle-headed, with the abilities of an intellectual, who is often conceited, without the vices of either.

Key ideas

The defence of common sense and proof of the external world

According to the doctrine of absolute idealism, deriving from the views of the German philosopher G. W. F. Hegel, reality is monistic and is explicable in terms of an absolute oneness or absolute mind, with individual perceptions and experience being ultimately grounded on this underlying mental or spiritual reality. Alternatively, subjective idealism, as expounded by Berkeley, focuses on individual perception: *esse est percipi*; and the objects we perceive, which we believe to have an independent existence, exist only in that we perceive them. Their key common feature is that, contrary to the common sense view that there is an external, material world of which we with our thoughts are part, and which constitutes (if there is no God) the whole of reality, reality is, in fact, essentially mental or spiritual.

In 'A Defence of Common Sense', Moore mounts a robust defence of the common sense view of the world and sets out what may be called a realist philosophical standpoint: if certain philosophical doctrines conflict with what common sense tells us, the common sense position is more likely to be correct. He takes a number of propositions or truisms, which, he says, can be regarded as certainly true, such as that he is a human being, with a human body, who has existed for a number of years. Further, propositions referring to the earth having existed for many years, or to the reality of space and the external world, are equally true, as common sense indicates.

He rejects the halfway-house, proposed by some philosophers, who maintain that, although propositions of the first kind may be true, those of the second kind are at least partially false. While we may know that we exist, in some sense, through awareness of ourselves, there can be no certainty that an external world exists, as we cannot get beyond our perceptions of it. Moore concentrates on the inconsistencies within such arguments: they depend on the very things which they purport to deny. For example, their use of the term 'we' indicates a belief in the existence of other human beings, even as they question it.

Moore's point is that there is no basis whatsoever for holding that physical facts are either logically or causally dependent on mental facts, in the way that subjective and absolute idealism assert; and that any form of idealism ultimately produces such counter-intuitive and common-sense defying propositions as that time or space are unreal. If reality is actually one unified spiritual substance, to be identified with the absolute mind or spirit, or a system of sensations, which do not exist beyond the individual's perception of them, then propositions that refer to, or presuppose, an external world, existing independently of us, and containing distinct material objects, are very wide of the mark. However, if we take the view that the external world and its features are as common sense indicates them to be, we avoid many unnecessary problems.

In his 'Proof of an External World', Moore offers a simple and rigorous proof that objects external to ourselves exist, by holding up and indicating one of his hands, then the other. From this premise, the conclusion follows that two human hands exist at this moment, and so external things exist. And, it would be absurd, Moore insists, for anyone to claim that he did not know, but only believed, that the premise of his argument (that there was one of his hands in a certain place, then another) was true. So, why do some philosophers find this proof inadequate? It is because they want a proof of his premise, that what he asserts now, when he holds up his hands, and so on, is true. But, this is both impossible and unnecessary because our being unable to prove something does not mean that we do not know it.

However, while Moore holds with certainty that propositions which assert the existence of material things are true, he is less sure about how to analyse them correctly. He believes that analysis should involve reference to sense-data, but does not think that an adequate analysis is attainable. It is clear, though, where the idealist philosophers go wrong: they question the existence of an external world, when the problem lies in developing a satisfactory analysis of propositions about it.

The naturalistic fallacy and the open question argument

Moore accuses other moral philosophers, including Bentham and Mill, of committing a logical error, in relation to what he regards as the fundamental question of ethics: how 'good' and other moral terms are to be defined. Their ethical naturalism has led them to try to define or analyse 'good' in terms of a natural property, and to hold that it simply means that property. For the utilitarians, the natural property is pleasure or happiness. Not everyone agrees that Bentham and Mill commit this error. However, Bentham does suggest that the only people who challenge the principle of utility are those who do not appear to know what 'right' or 'good' means.

Moore calls defining 'good', or any moral term, as a natural property, the 'naturalistic fallacy'. In fact, he holds that 'good' cannot be defined. It is a simple, indefinable, unanalysable, non-natural property or quality of things known by intuition. To say that something is 'good' is to say it has this simple, unanalysable property. Complex things, such as a horse, can be analysed or broken down into their simple or most basic constituent parts. However, these basic constituent parts will all be objects of thought which cannot be defined, because they are ultimate terms of reference, in relation to which whatever is capable of definition must be defined. Like 'yellow', 'good' is one of these ultimate terms of reference.

Moore points out that philosophers who define 'good' as a natural object do not agree among themselves about which one it is to be defined in terms of. Some say it is pleasure or happiness; others what people desire; and so on. But, if we just define pleasure as this or that natural (or supernatural) object, how can we prove that any of these definitions is right or wrong? Moore hammers this point home in another way. However 'good' is defined, it can always be asked intelligibly, of the thing so defined, whether or not it is itself good. But, if 'good' just means, for example, 'pleasure', it would not make any sense to ask whether pleasure is good. Whether or not pleasure is good would not be the open question that it obviously is.

Even if Moore's own definition of 'good' seems odd, he makes a very important point. Some philosophers do seem to define 'good' and other ethical terms as a natural property, such as pleasure, holding that it simply means that natural property. But, this is clearly a fallacy. Unless good and, for example, pleasure, are different, there is no point in saying pleasure is good, as it just states a tautology: 'pleasure is pleasure'. When people say pleasure is 'good', they do not think they are uttering a tautology. They believe they are evaluating or commending it. Thus, 'good' cannot just mean pleasure. Again, whatever people claim to be good, it is always an open question (one that can be asked meaningfully) whether it actually is.

Impact

- As a founding father of the analytical approach to philosophical questions, Moore played a central role in shaping the course philosophy would take in Britain and America during the twentieth century.

G. E. Moore (1873–1958)

- His robust defence of common sense opinions, particularly in relation to knowledge of the external world, helped to discredit all forms of philosophical idealism and attempts at speculative metaphysics.
- His focus on metaethics, as a means of clarifying, and trying to resolve, ethical problems, had a lasting effect on the direction taken by twentieth-century moral philosophy.
- His identification of the naturalistic fallacy and the open question argument are invaluable tools for analysing and refuting muddled ethical theories involving ethical naturalism or supernaturalism.

Further reading

A. J. Ayer, *Russell and Moore: The Analytical Heritage*, London: Macmillan, 1973.

T. Baldwin, 'George Edward Moore' (2004), in E. N. Zalta (ed.), *Stanford Encyclopaedia of Philosophy*, at http://plato.stanford.edu.

W. D. Hudson, *Modern Moral Philosophy*, second revised edition, London: Palgrave Macmillan, 1983.

D. Mills Daniel, *Moore's Principia Ethica*, London: SCM Press, 2007.

G. E. Moore, 'A Defence of Common Sense', in G. E. Moore, *Philosophical Papers*, London: Allen & Unwin, 1959.

G. E. Moore, *Principia Ethica*, ed. T. Baldwin, revised edition, Cambridge: Cambridge University Press, 1993.

G. E. Moore, 'Proof of an External World', in G. E. Moore, *Philosophical Papers*, London: Allen & Unwin, 1959.

G. E. Moore, *Some Main Problems of Philosophy*, London: Allen & Unwin, 1953.

Further reading

G. E. Moore, 'The Refutation of Idealism', in G. E. Moore, *Philosophical Studies*, London: Kegan Paul, Trench, Trubner & Co., 1922.

A. Preston, 'George Edward Moore' (revised 2005), in J. Fieser and B. Dowden (eds), *Internet Encyclopedia of Philosophy*, at www.iep.utm.edu.

P. Schlipp, *The Philosophy of G. E. Moore*, La Salle: Open Court Publishing, 1977.

G. Warnock, *English Philosophy since 1900*, Oxford: Oxford University Press, 1969.

23

Ludwig Wittgenstein
(1889–1951)
The picture theory of meaning
Language-games and forms of life

Context

Why is Ludwig Wittgenstein regarded as the twentieth century's most charismatic philosopher? Perhaps it is because
he exudes the angst, and intense earnestness in pursuit of
truth, considered obligatory in twentieth-century intellectuals:
indeed, he seems to have approached philosophy as a quasi-
religious vocation. There is the fact that, having developed a
theory which he believed would solve all philosophical problems, he changed his mind. Then, there is the mystery with
which he surrounded his later work, refusing to publish it
himself and trying to prevent others from publicizing it; his
lack of sociability and desire for solitude; and the variety of
jobs he did, from Austrian elementary school teacher to
Cambridge professor of philosophy. And, while charisma does
not make ideas more valid or valuable, it helps to draw attention
to them.

Broadly, Wittgenstein's position was that almost all of philosophy's many and seemingly insoluble problems boil down

to confusions arising from language. Religious statements provide numerous examples of the sort of thing he is talking about. Confusion about the nature and status of existential statements led Anselm and Descartes to believe that they had formulated a proof of God's existence. Similarities in what Wittgenstein later described as their surface grammar (they both contain subject, verb, object and adverb and use almost identical words), between such statements as 'Graham loves all his children equally', and 'God loves all his children equally' conceal the major differences between them. We know who Graham is, and can test the truth of the first statement by observing how he behaves towards his offspring. But how do we check the second? Do we even agree about its meaning? Even theists have different and differing concepts of God; and who exactly are his 'children'?

In moral philosophy, Wittgenstein's Cambridge colleague G. E. Moore had focused on metaethical problems, which almost invariably arise from imprecision or confusions of language, as with the application of the language of perception to ethical statements. Take the statements, 'everyone who looks at Kate's car can see that it is rusting', and 'everyone who looks at Kate's conduct can see that it is wrong'. All who look at Kate's car will see the rust on it, but what about her conduct? Will there be the same unanimity about that? Obviously, the verb 'see' is not being used in the same way in the two statements.

Wittgenstein talks about our intelligence being bewitched by language. What is needed is rigorous investigation of the language in which philosophical problems are expressed, to find the means of removing the spell it casts over us. Thus, Wittgenstein does not seem to have regarded philosophy as a separate branch of knowledge or distinct academic discipline, like physics or history, with its own subject matter. It is a process of spell-breaking, which, once complete, will no longer have a job to do. Indeed, Wittgenstein believed he had reached this point after publication of his *Tractatus Logico-Philosophicus*.

In the *Tractatus*, Wittgenstein, influenced by the logical atomism of his other great Cambridge mentor, Bertrand Russell, expounds a referential theory of meaning. This type of theory holds that the meaning of language derives from that to which it refers in the world (an object or referent), or the relationship between words and their referents. In Wittgenstein's version, language is meaningful because its logical form pictures that of reality; and the picture theory of meaning is one of the key ideas discussed below. Wittgenstein did not claim that his theory depicts people's everyday use of language; the *Tractatus* was designed to reveal the essence of language. But does he penetrate to language's inner core or present a fanciful theory, as its failure to correspond to the way language is actually used suggests?

This is Wittgenstein's own conclusion, set out in *Philosophical Investigations*. He came to see himself as having been fixated by the idea of the logical form of language picturing reality, producing the conviction that there is an essence of language and that meaning is explicable in only one way. But, this was the wrong approach. Instead of theorizing, and trying to impose a logical structure on language, the philosopher needs to look at the actual use of language in everyday life. He then begins to see that it does not have a single purpose or function. It is more like the tools in a tool-box, with different kinds of sentence performing different tasks. The language game and the form of life are the other key ideas discussed in this chapter.

Life

Born into a wealthy Viennese family, Wittgenstein was the youngest of eight children, three of whom later committed suicide. Though there were Jewish antecedents on both sides, his father Karl had been brought up as a Protestant and his mother Leopoldine as a Roman Catholic. Wittgenstein did not associate himself with any religion or denomination during his life, although he was very interested in religious questions. From an early stage, he showed an interest in science and technology, and in 1906, he became a student at the Technische Hochschule in Berlin, where he studied mechanical engineering, going from there to the University of Manchester in 1908.

Through his work in aeronautical engineering at Manchester, he became interested in mathematics and, through reading Russell's *Principles of Mathematics*, in its foundations. A visit to the philosopher and mathematician Gottlob Frege led to a change of direction; in 1911, he transferred to Trinity College, Cambridge, to work with Russell on mathematical logic, and also came into contact with G. E. Moore. Although very successful in his studies, he found Cambridge life and academics uncongenial and sought escape and solitude in Norway, where he worked on the ideas for his great work on logic and language, the *Tractatus Logico-Philosophicus*, completing the book during the First World War while serving in the Austrian army. Published first in German in 1921, and then in English, with an introduction by Russell, in 1922, this was the only book he published during his lifetime.

Wittgenstein believed that he had now contributed all that he could to philosophy and had nothing further to say. Having given away his large inheritance before the start of the First

World War, he spent the early 1920s teaching in elementary schools in Austria and then took a number of casual jobs. But, by 1929, he had become convinced that the *Tractatus* was not the final word on philosophy, and Frank Ramsey persuaded him to return to Cambridge. After completing a PhD, he became a fellow of Trinity and lecturer in philosophy, succeeding Moore as professor of philosophy in 1939. Focusing increasingly on ordinary language, rather than formal logic, he worked on the ideas that were later to appear in *Philosophical Investigations*.

During the Second World War, Wittgenstein worked as a hospital porter and technician in London and Newcastle, returning to Cambridge in 1944. But, depressed and suicidal, he resigned from his professorship after three years and retired to Ireland. In 1949, he was diagnosed with cancer, dying in Cambridge two years later. Although he prepared *Philosophical Investigations* for publication, he decided not to do so, and it did not appear until two years after his death.

Key ideas

The picture theory of meaning

In the *Tractatus*, Wittgenstein propounds a sophisticated version of the referential theory of meaning, designed to resolve the problems of its existing formulation. A difficulty with any theory that language derives its meaning from the objects in the world to which it refers, or the relationship between words or propositions and their referents, is that expressions appear to be meaningful, even if what they denote does not exist. 'The Archbishop of Canterbury is head of the Roman Catholic Church' does not refer to an actual state of affairs; but, though false, the proposition seems to be meaningful. So, while the referential theory appears to indicate that the meaningfulness of a sentence cannot be known, unless certain objects or facts exist in the world, the question of whether such objects or facts actually exist cannot be raised, unless the words of the sentence already make it clear what kind of objects or facts it refers to. Again, the referential theory of meaning is unable to account for such propositional connectives as 'and', 'or' and 'not'. They have no referent; are they meaningless?

Wittgenstein's picture theory is intended to show that these problems arise from a misunderstanding of the logic of language. The basic form of the referential theory fails to capture the true logical structure of language, which reflects that of reality. Full analysis reveals that language pictures reality in the way that a model does. Wittgenstein had a particular example in mind: a case in the Paris law-courts where models were used to represent a motor accident. He maintains that a proposition refers to the world in the same way that the models represent the motor accident, thus producing a logical picture of the world.

The book consists of numbered propositions, which are developed from seven basic ones, such as: the world is all that is the case; what is the case, a fact, is the existence of states of affairs; a logical picture of facts is a thought; a thought is a proposition with sense; and a proposition is a truth function of elementary propositions, the latter being truth functions of themselves. Their terse nature does not aid understanding of the propositions. Wittgenstein's contention is that the world contains objects, which language denotes by names, and we need to learn these names. However, the objects do not exist by themselves, but in combination with others. These are states of affairs or atomic facts, to which, in language, there are corresponding elementary propositions: collections of names, which have 'sense' (they convey information). Just as, in the world, there are facts of varying degrees of complexity (combinations of atomic facts), in language there are (compound) propositions of varying degrees of complexity (combinations of elementary propositions). While the truth-value of the compound propositions is determined by that of its constituent elementary propositions, the latter, by having the same logical form as reality and picturing it, have their own truth-value. Thus, through analysis, compound propositions can be reduced to elementary propositions, consisting of names, each of which has its referent in the world.

Locating meaning in the overall logical picture of reality, which propositions provide, does remove the need for propositional connectives to have a referent in order to be meaningful: their meaning derives from the way they function within the proposition. While individual words have their objects or referents, which we must learn, this is not the case with propositions, as they communicate a new sense or picture of reality to us. Although the objects, picked out by individual words, are fixed and unalterable, propositions enable us to build up a picture of the world experimentally by configuring objects in a variety of situations. However, though some of these propositions may be false, they are still meaningful.

Wittgenstein also clearly distinguishes between logical and empirical propositions. The laws of logic, such as that of contradiction, mark the boundary between propositions which have sense, and those which, by breaching them, are nonsense. However, logical propositions themselves, though they provide the framework within which meaning is possible, cannot be proved: they must just be accepted. Whereas the hallmark of a logical proposition is that its truth is self-evident, the truth or falsehood of non-logical propositions is not: it must be discovered empirically.

Wittgenstein became increasingly aware of his theory's failure to give a satisfactory account of language and meaning. By suggesting that language's sole purpose and function is to state propositions, and that the world consists of atomic facts, which can ultimately be broken down into simple objects, his theory ignores both the wide diversity of uses to which language is put and the complexity of the world it is supposed to picture. The last of the *Tractatus'* basic propositions is to the effect that what we cannot speak about, we must pass over in silence. However, this silence seems to include, for example, all ethical and religious statements.

Language-games and forms of life

The *Tractatus* set out a single comprehensive theory of meaning. Wittgenstein came to realize that this was the wrong approach. The logician's preference for a single theory must be abandoned. He must look at how language is actually used in the world and learn from observation. This suggests that there is no single purpose or function; language is more like a tool-box with tools to suit a multiplicity of purposes and functions. In the *Philosophical Investigations*, he reflects on the countless different kinds of sentence that exist in language, and which can (among a myriad possibilities) assert, question, command, describe, report, speculate, tell stories or jokes, thank, greet, pray and so on. Further, these diverse ways of using sentences and words are not fixed: different uses emerge and disappear in response to our changing everyday needs. Wittgenstein calls these different ways of using language, and the variety of contexts in which it is used, 'language-games'.

The term conveys the fact that language is always part of an activity, and varies from activity to activity, even though the uses of particular words or phrases may have a lot in common across different language-games. For example, the sentences, 'Thank you, Jane, for giving me enough money for my fare,' 'Thank you, God, for making sure that I had enough money for my fare,' and 'Thank God I had enough money for my fare,' have a lot of words in common, but relate to different if overlapping language-games. The first language-game is a straightforward expression of thanks to another person; the second, a prayer of thanksgiving to a transcendent being; while the third is not about addressing God, but recording relief at having necessary funds.

Wittgenstein calls the rules that govern the construction of sentences within the various language-games, 'grammar'. This is developed by and known to those who share these activities and who therefore understand what it does or does not make sense to say within a particular language-game. In the wrong context, words or particular uses of them may make no sense because they are being used incorrectly or inappropriately.

Wittgenstein also relates language to what he calls a 'form of life', to emphasize his view that not only is meaning determined by use, but also that language's very intelligibility is deeply embedded within our way of life as human beings or members of particular societies or cultures. Consensus about the meaning of the language we use does not reflect agreement in opinions but a shared form of life. Wittgenstein says that, if we came across a speaking lion, we could not understand him, even if he appeared to speak our language, because we do not share a lion's form of life.

Impact

- Wittgenstein's picture theory resolved some of the problems of the referential theory of meaning, but also highlighted its shortcomings.
- His focus on and clear distinction between empirical propositions and the propositions of logic in the *Tractatus* were well received by the logical positivists.
- He stressed the crucial point that philosophers should not try to impose a logical structure on language, but look at how language is actually used in everyday life.
- His view that language has a multiplicity of purposes and functions, expressed in the notions of the language-game and the form of life, had a major impact on the course of philosophy in the second half of the twentieth century and on the development of ordinary language philosophy.

Further reading

A. Biletzski and A. Matar, 'Ludwig Wittgenstein' (revised 2009), in E. N. Zalta (ed.), *Stanford Encyclopaedia of Philosophy*, at http://plato.stanford.edu.

A. Flew, *An Introduction to Western Philosophy*, London: Thames and Hudson, 1971.

W. D. Hudson, *Modern Moral Philosophy*, second revised edition, London: Palgrave Macmillan, 1983.

A. Kenny, *Wittgenstein*, revised edition, Oxford and Malden, MA: Blackwell Publishing, 2006.

J. C. Klagge (ed.), *Wittgenstein: Biography and Philosophy*, Cambridge: Cambridge University Press, 2001.

D. J. Richter, 'Ludwig Wittgenstein' (updated 2004), in J. Fieser and B. Dowden (eds), *Internet Encyclopedia of Philosophy*, at www.iep.utm.edu.

G. Warnock, *English Philosophy since 1900*, Oxford: Oxford University Press, 1969.

Ludwig Wittgenstein, *Notebooks 1914–16*, trans. G. E. M. Anscombe and ed. G. H. von Wright and G. E. M. Anscombe, second edition, Oxford and Malden, MA: Blackwell Publishing, 1981.

Ludwig Wittgenstein, *Philosophical Investigations*, trans. G. E. M. Anscombe, Oxford: Basil Blackwell, 1953.

Ludwig Wittgenstein, *Tractatus Logico-Philosophicus*, trans. B. McGuiness and D. Pears, second edition, London: Routledge, 2001.

24

Jean-Paul Sartre
(1905–80)
Consciousness and existence
Bad faith

Context

Why does one particular intellectual or writer manage to capture and embody the mood of a particular era and to become
its representative thinker, even for those who do not share
(all of) his views? Perhaps, it is a phenomenon that is more
likely to occur in France, where (or so it is claimed!) intellectuals command more respect than elsewhere. Certainly, it was
true of Sartre, who seems to have been regarded with pride
by many French people, whatever they thought of his philosophical ideas or political views, in a way that was not the case
with such contemporary figures as Russell or Ayer in Britain.
Hence the comment that, with Sartre's death, France lost its
conscience.

Existentialism, as propounded by Sartre, was certainly the
fashionable philosophy in continental Europe during the
1950s and 1960s and had plenty of followers in Britain and
America. And, due to his fame, Sartre and existentialism
seem to be one and the same. However, a distinction needs to
be made between existentialism and Sartre's conception of it.

Jean-Paul Sartre (1905–80)

He is not the only existentialist philosopher, and there is nothing monolithic about existentialism. Kierkegaard and Sartre were both existentialists, but their views were far from identical: for example, while Sartre was an atheist, Kierkegaard was passionately committed to Christianity. Clearly, existentialism is not a fixed set of ideas; but then neither is rationalism or empiricism. Locke and Berkeley were both empiricists and Descartes and Spinoza both rationalists, but there are many points of difference between these two pairs of philosophers.

So, what do existentialists have in common, if they can disagree about something as fundamental as whether or not there is a God? Perhaps, existentialism is best understood as a way of looking at and approaching the world and human beings and the latter's nature and responsibilities, with existentialist philosophers, whatever their points of difference, emphasizing certain common themes. There is a focus on the individual, individual experience and individual choice. There is also the insistence that no one creed or ideology should be adopted without question, in the way that those brought up within certain religious traditions may do. As we look around the world, it seems to lack any clear purpose and often seems absurd; therefore, it does not dictate any particular set of beliefs or values. We must choose our fundamental principles; what matters is making the choice ourselves, however absurd it may seem (and Kierkegaard highlights the apparent absurdity of Christian teaching, when measured against worldly standards), and not allowing others to do it for us. By taking responsibility, choosing our fundamental principles for ourselves, and following them, we can lead lives that are genuine and authentic.

Sartre focuses on the nature of human existence and human consciousness. His ontology identifies two distinct kinds of being: 'being-in-itself' and 'being-for-itself'. The first is the mode of being of material objects, which are unconscious, inert and inanimate. They comply with the law of identity: they are what they are and are identical with themselves. Being-for-itself is conscious, alert, active and, by being its opposite, the negation of being-in-itself. As human beings, we unite both kinds of being, but our consciousness enables us to transcend the limitations of being-in-itself. At one level, this sounds like Cartesian dualism, with its distinction between mind, the essence of which is to think, and body, the essence of which is extension. But, for Sartre, being-for-itself is too elusive to be pinned down in this way. What we are conscious of is x, y or z, not consciousness itself, so it cannot be comprehended and neatly defined as a thinking thing or substance.

As we can transcend the limitations of being-in-itself, our existence precedes our essence, so we have freedom and choice. Therefore, we cannot invoke background, upbringing or other external factors as legitimate excuses for not taking responsibility for our own lives. Life is about making choices, and taking responsibility for them. Those who accept the roles that society, their family or other people impose on them, whether the straitjacket of a religious orthodoxy or a rigid political ideology, which precludes adherents from choosing their beliefs for themselves, or the role of a submissive wife and mother, who refuses to challenge her overbearing spouse, to that extent become things-in-themselves. What Sartre calls 'bad faith' occurs when individuals fail to take responsibility for themselves or their decisions, or seek to shift responsibility for their choices onto other people, or their circumstances. Sartre insists that we can always make something out of what we have been made into. Thus, like Kant, he is a libertarian: he rejects any form of determinism in relation to the human will and our ability to make genuinely free choices.

Sartre's ideas about consciousness and existence and bad faith are explored below.

Most philosophers expound their arguments in systematic treatises. But, this is not the only way that philosophical ideas can be presented. Plato explored his ideas in dialogues, while Kierkegaard used pseudonyms, so that he could take up conflicting views. Rousseau used the dialogue form and the novel. While Sartre sets out the main elements of his philosophy in *Being and Nothingness* (his major philosophical work), *Existentialism Is a Humanism* and *Critique of Dialectical Reason*, he also uses novels and short stories, such as *Nausea* and *The Wall*, and plays, such as *The Flies*, to put across his ideas in a vivid fashion.

Life

Born in Paris, Sartre's father died while he was a baby and he was brought up by his mother, Anne-Marie, and his maternal grandfather, Karl Schweitzer, a professor at the Sorbonne (they were related to the theologian and medical missionary Albert Schweitzer). After attending the Lycée Henri IV and the Lycée Louis-le-Grand in Paris, he studied philosophy at the École Normale Supérieure (1924–9). He formed friendships with a number of future French intellectual leaders, including the philosopher and feminist writer Simone de Beauvoir, with whom he had a lifelong, but not exclusive, relationship, the philosopher and theologian Simone Weil, the philosopher and sociologist Raymond Aron and the anthropologist Claud Lévi-Strauss.

After military service, Sartre taught philosophy in Le Havre and spent a year in Germany, studying the work of the philosopher and mathematician Edmund Husserl and the existentialist philosopher and Nazi supporter Martin Heidegger. For the rest of the 1930s, he taught in lycées in Laon and Paris. His novel *Nausea*, in which he explores the question of life's purposelessness, and *The Wall*, a collection of stories which address the issue of bad faith, were published in 1938.

While serving in the French Army, at the beginning of the Second World War, he was captured and imprisoned by the Germans. After his release, he returned to teaching and was active in the French Resistance. *Being and Nothingness*, in which he expounds his existentialist philosophy in detail, was published in 1943 and, in 1945, with Simone de Beauvoir and Raymond Aron, he started a radical literary, political and philosophical magazine, *Modern Times*, which he edited. In 1946, Sartre delivered his famous lecture 'Existentialism Is a Humanism', in which he set out the key existentialist principles.

From the late 1940s, Sartre concentrated on literary and political subjects, rather than philosophy. A leading left-wing thinker, he espoused Marxist views and, until the mid 1950s, seemed loath to attack the policies and actions of the Soviet Union in the way he did those of the United States. But, he showed he was not an unqualified admirer of Soviet communism, especially its suppression of individual freedom, by condemning Soviet intervention in Hungary in 1956 and in Czechoslovakia in 1968. A consistent critic of US involvement in Vietnam, he was a member of Bertrand Russell's War Crimes Tribunal, set up in 1967, to investigate US war crimes in Vietnam. He also supported the 1968 student uprisings in Paris.

Sartre's output of books and articles, from the 1930s up to the time of his death, was considerable. In addition to works of philosophy, which also include *Critique of Dialectical Reason* (1960) and literary criticism, such as *What is Literature*

(1947), he wrote a three-volume biography of Gustav Flaubert, *The Family Idiot: Gustav Flaubert from 1821 to 1857* (1971–2) and plays, such as *The Flies* (1943) and *In Camera* (1944), which deal with existentialist themes. In 1964, he rejected the Nobel Prize in Literature. Sartre travelled extensively, often with Simone de Beauvoir, and met such political leaders as Nikita Khrushchev and Fidel Castro.

Key ideas

Consciousness and existence

Sartre maintains that, as our existence precedes our essence, we must reject any predetermined image of what we are or should be as human beings, or how we should behave. Yet, not only do religious believers do so, when they hold that God has made us in his image, but non-religious thinkers also impose on humanity the limitations arising from the concept of a shared human nature that is believed to define all that human beings are and can be. For Sartre, our existence is absurd and inexplicable; there can be no predetermined or predetermining image of what human beings are or can become. We must decide life's meaning and value for ourselves and embrace our immense individual freedom with all its implications and responsibilities. We must appreciate that, in choosing, we do so not only for ourselves as individuals but also for the whole of humanity. Whenever we make a choice of one thing, rather than another, we are affirming a particular image of human life and its significance and suggesting that this is how others should behave.

For Sartre, our capacity for freedom derives from our consciousness. We are beings-for-themselves, as distinct from beings-in-themselves, all those things in the material world, such as trees or bricks, which lack consciousness and are its objects. However, as conscious beings, we have a problem: our existence is dominated by negatives. As we look at an object, we can say what it is, because its existence is determinate, fixed and unchanging; and we understand that we are not it. However, because, as beings-for-themselves, we are conscious, active and indeterminate, we can only say what we are not. We cannot give a positive definition of what we are, nor even exactly define our ever-changing relationship to the objects of which we are conscious.

As individual, conscious human beings, therefore, we experience great anxiety or existentialist dread; our freedom and responsibility are burdensome. We know we are not the objects in the material world, but this does not tell us what we are. We must decide for ourselves. However, our choosing does not dispel our anxiety. As we reflect on our past, we recognize only that it is not the present, and that we are no longer that past. Looking towards the future, we realize that it has not yet happened, and that we will not be the same then as now. Thus, our present or future are not determined by our past or present. We are always free to choose our course, no matter what our previous choices; but, unlike an object in the world, we cannot avoid choosing, and are always responsible for the choices we must keep on making.

Bad faith

Sartre believes that we may wish to be beings-in-themselves, not beings-for-themselves, because objects without consciousness have no awareness of choice and possibility and so escape anxiety or dread. As conscious beings, we will always define ourselves by what we are not and be unable to escape the freedom and responsibility to make choices. However, instead of trying to turn themselves into objects in the world, some human beings strive vainly to become God and thus beings who have a meaning that does not depend on the decisions they make. As a being whose essence precedes his existence, God is not defined by his actions, which proceed from his nature, and he can be known positively by what he is, rather than what he is not. Individual human beings aim to be like God, or mere objects, in order to overcome the dilemma we face in the world, where we find ourselves positioned between objects, which are unresponsive to human consciousness, and other individual human beings, who confuse and unnerve us by confronting us with the gaze of other conscious beings, who can judge us, although it is not immediately clear how we are connected to them. For Sartre, to strive to become God (who does not exist) is just as hopeless as striving to become a tree, thus adding to our sense of isolation and desperation, as we try to satisfy desires that cannot possibly be fulfilled.

However, some human beings approach closely to being-in-itself, through what Sartre calls 'bad faith'. They convince themselves that they do not have the freedom to choose and that they can disengage from the responsibilities of their existence. For example, a woman may wilfully ignore a man's intentions towards her. She may agree to go out with him, but does not think that she has to decide what her feelings towards him are. He may take her hand, and she may respond by holding his. But, she can pretend they are things-in-themselves, and that she is not accountable in or responsible for the situation. She is guilty of bad faith. Similarly, a waiter immerses himself in the routine of his work: he must rise at five in the morning and walk, talk and relate to others in the way his job dictates. However, in so doing, the waiter attempts to become the being-in-itself of the waiter: his mode of existence is prescribed by his role and he denies himself the freedom to be anything else. But, the waiter is free to behave in any way he wishes, and it is bad faith to say that he is bound to do this or that. He is not only free not to get up at five, but he must accept that every time he does rise at five, and go through his routine, this is a choice he has made and for which he is responsible.

Thus, Sartre confronts every human being with their freedom to act and their responsibility for their actions. Our social class, job or past conduct do not determine our actions, whatever we tell ourselves. All that we do, we do freely. If it is not what we would wish, we must confront our freedom and choose something else. Sartre is aware of the terrifying nausea that the reality of our freedom to choose and act engenders. By accepting our freedom and its accompanying responsibility, we come face to face with existence and the fundamental obligations of authentic human life.

Impact

- Sartre identifies two distinct kinds of being: being-in-itself, the mode of being of material objects, which are unconscious, inert and inanimate; and being-for-itself, which is conscious, alert, active, and the negation of being-in-itself.
- As human beings, we unite both kinds of being, but our consciousness enables us to transcend the limitations of being-in-itself.
- As there is no predetermined or predetermining image of what human beings are, or can become, we must decide for ourselves what the meaning and value of life is, and

embrace our immense individual freedom with all its implications and responsibilities.

- Bad faith occurs when individuals refuse to take responsibility for themselves or their decisions, or seek to shift responsibility for their choices onto other people or their circumstances, and fail to lead authentic lives.

Further reading

S. de Beauvoir, *Adieux: Farewell to Sartre*, new edition, Harmondsworth: Penguin, 1985.

P. Caws, *Sartre*, London: Routledge and Kegan Paul, 1979.

T. Flynn, 'Jean-Paul Sartre' (2004), in *Stanford Encyclopaedia of Philosophy*, at http://plato.stanford.edu.

D. Law, *Briefly: Sartre's Existentialism and Humanism*, London: SCM Press, 2007.

C. J. Onof, 'Sartre's Existentialism' (updated 2010), in J. Fieser and B. Dowden (eds), *Internet Encyclopedia of Philosophy*, at www.iep.utm.edu.

Jean-Paul Sartre, *Being and Nothingness*, trans. H. E. Barnes, second edition, London: Routledge, 2003.

Jean-Paul Sartre, *Existentialism Is a Humanism*, trans. C. Macomber, New Haven: Yale University Press, 2007.

Jean-Paul Sartre, *Nausea*, trans. R. Baldick, reprinted with Introduction by J. Wood, London: Penguin, 2000.

Jean-Paul Sartre, *The Wall* (And Other Stories), trans. L. Alexander, third revised edition, New York: New Directions, 1969.

P. A. Schlipp (ed.), *The Philosophy of Jean-Paul Sartre*, La Salle, IL: Open Court Publishing, 1981.

M. Warnock, *Existentialism*, Oxford: Oxford University Press, 1970.

25

A. J. Ayer
(1910–89)
The verification principle and the
elimination of metaphysics
Ethical emotivism

Context

Why are today's academics totally unknown to the general public? Is it because they immure themselves in university departments in order to write papers that only their peers will understand or want to read? Or is it because our national broadcasters think we are incapable of digesting expert views and only interested in the empty vapourings of the latest 'celebrity'? It was not the case with Alfred Jules Ayer, who, like C. S. Lewis and A. J. P. Taylor, brought his subject to a wider audience through radio and television and was actively involved in political and social issues. And, he started early. His first book, *Language, Truth and Logic*, written when he was 26, had a tremendous impact when it was published in 1936. As Ayer notes in the Appendix, written for the book's republication in 1946, he was a young man when it first appeared and it was written with more passion than most works of philosophy.

For, Ayer had a mission. Influenced by Bertrand Russell, Ludwig Wittgenstein, the logical positivists of the Vienna Circle,

A. J. Ayer (1910–89)

G. E. Moore's analytical philosophy and, in particular, the empiricism of David Hume, he provides a robust statement of his version of logical positivism: the view that, to be significant, propositions must either be tautologies, which it would be self-contradictory to deny, or (conclusively) verifiable in experience. Ayer's treatment of the verification principle is a key idea discussed below. He maintains that philosophy should avoid metaphysical and theological speculation and confine itself to analysis. Its role does not include attempting to attain knowledge of a world that transcends those of science and common sense, in order to discover the nature of ultimate reality. Philosophers are beguiled into a metaphysical view of truth, because the grammatical form of sentences, in which the word 'truth' appears, suggests that it stands for some metaphysical entity.

He maintains that a sentence can only express a genuine proposition about a matter of fact if it is verifiable, such that the observations relevant to determining its truth or falsehood are known. The philosopher's task is analysis. By exposing the logical complexity of the sentences, in which facts and notions are expressed, he can clarify their meaning, facilitate scientific enquiry and ordinary discourse, and remove the confusions that give rise to metaphysics.

However, although the notion that there should be a defined relationship between a proposition's meaning and the evidence for it seems clear enough, it is harder to hit on a satisfactory formulation of it and to provide an absolutely clear empiricist criterion of meaning. After all, metaphysical statements are not incomprehensible gibberish; Ayer does concede that statements which are not empirically verifiable may be meaningful in some sense, though, lacking factual content, they are not literally so.

What about the problems of induction and perception? What is the philosophical justification for our reliance on inductive reasoning and the evidence we receive through our senses? In *The Problem of Knowledge*, Ayer defines an inductive inference as any factual inference in which the premises do not entail the conclusion. When we make inductive inferences, we assume the uniformity of nature and that the future will resemble the past. Philosophy is unable to solve the problem of induction. However, there is no need to do so: the only relevant test is that it works.

What justifies our common sense belief in material things is that we have sensations. Sense experience is the sole basis of the validity of perceptual judgements. The mistake philosophers make, when trying to describe the nature of material things, is to think that they are dealing with a factual question about the properties of things, not one about definitions and the relationship of symbols standing for sense-contents. Through not being aware of the logical complexity of a sentence like, 'This is a table', they may adopt a metaphysical belief about the existence of material substances.

One of the most controversial aspects of *Language, Truth and Logic* (1936) is Ayer's treatment of moral and religious issues. He maintains that we cannot say it is even probable that God exists, as 'God' is a metaphysical term, and no metaphysical utterance can be either true or false. He also holds that ethical judgements are non-cognitive. Adding an ethical symbol, such as 'good' or 'right', to a statement adds nothing to its factual content, and there is no way of deciding whether an ethical statement is true or false.

Ayer's emotivist theory of ethics, which holds that ethical terms have the purely emotive function of expressing and arousing feelings, stimulating action and operating as commands, is the second key idea discussed in this chapter. Ayer argues that, as there is no objective way of determining the validity of any ethical system or principles, moral philosophy should confine itself to metaethics.

Life

Alfred Jules Ayer was born in London, the son of Jules Louis Cyprien Ayer and his wife Reine (née Citroen). After preparatory school in Eastbourne, he won a King's Scholarship to Eton, where he displayed outstanding intellectual ability, excelled at classics and also competed successfully in games. However, he was not particularly popular with his fellow pupils. Towards the end of his school career, he met his future first wife Renee Lees, whom he married in 1933, during a visit to Paris.

He won a scholarship to Christ Church, Oxford, which he attended from 1929, where he was tutored by the philosopher Gilbert Ryle, author of *Concept of Mind*, and gained a first in Greats. At both Eton and Christ Church, he studied the writings of the great Cambridge philosophers, G. E. Moore, Bertrand Russell and Ludwig Wittgenstein.

After studying at the University of Vienna, where he got to know the leading logical positivists of the Vienna Circle, such as Moritz Schlick, Rudolf Carnap and Friedrich Waismann, Ayer lectured in philosophy at Christ Church, where he was elected to a research studentship (fellowship) in 1935. He also completed his controversial and widely read first book, *Language, Truth and Logic*.

In 1940, Ayer joined the Welsh Guards, publishing his *The Foundations of Empirical Knowledge* in the same year. During the war, Ayer served in the Special Operations Executive (SOE), which included a period in the United States, and after the liberation of France as an attaché at the British Embassy in Paris, which gave him the opportunity to study existentialism.

After a year (1945–6) as fellow and dean of Wadham College, Oxford, Ayer became Grote Professor of the Philosophy of Mind and Logic at University College, London in 1946. In 1959, he was appointed Wykeham Professor of Logic at Oxford (and a fellow of New College), a post he held until 1978. Ayer is thought to have wanted to debate issues about which they disagreed with the linguistic philosopher J. L. Austin, White's Professor of Moral Philosophy, but Austin's early death ruled this out.

Outside philosophy, Ayer was interested in a wide range of social and political issues. Active in the Labour Party from the 1930s, he stood as a Labour candidate for Westminster Council, although he left the party in the early 1980s to support the SDP (Social Democratic Party). A supporter of the Abortion Law Reform Association, he was active in the campaign that led to the Abortion Act, 1967. He served as President of both the British Humanist Association and the Homosexual Law (later Sexual Law) Reform Society, which helped to secure the passing of the 1967 Sexual Offences Act.

A member of the Central Advisory Council for Education (England), which produced the Plowden report on primary education, Ayer appeared regularly on radio and television, and gave lectures around the world. Knighted in 1970, his other books include *The Problem of Knowledge* (1956), *Logical Positivism* (1959), *Russell and Moore: The Analytical Heritage* (1971) and two volumes of autobiography, *Part of My Life* (1977) and *More of My Life* (1984). He was married three times.

A. J. Ayer (1910–89)

Key ideas

The verification principle and the elimination of metaphysics

Philosophers from Plato onwards have regarded metaphysics, discovering the nature of ultimate reality, as a major philosophical activity. What is Ayer's view? In *Language, Truth and Logic*, he totally rejects it. Indeed, he thinks that metaphysicians' claims to have access to facts that cannot be known from sense experience are excluded by the rule determining language's literal significance. A sentence can only express a genuine proposition about a matter of fact, if it is empirically verifiable: if it is known what observations are relevant to determining its truth or falsity.

Ayer uses the example of a supposed metaphysical proposition from the writings of the idealist philosopher F. H. Bradley to prove his point. Bradley had referred to the Absolute as entering into, but itself being incapable of, evolution and progress. Ayer asks what such a sentence can mean. The grammatical structure is similar to, for example, a sentence about a man entering a house through a door, but being incapable of getting in by the window. However, the all-important difference is that it is obvious what observations would decide the truth of the second, whereas no observations could determine the truth or falsity of the first. Bradley's supposed proposition is not empirically verifiable. For Ayer, it is a metaphysical pseudo-proposition.

What exactly does Ayer mean by 'verifiability'? There are propositions about matters of fact, which there are no known practical means of verifying, but they are significant, because we know what observations would determine their truth. Therefore, they are verifiable in principle. It is also important to distinguish between strong and weak senses of verifiability. The first refers to conclusive verification, advocated by some logical positivists, but which Ayer rejects. General propositions, like 'all human beings are mortal', cannot be conclusively verified by any finite series of observations, so adopting conclusive verifiability, as the criterion of significance, would mean treating them like metaphysical statements.

He prefers a weaker form of the verification principle. A proposition is genuinely factual if any observations are relevant to determining its truth or falsity. Thus, the supposed propositions of monists, who say reality is one substance, or pluralists, who say it is many, are both strictly nonsensical. We can form some idea of what these statements mean, but no possible observations could determine their truth. They lack factual content, and so are not literally meaningful. The only other literally meaningful propositions are the *a priori* ones of logic and pure mathematics, the truth of which can be determined analytically. Ayer stresses the nature and purpose of factual propositions. They are empirical hypotheses that provide a rule for anticipating experience, so some actual or possible experience must be relevant to them.

As metaphysics is a fruitless enterprise, why are philosophers so prone to it? Ayer does not accuse metaphysicians of intending to write nonsense. Linguistic ambiguities beguile them into reasoning errors. For example, sentences that express existential propositions can be confusing. 'Martyrs exist' has the same grammatical form as 'martyrs suffer', so may also be thought to attribute a property to them. It is said that, to be fictitious, such creatures as unicorns must exist, but that, as it is self-contradictory to maintain that fictitious objects exist, they exist in some special, non-empirical sense. He does not deny that some metaphysical writings may express genuine mystical feeling, but they are not literally meaningful and so can be no part of philosophy.

A. J. Ayer (1910–89)

Ethical emotivism

What are we doing when we make ethical statements that say what we ought to do? Moral philosophers have given different answers to this question. Ayer agrees that ethical subjectivists, who define goodness and rightness in terms of people's subjective feelings of approval or disapproval, and utilitarians, who define them in terms of pleasure or happiness, and who both commit the naturalistic fallacy, believe that statements of ethical value can be translated into non-ethical ones, about whether the things in question are approved of or pleasant.

However, he points out that, generally, ethical terms, like 'good' and 'right', are not used in this descriptive way. Most ethical statements are normative, expressing judgements of value and/or prescribing conduct. Therefore, as it is always an open question (it can be asked intelligibly) whether anything that is said to be good or right actually possesses ethical value, ethical statements cannot be reduced to non-ethical ones. It is certainly not self-contradictory to hold that things or actions that are generally approved are not right or good, or to say that an action that would probably maximize happiness is wrong.

So what is Ayer's analysis? He thinks ethical statements are not literally meaningful, because they just express emotions. For example, adding an ethical term, like 'wrong', to a statement about stealing money, adds nothing to its factual content. It just expresses our moral disapproval of the action, and cannot be true or false. This emotivist theory of ethics holds that ethical terms have a purely emotive function: that of expressing and arousing feelings, stimulating action, and functioning as commands.

But, if ethical statements just express or arouse feelings, why are there disputes about questions of value? Ayer denies that these disputes concern ethical values as such. Ethical disputes are about facts, not values. Disputants hope, by securing their opponent's agreement about the facts of, or the motives behind, a (proposed) action, to influence their feelings about it. They use ethical terms to express their own feelings about their opponent's point of view, and to try to change it.

Ayer believes the major causes of moral behaviour and debate are fear of God's displeasure or of society's disapproval, which is why moral precepts are often regarded as categorical commands. Moral sanctions are invoked to promote or prevent behaviour that increases or diminishes society's wellbeing. However, there is no objective way to determine the validity of any ethical principles. Instead of trying to do so, moral philosophy should confine itself to metaethics and focus on analysing moral terms and their use.

Even if we agree with Ayer that normative ethical statements are not ordinary empirical propositions, and accept that they have an emotive function, does his account do justice to the complexity of ethical debate? This will involve facts, but may not be confined to them. It could move from the facts of a particular situation, and different views of the facts, to different opinions about which course of action would be most likely to maximize happiness and a clash of values about whether happiness is the ultimate good. Again, those who believe that morality is grounded in the needs of intrinsically valuable human beings will regard statements that murder or torture is wrong as clearly true.

Impact

- Ayer presented his version of radical empiricism and logical positivism in a form that made it comprehensible to the wider public and stimulated debate.

A. J. Ayer (1910–89)

- He makes it clear that metaphysical and ethical propositions are not ordinary empirical propositions, the truth or falsehood of which can be determined by sense-experience, forcing those who do not agree that they are pseudo-propositions at least to reflect on their status.
- Ethical emotivism recognizes the dynamic nature and persuasive purpose of moral language and that it is used to influence behaviour.
- Whatever their weaknesses as a metaethical theory and tendency to debase moral argument to the level of propaganda, Ayer's ideas made an important contribution to the lively metaethical debate of the twentieth century, which involved such philosophers as C. L. Stevenson, R. M. Hare and G. J. Warnock.

Further reading

A. J. Ayer, *Language, Truth and Logic*, reprinted with an Introduction by Ben Rogers, London: Penguin, 2001.

A. J. Ayer, *The Foundations of Empirical Knowledge*, London and New York: Macmillan, 1969.

A. J. Ayer, *The Problem of Knowledge*, Harmondsworth: Penguin, 1971.

R. M. Hare, *The Language of Morals*, Oxford and New York: Oxford University Press, 1952.

G. Macdonald, 'Alfred Jules Ayer' (2005) in E. N. Zalta (ed.), *Stanford Encyclopaedia of Philosophy*, at http://plato.stanford.edu.

G. Macdonald and C. Wright (eds), *Fact, Science and Morality: Essays on A. J. Ayer's 'Language, Truth and Logic'*, Oxford: Oxford University Press, 1986.

Further reading

D. Mills Daniel, *Briefly: Ayer's Language, Truth and Logic*, London: SCM Press, 2007.

New World Encyclopedia contributors, 'A. J. Ayer', *New World Encyclopedia*, 3 April 2008, at www.newworldencyclopedia. org/entry/A._J._Ayer?oldid=684994.

B. Rogers, *A. J. Ayer: A Life*, London: Chatto and Windus, 1999.

C. E. Stevenson, *Ethics and Language*, New Haven and London: Yale University Press, 1965.

G. J. Warnock, *The Object of Morality*, London: Methuen, 1971.

Glossary of Philosophers and Thinkers

Addison, Joseph (1672–1719). British politician, Whig MP, classical scholar, author and journalist, who was a chief secretary for Ireland and co-founder of *The Spectator*.

Albert the Great, Saint (Albertus Magnus) (*c*. 1200–80). German-born Dominican philosopher and theologian, author of commentaries on Aristotle's works and bishop of Ratisbon. Aquinas' teacher and, like his student, interested in bringing together Christian teaching and Greek philosophy.

Ambrose of Milan (*c*. 339–97). German-born bishop of Milan and one of the four Doctors of the Church.

Anscombe, Gertrude Elizabeth Margaret (G. E. M.) (1919–2001). British philosopher, professor of philosophy at the University of Cambridge, disciple of Ludwig Wittgenstein and one of his literary executors. Her publications include a translation of Wittgenstein's *Philosophical Investigations* (1953) and *An Introduction to Wittgenstein's Tractatus* (1959).

Arnauld, Antoine (1612–94). French philosopher, theologian, disciple of Descartes and co-author of *Logic, or the Art of Thinking* or *Port-Royal Logic* (1662), who rejected Malebranche's view that knowledge requires the existence of the archetypes of objects in the mind of God. A Jansenist, he was forced to take refuge in Belgium in 1679.

Aron, Raymond (1905–83). French writer, journalist, philosopher, philosopher of history and professor at the Sorbonne. A critic of Marxism and defender of individual liberty, his works include *Introduction to the Philosophy of History* (1938) and *The Opium of Intellectuals* (1955).

Ashley Cooper, Anthony, first Earl of Shaftesbury (1621–83). English politician, chancellor of the exchequer (1661–72) and lord chancellor (1672–3). Founder and leader of the Whig party during the reign of Charles II and advocate of religious toleration, whose attempts to exclude Charles' Roman Catholic brother, James, Duke of York from the succession led to exile in Holland. Patron of John Locke, who was his physician and political adviser.

Augustine of Hippo (354–430). North African-born philosopher and theologian and one of the original Doctors of the Church, bishop of Hippo in North Africa and author of the *Confessions* (400) and *The City of God* (412–27).

Austin, John Langshaw (1911–60). British analytic and linguistic philosopher and White's Professor of Moral Philosophy at Oxford, who played a major role in British intelligence during the Second World War. He published little during his lifetime, but his views and posthumous books, including *Sense and Sensibilia* (1962) and *How to Do Things with Words* (1962), had a tremendous impact on the study of philosophy in Britain and the United States during the second half of the twentieth century.

Averröes (Ibn Rushd) (1126–98). Spanish-born Islamic philosopher, scientist and lawyer, who sought to bring together Western philosophy and Islamic theology and traditions, through his commentaries on the works of Aristotle and Plato's *The Republic*.

Bayle, Pierre (1647–1706). French philosopher and proponent of scepticism, the limitations of reason in religious matters, and religious toleration. Best known for his *An Historical and Sceptical Dictionary* (1690s). Raised as a Protestant, he became a Roman Catholic, but then lapsed. After teaching at a Calvinist academy in Sedan, Bayle sought refuge in Holland, to avoid persecution in Louis XIV's France, spending the rest of his life there.

Beauvoir, Simone de (1908–86). French philosopher, feminist writer and long-time companion of Sartre, who accompanied him on many of his visits to meet world leaders. Her books include *The Second Sex* (1949), *Memoirs of a Dutiful Daughter* (1958) and *Adieux: A Farewell to Sartre* (1981).

Blackstone, Sir William (1723–80). British lawyer, Vinerian Professor of (Common) Law at the University of Oxford, judge of the Court of Common Pleas and author of the authoritative *Commentaries on the Laws of England* (the first volume was published in 1765), which set out and made intelligible to lay readers the English system of common law.

Boyle, Robert (1626–91). Anglo-Irish chemist and son of the first earl of Cork, who became famous through his research into gases and for the development of Boyle's Law. Author of *The Sceptical Chemist* (1661) and one of the founders of the Royal Society in 1660.

Bradley, Frances Herbert (1846–1924). British idealist philosopher, fellow of Merton College, Oxford, and brother of the Shakespearean scholar A. C. Bradley (1851–1935). His books include *Principles of Logic* (1883) and *Appearance and Reality* (1893). Bradley's philosophical idealism, which was strongly influenced by the writings of Hegel, had a huge influence on British philosophy in the late nineteenth and early twentieth centuries, but fell out of favour following criticisms by Moore and Russell, in particular.

Bramhall, John (1594–1663). English theologian and writer, and archbishop of Armagh (1661–3), who criticized Hobbes' *Leviathan* and its physicalism, and defended Anglicanism against Roman Catholicism.

Broad, Charlie Dunbar (1887–1971). British philosopher and fellow of Trinity College, Cambridge, who taught philosophy at St Andrews, Bristol and Cambridge, before becoming Knightbridge Professor of Philosophy at Cambridge in 1933, a post he held for 20 years. Interested in the philosophy of science and psychical research, his books include *Scientific Thought* (1923), *Mind and its Place in Nature* (1925) and *Examination of McTaggart's Philosophy* (1933–8).

Buber, Martin (1878–1965). Austrian-born Jewish philosopher, theologian and existentialist. After emigrating to Palestine in 1938, he became professor at the Hebrew University in Jerusalem and played a major part in the educational developments in the new State of Israel. His best-known book is *I and Thou* (1922).

Bultmann, Rudolf (1884–1976). German Lutheran theologian, New Testament scholar and professor of theology at the University of Marburg, who was influenced by existentialist thought, particularly that of Martin Heidegger. His focus was on what it means for the individual to profess Jesus Christ and how Christian belief can transform lives. His books include *History of the Synoptic Tradition* (1921), *The Gospel of St John* (1941) and *Theology of the New Testament* (1948–53).

Burke, Edmund (1729–97). Anglo-Irish Whig politician, MP and political philosopher, who held ministerial office under the Marquess of Rockingham. Originally a radical and ally of Charles James Fox, who supported the American colonies in their struggle with George III's government, Burke was an opponent of democracy, which he believed would lead to inefficient government, dominated by demagoguery and mob rule and the destruction of established institutions and religion. He was a severe critic of the French Revolution, which he condemned in his *Reflections on the Revolution in France* (1790).

Calvin, John (1509–64). French-born theologian, leader of the Reformation and author of the *Institutes of the Christian Religion* (1536), who emphasized original sin and predestination, and established a theocratic form of government in the Swiss city of Geneva.

Camus, Albert (1913–60). French writer, political journalist and playwright and winner of the Nobel Prize in Literature (1957), whose works, which include the essay *The Myth of Sisyphus* (1942) and the novel *The Stranger* (1942), deal with existentialist issues and the idea of the absurd.

Carnap, Rudolf (1891–1970). Austrian philosopher and exponent of logical positivism, who was professor at Prague, Chicago and Los Angeles. Author of *The Logical Structure of the World* (1928) and *Logical Foundations of Probability* (1950).

Chrysippus of Soli (*c.* 279–206 BCE). Ancient Greek philosopher and a leading Stoic thinker and student of Cleanthes, none of whose many books survive.

Cicero, Marcus Tullius (106–43 BCE). Roman lawyer, statesman, philosopher and champion of the Roman Republic, who was murdered on the orders of Mark Anthony. Author of *On the Nature of the Gods* and *On the Laws*.

Clarke, Samuel (1675–1729). British theologian, philosopher and Anglican clergyman, who was rector of St James Westminster. Clarke was a proponent of natural theology, including the cosmological proof of God's existence, and of the view that moral truths can be discovered by reason. He corresponded with Leibniz in defence of his friend Isaac Newton, and his writings include *A Demonstration of the Being and Attributes of God* (1705).

Cleanthes of Assos (*c.* 330–231 BCE). Ancient Greek Stoic philosopher, who believed that the best way of life is one lived in harmony with nature.

Copernicus, Nicolaus (1473–1543). Polish mathematician and astronomer, who propounded the theory that the earth rotates around the sun (heliocentric theory). Though very controversial in the sixteenth century, Copernicus' work led to a revolution in human understanding of the nature of the universe.

Copleston, Frederick Charles (1907–94). British philosopher and Jesuit priest, whose books include *Aquinas* (1955) and the multi-volume *A History of Philosophy* (1946–75).

Cratylus (fifth century BCE). Ancient Greek philosopher and reputed early teacher of Plato, who maintained that the ever-changing nature of the world makes it impossible to make any definite statements about it.

Cudworth, Ralph (1617–88). English philosopher who was influenced by Plato's writings, he was one of the Cambridge Platonists and became master of Christ's College, Cambridge, in 1654. An opponent of deism and atheism, he argued (against Locke) for innate knowledge and reason's ability to give access to moral and religious truth. The father of Damaris Masham, he wrote *The True Intellectual System of the World* (1678) and the posthumously published *A Treatise Concerning Eternal and Immutable Morality* (1731).

Democritus of Abdera (*c.* 460–370 BCE). Ancient Greek philosopher, who held that the universe consists of atoms which move about in space and form bodies; that human beings consist of a body and a soul, both of which are made up of atoms; that the bodies perish, but the atoms do not; and that moderation and the curbing of desire are the keys to happiness.

Derrida, Jacques (1930–2004). French postmodernist and deconstructionist philosopher, who rejected the idea that language has a definite meaning or significance which is determined by what the speaker or writer intends or its relationship to the world/objects to which it refers, holding that what is written or spoken is capable of limitless different and differing interpretations. Professor at the École Normale Supérieure, his publications include *Of Grammatology* (1967).

Diderot, Denis (1713–84). French philosopher and writer, and exponent of Enlightenment ideas, who championed freedom of thought and expression, an understanding of the world based on scientific knowledge, and anti-clericalism. For more than a quarter of a century, he was the principal editor of the *Encyclopédie*, which sought to bring together all available knowledge, and was also the author of such works as *Thoughts on the Interpretation of Nature* (1754) and the controversial novel *The Nun*, which was published in 1796.

Dumont, Etienne (1759–1829). Swiss writer and politician, who edited and published Bentham's writings.

Elizabeth of Bohemia, Princess (1618–80). German-born daughter of the Elector Palatine, Frederick V (briefly King of Bohemia) and Elizabeth Stuart (daughter of James I). Elder sister of Sophia, the future Electress of Hanover and mother of George I. Following her father's expulsion from the Palatinate, she and her parents were exiled in Holland, where she received a thorough education in classical languages and became interested in philosophy. After reading Descartes' *Meditations on First Philosophy* in the early 1640s, she began a correspondence with Descartes, who was also living in Holland, which lasted until his death and in which she challenged aspects of his philosophy.

Elizabeth Tudor, Queen Elizabeth I of England (1533–1603). Daughter of Henry VIII and Anne Boleyn, she succeeded her half-sister, Mary, as monarch in 1558. Tutored by the classical scholar Roger Ascham (1515–68), her great intellectual ability, courage and political skill enabled her to establish Protestantism securely in the country, to overcome the many attempts to overthrow her, including the Spanish Armada (1588) and to restore England's prestige in Europe.

Epictetus of Hierapolis (*c.* 55–135). Stoic philosopher from Asia Minor, who believed that events outside ourselves are determined by fate, so we should learn to accept them calmly, while at the same time taking responsibility for our own actions which we can control.

Epicurus of Samos (*c.* 341–270 BCE). Ancient Greek philosopher who adhered to the atomistic theory of Democritus (see above); he believed that knowledge comes through the senses, that superstition should be eliminated, and that pleasure (as the only one known to the senses) is the sole good.

Euclid of Megara (fifth/fourth century BCE). Ancient Greek philosopher and disciple of Socrates, who taught that there is one universal reality or existence, which manifests itself in various forms, and who developed the process of dialectic(s).

Foot, Michael (1913–2010). British politician, journalist and writer, who was Labour MP for Plymouth Devonport (1945–55) and Ebbw Vale (1960–92), editor of *Tribune* (1948–52), secretary of state for employment (1974–6), leader of the House of Commons (1976–9), leader of the Labour Party (1980–3) and author of the two-volume *Aneurin Bevan* (1962, 1973) and *Debts of Honour* (1981).

Foucault, Michel (1926–84). French philosopher and historian of ideas, and professor at a number of universities in France and the Collège de France, who argued that the relationships between the different groups and categories of people in society, such as the sane and the insane, or the law-abiding and the criminal, should be understood in terms of the power that one group exercises over another, in order to achieve and maintain political/social control. His books include *The Order of Things* (1966) and the *History of Sexuality* (1976–88).

Franklin, Benjamin (1706–90). American printer, publisher, journalist, entrepreneur and inventor, who was the American colonies' agent in England. He helped to draft the American Declaration of Independence, represented the American colonies in France during the War of Independence, was one of the signatories of the Constitution of the United States, and served as president of the executive council of Pennsylvania.

Frege, Gottlob (1848–1925). German mathematician and philosopher, and teacher at the University of Jena, whose studies, which included the formulation of such concepts as the 'quantifier' and the 'variable', helped to lay the foundations of modern logic and influenced the work of Bertrand Russell. His books include *The Foundations of Arithmetic* (1884) and *The Basic Laws of Arithmetic* (1893).

Glossary of Philosophers and Thinkers

Galileo Galilei (1564–1642). Italian astronomer and scientist, who maintained that scientific knowledge derives from observation and experiment, not reliance on tradition or the authority of previous thinkers. His championing of the ideas of Copernicus led to his being persecuted by the Roman Catholic Church.

Gaunilo (eleventh century). French Benedictine monk from the abbey of Marmoutier near Tours in France, who put forward powerful arguments against Anselm's ontological argument shortly after publication of the *Proslogion*.

Gladstone, William Ewart (1809–98). British statesman and prime minister. Originally a Conservative, and subsequently a Liberal MP and leader of the Liberal Party, he was president of the board of trade and secretary for war and colonies under Peel, chancellor of the exchequer under Aberdeen, Palmerston and Russell, and prime minister four times (1868–74; 1880–5; 1886; 1892–4). His first ministry laid the foundations of a national education system, introduced the secret ballot, reorganized the legal system, reformed the army and brought in competitive examinations for the civil service. Editor of Butler's *Analogy* (1895), his other books include *The State in its Relations with the Church* (1838) and *Studies on Homer and the Homeric Age* (1858).

Gregory the Great (*c.* 540–604). Italian ecclesiastic and one of the original four Doctors of the Church; Pope Gregory I (590–604).

Hare, Richard Mervyn (R. M.) (1919–2002). British philosopher, White's Professor of Moral Philosophy at the University of Oxford and the leading proponent of the metaethical theory of ethical prescriptivism; his publications include *The Language of Morals* (1952), *Freedom and Reason* (1963) and *Moral Thinking: Its Levels, Methods and Point* (1981).

Hegel, Georg Wilhelm Friedrich (G. W. F.) (1770–1831). German philosopher and exponent of absolute idealism, whose philosophical doctrines had a major impact on the course of philosophy in the nineteenth century. Professor of philosophy at Heidelberg and Berlin, his works include *The Phenomenology of Mind* (1807), *Science of Logic* (1812 and 1816) and *The Philosophy of Right* (1821).

Heidegger, Martin (1889–1976). German existentialist philosopher and professor at Marburg and Freiburg, whose books include *Being and Time* (1927) and *Identity and Difference* (1955–7).

Heraclitus of Ephesus (sixth/fifth century BCE). Ancient Greek philosopher, who distinguished between the ever-changing nature of the world of the senses, such that it is impossible to enter the same river twice, and the eternal *logos* or law, which unifies everything.

Husserl, Edmund Gustav (1859–1938). German philosopher and mathematician, who taught at the universities of Göttingen and Freiburg, developed phenomenology, which makes examination of mental/intellectual activities the focus of philosophical enquiry, and whose books include *Logical Investigations* (1913).

Huygens, Christiaan (1629–95). Dutch mathematician, scientist and astronomer, who propounded the wave theory of light, improved the design of astronomical instruments, by means of which he discovered the ring of Saturn and observed the surface of Mars, and developed a highly accurate pendulum clock.

Israel, Manasseh ben (1604–57). Dutch theologian and rabbi. Originally from Portugal, his family fled to Holland to escape the Inquisition, and he became a popular preacher and

Jewish leader in Amsterdam. Widely respected by non-Jews for his scholarship and expertise in secular matters, he was an effective defender of Judaism and biblical teachings, and led the efforts to find places where Jews could live in safety, which included a mission to Cromwell's England in 1655.

Jefferson, Thomas (1743–1826). American politician and champion of individual liberty and religious freedom, who drafted the Declaration of Independence, which was adopted by the Continental Congress of the 13 colonies in 1776, and was the third President of the United States (1801–9).

Jerome (*c.* 342–420). Italian theologian and biblical scholar, one of the original Doctors of the Church, who produced the first Latin translation of the Bible.

Jesus (Christ). (*c.* 5–6 BCE–*c.* CE 30). Founder of Christianity, whose life of preaching, teaching and healing is described in the New Testament and who is believed by Christians to be the incarnate Word of God and the second person of the Trinity.

Keynes, John Maynard (Baron Keynes of Tilton) (1883–1946). British economist and fellow of King's College, Cambridge, whose economic theories were a major influence on the development of post-Second World War economic policies and who advocated establishment of the International Monetary Fund. His books include *A Treatise on Probability* (1921), *Treatise on Money* (1930) and *The General Theory of Employment, Interest and Money* (1936).

Knutzen, Martin (1713–51). German rationalist philosopher and scientist, who was professor at the University of Königsberg and one of Immanuel Kant's teachers.

Lanfranc (*c.* 1010–89). Italian-born theologian and abbot of Caen in Normandy, who, following the Norman conquest of England, was invited to become Archbishop of Canterbury by William I in 1070. Loyal to both William I and William II (William Rufus), he reformed and reorganized the Church in England.

Lévi-Strauss, Claud (1908–2009). French anthropologist, philosopher, professor of social anthropology at the Collège de France and author of *The Elementary Structures of Kinship* (1949) and *The Savage Mind* (1966), who developed the theory of structuralism, which holds that social relationships and institutions reflect the basic structures of the human mind.

Lewis, Clive Staples (C. S.) (1898–1963). British academic, writer and specialist in medieval and renaissance literature, who spent most of his academic career at Oxford, where he was fellow of Magdalen College, before becoming Professor of Medieval and Renaissance English at Cambridge. An active Christian, Lewis was a popular writer and broadcaster about Christianity and the author of children's books. His books include *The Allegory of Love* (1936), *The Screwtape Letters* (1942), *Mere Christianity* (1952) and the *Chronicles of Narnia* (1950–6).

McTaggart, John McTaggart Ellis (J. M. E. McTaggart) (1866–1925). British idealist philosopher and follower of Hegel, fellow of Trinity College, Cambridge, and author of 'The Unreality of Time' (1908), in which he maintained that the way we perceive time is an illusion, and *The Nature of Existence* (1921–7), in which he developed his metaphysical system, which includes the immortality of the soul.

Malebranche, Nicholas (1638–1715). French rationalist philosopher, disciple of Descartes and author of *Of the Search for Truth* (1674–5), who held that attainment of knowledge of objects in the world requires that there be archetypes of them in the mind of God, and that only God, not bodies, could be an efficient cause.

Masham, Damaris, Lady (1658–1708). English philosopher, daughter of the Cambridge philosopher Ralph Cudworth, and friend of John Locke, who lived at her home in Essex for the final 13 years of his life. Author of *A Discourse Concerning the Love of God* (1696) and *Occasional Thoughts in Reference to a Virtuous or Christian Life* (1705), she also corresponded with Leibniz.

Mersenne, Marin (1588–1648). French philosopher and author of *The Truth of the Sciences Against the Sceptics or Pyrrhonians* (1625), whose main concern was to defend the adequacy of scientific knowledge and to refute extreme or Pyrrhonian scepticism.

Mill, James (1773–1836). British utilitarian philosopher and historian, father of John Stuart Mill, friend and collaborator of Jeremy Bentham and chief examiner for the East India Company, his books include *The History of British India* (1818) and *An Analysis of the Phenomena of the Human Mind* (1829).

Newman, John Henry (J. H.) (1801–90). Theologian, author and fellow of Oriel College, Oxford, whose books include *The Idea of a University* (1852) and *An Essay in Aid of a Grammar of Assent* (1870). An Anglican clergyman, and one of the leaders of the Oxford Movement which sought to promote Anglo-Catholicism in the Church of England, he became a Roman Catholic convert and priest, and was created a cardinal in 1879.

Newton, Sir Isaac (1642–1727). British physicist and mathematician, who carried out groundbreaking experiments into the composition of light and identified the force of gravity. Author of *Philosophiae Naturalis Principia Mathematica* (1687), Newton was Lucasian Professor of Mathematics at the University of Cambridge (1669–1702), Master of the Mint (1700–27), President of the Royal Society (1703–27) and an MP for the University of Cambridge. He engaged in an acrimonious dispute with Leibniz about the discovery of the differential calculus.

Parmenides of Elea (born *c.* 510 BCE). Ancient Greek philosopher, who believed that the universe is eternal and unchanging, and that things which are changing and perishable cannot be objects of knowledge. He features in Plato's dialogue of that name.

Peirce, Charles Saunders (C. S.) (1839–1914). American philosopher and logician, whose groundbreaking work in logic was very influential, but was not published until after his death.

Pope, Alexander (1688–1744). British essayist and satirist, and author of *Essay on Criticism* (1711) and *Essay on Man* (1733).

Price, Dr Richard (1723–91). British philosopher, Unitarian minister and economic commentator. An advocate of civil and religious freedom and a friend of Joseph Priestley, Benjamin Franklin and the Earl of Shelburne, Price supported both the American and French Revolutions, expressing his views in the pamphlet 'Observations on the Nature of Civil Liberty, the Principles of Government and the Justice and Polity of the War with America' (1776) and the controversial sermon 'A Discourse on the Love of Our Country' (1789). His major publications include *Review of* the Principal Questions in Morals (1757) and *An Appeal to the Public on the Subject of the National Debt* (1772).

Pyrrho of Elis (*c.* 360–270 BCE). Ancient Greek philosopher who established a profoundly sceptical approach to philosophical enquiry. His ideas became influential in France from the mid-sixteenth century, following publication of the works of Sextus Empiricus.

Ramsey, Frank Plumpton (1903–30). British mathematician, logician, philosopher, economist and fellow of King's College, Cambridge, who worked with Moore, Russell, Wittgenstein and Keynes and made important contributions to all their areas of enquiry, including the Ramsey theorem. His major articles were published posthumously in *The Foundations of Mathematics and Other Logical Essays* (1931).

Rhees, Rush (1905–89). American philosopher, who became a friend of Ludwig Wittgenstein while a research student at Cambridge and taught philosophy at University College, Swansea (Swansea University). He was Wittgenstein's literary executor, co-editor of his *Philosophical Investigations* (1953) and author of *Without Answers* (1969) and *Wittgenstein and the Possibility of Discourse* (1988).

Ricardo, David (1772–1823). British stockbroker and investor, independent MP, influential economist and advocate of the labour theory of value and free trade, whose major works include *On the Principles of Political Economy and Taxation* (1817).

Ritschl, Friedrich Wilhelm (1806–76). German classicist and philologist, who was professor at the universities of Halle, Breslau, Bonn and Leipzig.

Russell, Lord John, first Earl Russell (1792–1878). British statesman and younger son of the sixth Duke of Bedford.

Whig/Liberal MP and advocate of parliamentary reform (he had a major responsibility for the Great Reform Act of 1832) and religious toleration. Successively, paymaster-general, home secretary and secretary for war and colonies under Earl Grey (prime minister 1830–4) and Viscount Melbourne (prime minister 1835–41), he was prime minister (1846–52), foreign secretary and lord president of the council under the Earl of Aberdeen (1852–5), secretary for the colonies and foreign secretary under Viscount Palmerston (1855 and 1859–65) and prime minister (1865–6).

Ryle, Gilbert (1900–76). British philosopher, Waynflete Professor of Metaphysical and Philosophy at Oxford and editor of *Mind*, who was A. J. Ayer's tutor. His books include *The Concept of Mind* (1949) and *Dilemmas* (1953).

Schlick, Moritz (1882–1936). German-born philosopher and logical positivist, professor of philosophy at the University of Vienna and author of *General Theory of Knowledge* (1918).

Schopenhauer, Arthur (1788–1860). German philosopher who taught at the University of Berlin. A disciple of Kant, a severe critic of Hegel and noted for his philosophical pessimism, his works include *The World as Will and Idea* (1818).

Schweitzer, Albert (1875–1965). Alsace-born theologian, philosopher, musicologist, organist, physician and medical missionary. While principal of the Theological College of St Thomas and lecturer at the University of Strasbourg, he published his *J. S. Bach, the Musician–Poet* (1905) and his major theological work, *The Quest of the Historical Jesus* (1906). After studying medicine, he established (1913) a hospital mission in Lambaréné, in French Equatorial Africa, where he spent most of the rest of his life. Awarded the Nobel Peace Prize in 1952, his other publications include

On the Edge of the Primeval Forest (1920), *The Mysticism of Paul the Apostle* (1930) and *Indian Thought and its Development* (1935).

Seneca, Lucius Annaeus (*c.* 1 BCE–65 CE). Roman statesman, Stoic philosopher and playwright, who was adviser to Nero, and who was forced to commit suicide for alleged complicity in a plot against the emperor. Author of *Moral Epistles and Natural Questions.*

Sextus Empiricus (first/second century CE). Ancient Greek medical practitioner and philosopher, whose writings include *Outlines of Pyrrhonism.*

Smith, Adam (1723–90). British philosopher and economist and professor of logic, then moral philosophy, at the University of Glasgow, whose philosophical and economic ideas, including the ideal observer, the invisible hand and how pursuit of self-interest can promote the common good, expressed in his books *Theory of the Moral Sentiments* (1759) and *An Enquiry into the Nature and Causes of The Wealth of Nations* (1776), continue to be extremely influential.

Socrates (*c.* 470–399 BCE). Ancient Greek philosopher and teacher of Plato, who devoted his life to the pursuit of truth, particularly in the field of moral philosophy; he was executed on charges of undermining belief in the Greek gods and corrupting youth.

Spengler, Oswald (1880–1936). German historian and philosopher, who in his *The Decline of the West* (1918), argues that the course of history is cyclical not linear; cultures rise and fall; and that no rational principle governs the process, nor is there inevitable progress.

Stevenson, Charles Leslie (C. L.) (1908–79). American analytical philosopher and ethicist, who made a major contribution to the metaethical theory of emotivism, and who was professor of philosophy at Yale and the University of Michigan. Author of *Ethics and Language* (1944) and *Facts and Values* (1963).

Strachey, Giles Lytton (1880–1932). British intellectual, biographer and literary critic of *The Spectator*, whose books include *Eminent Victorians* (1918), *Queen Victoria* (1921) and *Elizabeth and Essex* (1928).

Swift, Jonathan (1667–1745). Anglo-Irish writer, ecclesiastic and political controversialist, who was dean of St Patrick's, Dublin, and author of many pamphlets on political, church and Irish questions, as well as *Gulliver's Travels* (1726).

Taylor, Alan John Percivale (A. J. P.) (1906–90). British historian, writer and broadcaster, fellow of Magdalen College, Oxford, and author of *The Struggle for Mastery in Europe 1848–1918* (1954), *Bismarck: The Man and Statesman* (1955) and *The Origins of the Second World War* (1961).

Theophrastus of Eresus (*c.* 370–287 BCE). Ancient Greek philosopher and scientist, and a student of Aristotle. More sceptical and empirically minded than Aristotle, he succeeded him as director of the Lyceum, which he ran for over 30 years.

Thucydides (*c.* 460–400 BCE). Ancient Greek historian and an Athenian general during the Peloponnesian War, who in his *History of the Peloponnesian War* gives an account of the conflict between Athens and Sparta.

Tillich, Paul Johannes (1886–1965). German-born theologian, philosopher and Lutheran minister. Following dismissal from his post of professor of theology at the University of Frankfurt by the Nazis, he moved to the USA and held professorships at Union Theological Seminary, New York, and Harvard and Chicago Divinity Schools. His books include

Systematic Theology (1951–63), *The Courage to Be* (1952) and *Dynamics of Faith* (1957).

Tindal, Matthew (1657–1733). British deist thinker and writer, and author of *Christianity as Old as the Creation: The Gospel of a Republication of the Religion of Nature* (1730), which argues that reason must predominate in Christianity and that the true service of God consists in behaving morally towards other people.

Toland, John (1670–1722). Anglo-Irish philosopher and diplomat. Deist and freethinker, and author of *Christianity Not Mysterious* (1696) and *Letters to Serena* (1704).

Voltaire, François-Marie Arouet (1694–1778). French playwright, poet, satirist and philosopher, Voltaire embodied the Enlightenment spirit of free enquiry, tolerance and rigorous criticism of existing beliefs and institutions, including organized religion. Forced to take refuge in Holland and England, or to live outside Paris in order to avoid prosecution for his radical ideas, his works include *Essays on the Manners and Spirits of Nation* (1756) and *Candide* (1759), in which he ridicules Leibniz's view that this is the best of all possible worlds.

Waismann, Friedrich (1896–1959). Austrian philosopher and logical positivist, who was lecturer at Cambridge and Oxford. Author of *Introduction to Mathematical Thinking* (1936) and *The Principles of Linguistic Philosophy* (1965).

Wallis, John (1616–1703). British mathematician and Anglican clergyman, who was Savilian Professor of Mathematics at Oxford for 50 years.

Warnock, Geoffrey James (G. J.) (1923–95). British philosopher, principal of Hertford College, Oxford, and vice-chancellor of the University of Oxford, who prepared J. L. Austin's writings for publication after his death. A leading proponent of the metaethical theory of ethical descriptivism, his books include *Berkeley* (1953), *Contemporary Moral Philosophy* (1967) and *The Object of Morality* (1971).

Wasa, Kristina, Queen of Sweden (1626–89). Daughter of King Gustav II of Sweden, and Queen of Sweden from 1632 until her abdication in favour of her cousin, in 1654. Her extensive intellectual interests included philosophy, science and astronomy. After leaving Sweden, she travelled around Europe, converting from Protestantism to Roman Catholicism, and eventually settling in Rome. She was a controversial figure, due to the murder of her servant Gian Rinaldo Monaldeschi in her presence, and her attempts to make herself ruler of Naples and Poland.

Weil, Simone (1909–43). French philosopher, poet, religious mystic and political activist, who died in Britain while working for the Free French movement and whose articles and other writings were published posthumously in *Notebooks* (1951–6).

Whitehead, Alfred North (1861–1947). British philosopher and mathematician, who taught philosophy at Cambridge, London and Harvard. Russell's supervisor at Cambridge, he was co-author with him of *Principia Mathematica* (1910–13). His other books include *Enquiry Concerning the Principles of Natural Knowledge* (1919) and *Process and Reality* (1929).

Wolff, Christian (1679–1754). German rationalist philosopher, chancellor of the University of Halle and disciple of Leibniz, whose major philosophical work, *First Philosophy or Ontology* (1730), influenced Martin Knutzen and, though him, his student Immanuel Kant.

Woolf, Virginia (1882–1941). British experimental novelist and literary critic, whose books include *Mrs Dalloway* (1925), *To the Lighthouse* (1927) and *The Waves* (1931).

Wordsworth, William (1770–1850). British poet, whose works include *Lyrical Ballads* (1798), *Sonnets Dedicated to Liberty* (1807) and *Poems Chiefly of Early and Late Years* (1842), who was poet laureate from 1843 until his death.

Wright, Georg Henrik von (1916–2003). Finnish analytical philosopher and logician, who succeeded Wittgenstein as professor of philosophy at Cambridge and was one of his literary executors, and whose books include *The Logical Problem of Induction* (1941), *An Essay in Modal Logic* (1951) and A *Treatise on Induction and Probability* (1951).

Zeno of Citium (334–262 BCE). Cyprus-born ancient Greek philosopher, who taught in Athens and was the founder of Stoicism. He believed that human beings should live according to nature, and can become indifferent to suffering if they can master their emotions.

Glossary of Terms

Abraham. The story of Abraham, which consists of a number of legendary narratives, is found in Genesis 11.27–25.18. In response to God's call, Abraham left his home in Ur of the Chaldees and migrated to the land of Canaan, where he settled. He is seen as the father of the Hebrew race and also of Judaism, Christianity and Islam. For Kierkegaard, he is the exemplar of faith in and obedience to God, as shown by his willingness to sacrifice Isaac.

Abortion Law Reform Association. Founded in 1936, its campaign for clarification and reform of abortion legislation in Britain helped to bring about the 1967 Abortion Act, which permits termination of pregnancies under certain conditions.

Absolute idealism. System of philosophy, deriving from that of Hegel, which maintains that, contrary to the empiricist view of the world (that it consists of many different things, which we know through our senses), ultimate reality is unified and whole, and is to be identified with the one absolute mind or spirit.

Abstract ideas/abstraction (theory of). See Process of abstraction below.

Absurd (the). In the context of existentialist philosophy, this relates to the purposelessness and pointlessness of life and the lack of any compelling reason for choosing one set of beliefs over another. Kierkegaard emphasizes the absurdity of Christian teaching, when tested against supposedly rational standards.

Analogy. Drawing a parallel between two things on the basis of similarities between them, as in the analogy between the world/features of it and a human artifact in the design argument for the existence of God (see Design argument below); using the similarities between God and creatures (which are known) as a basis for statements about God, because there is a relation between God and creatures, that of cause and effect.

Analysis. The philosophical activity of breaking complex objects of thought down, until their simple/simplest parts are reached. This approach to philosophy is particularly associated with G. E. Moore.

Analytic (of propositions). One in which the concept of the subject contains the concept of the predicate, so that the predicate adds nothing to the subject. Such propositions are necessary and certain, because they say nothing about the empirical world.

Animal rights. The issues surrounding the question of whether and to what extent animals have moral status and the nature of human obligations towards them.

Anthropocentric ethics. Human-centred ethics, which are exclusively or primarily concerned with how we ought to behave towards other human beings and ourselves.

A posteriori. That which comes after, or is based on, experience.

A priori. That which comes before experience, does not depend upon experience, and which holds true (or is claimed to) irrespective of experience.

A priori **concepts/categories of the understanding**. In the *Critique of Pure Reason*, Kant argues that we do not derive the general categories of thought, such as causality, existence, substance, reality and so on, which make thinking possible, from experience; rather, our minds impose them upon experience, thus determining the way we think about the data we receive through the senses.

A priori **intuitions of time and space.** In the *Critique of Pure Reason*, Kant argues that we do not derive our concepts of space and time from sense experience, but impose them on experience, of which they are necessary conditions. They are forms of sensibility, which shape our sense experience.

A priori **moral laws.** According to Kant, moral laws or precepts are discovered *a priori* by the reason. So far from being based on experience of the world and/or human needs, they prescribe standards of conduct for human beings, irrespective of the human condition and general or particular human needs.

Arguments for the existence of God (traditional). The attempts to provide philosophical proofs of God's existence, such as the ontological, cosmological and design arguments. See below.

Aristotelianism. Aristotle's approach to philosophy, which emphasizes both empirical methods and the use of reason; medieval philosophy, such as that of Aquinas, which follows that of Aristotle and attempts to combine his philosophical ideas with Christian teaching.

Aristotelian logic. Aristotle's system of logic.

Aryanism. Racial doctrine propagated by Hitler and the Nazi Party that northern European/Germanic people are superior to/more civilized than other races/racial groups.

Atheist/atheism. One who is convinced/the conviction that there is no God.

Atomism/atomistic theory of the universe. See Glossary of Philosophers and Thinkers entry for Democritus of Abdera.

Attribute(s). A characteristic of, or that which constitutes the essence of, a substance. See Substance below.

Glossary of Terms

Attributes of God. See God below.

Averröes/Averroism. Philosophical ideas associated with the Islamic philosopher, Averröes, such as monopsychism (see below) and the view (which Averröes and his followers do not seem to have held) that there are different kinds of truth, such as those of philosophy and theology, so that something may be 'true' in theological terms, even though it is untenable philosophically.

Bad faith. Sartre's term for human self-deception, which denies freedom and individual responsibility.

Basic moral principles. The primary or fundamental moral principles, such as the categorical imperative (see below) or the principle of utility (see below), against which all other maxims or rules of conduct are tested, or on which a system of moral rules is based. See also Secondary principles below.

Being-for-itself. Conscious being, which is aware of itself, in contrast to things/objects.

Being-in-itself. Things/objects that lack self-awareness.

Best of all possible worlds. The view, propounded by Leibniz, that the world, as it is, is the best of all possible worlds, because the best of all possible worlds is the only world that an omnipotent and omnibenevolent God would have created.

British/English empiricism/empiricist tradition. The British tradition of empiricism, which originated in the work/writings of John Locke, George Berkeley and David Hume, and which includes such philosophers as John Stuart Mill, Bertrand Russell and A. J. Ayer.

Campaign for Nuclear Disarmament (CND). Organization, founded in 1958, which campaigns against nuclear weapons/weapons of mass destruction.

Cartesian doubt. Descartes' extreme and comprehensive doubt of everything he previously believed, in order to try to discover what we certainly know.

Cartesian dualism. The absolute distinction which Descartes makes between mind and body, the ability to think being the essence of mind and extension (see below) being the essence of body. This raises the issue, not satisfactorily resolved by Descartes, of how the two relate to each other.

Categorical imperative. Kant's term for the imperative of morality, which commands unconditionally. What it commands must be done for its own sake, and because it is right, not in order to accomplish some further purpose; and it may conflict with a person's inclinations. Kant gives five different formulations of the categorical imperative in his *Groundwork of the Metaphysics of Morals*, the first of which is: 'act only in accordance with that maxim through which at the same time you can will that it become a universal law'.

Cause/causation/causality. Causal relationships, the relation between two objects or events, such that when one is present, or occurs, it produces or leads to the other.

Central Advisory Council for Education (England). Advisory body established under the Education Act 1944 to advise the minister of education (later the secretary of state) on educational matters. The Plowden report considered the whole subject of primary education and the transition to secondary education.

Cogito ergo sum. I think, therefore I am. From Descartes' *Discourse on Method*; he regards it as absolutely certain and a secure base for all knowledge.

Common sense (views). Those which the majority of non-philosophical people have, such as the view that there is an external world, to which our senses give us access, and which is as we perceive it. In morality, the generally accepted ethical principles and rules of a particular society.

Conatus. The striving of everything in the universe, including human beings, to preserve its own existence.

Conclusive verifiability. The logical positivists' criterion for distinguishing between metaphysical utterances and genuine synthetic propositions: that the latter must be conclusively verifiable in experience.

Conscience. Generally, human beings' intuitive/instinctive awareness of what is right or wrong, which deters us from contemplating or performing certain actions.

Consequentialist ethics. Ethics/ethical system in which the rightness or wrongness of an action is determined on the basis of its consequences. The best-known consequentialist ethical system is utilitarianism. This judges actions to be right or wrong, according to whether or not they maximize pleasure/happiness, which utilitarians regard as the ultimate good. One major problem with any consequentialist system is the difficulty of calculating all the consequences, over time, of any action we perform.

Constitution/constitutional government. A statement (generally written) of the basic principles by which a country is governed, providing (usually) for a representative or democratic element and recognition of human/individual rights.

Continental rationalism. The approach to philosophy of philosophers such as Descartes, Spinoza and Leibniz, which holds that reason, not experience, is the source of knowledge, including such fundamental truths as the existence and nature of God.

Contingency/contingent things. That which could not-be, or which might not have occurred and depends on something else for its existence/occurrence.

Contraception. Artificial methods of preventing conception, which are opposed by some groups, such as the Roman Catholic Church.

Cosmological argument for the existence of God. One of the traditional arguments for the existence of God. In his *Summa Theologica*, Aquinas attempts to argue (the five ways: see below) from God's effects (the existence of the universe/world and/or how it exists) to God as its cause.

Deconstructionism. The view, propounded by Jacques Derrida, that the meaning of language is determined by its relationship to other language, and is capable of limitless different and differing interpretations; it has no fixed or objective meaning or significance, which is determined by what the speaker or writer intends, or its relationship to the world/objects to which it refers.

Deduction/deductive reasoning. Arguing from certain premises to conclusions from which they (may) follow necessarily.

Deductive system. A system of first or fundamental principles or premises, which, together with the conclusions deduced from them, would give a complete picture of reality. This approach to philosophy is associated with the rationalist philosophers, such as Descartes, Spinoza and Leibniz.

Deism. The approach to religious belief, particularly popular in the seventeenth and eighteenth centuries, which limits the concept of God to what it is believed can be established through natural theology. This results in the concept of an intelligent being who designed the world, but whose powers are limited, and who does not interfere in the natural order or answer prayers.

Democracy (direct). System of government where citizens vote directly on issues (as in a referendum), instead of electing members of a parliament/assembly to represent them, and legislate on their behalf.

Demonstration/demonstrative/demonstrative knowledge. That which can be proved and therefore known conclusively, such that its denial involves a contradiction.

Denoting. Referring to something. In 'On Denoting', Russell makes the point that some descriptive phrases, such as 'the present king of France', which appear to denote or name something, do not refer to an actually existing person/object.

Deontological ethics. An ethical system which holds that rightness has little or nothing to do with an action's consequences, and everything to do with the action itself; and that we have a duty to perform certain actions, such as keeping promises, telling the truth, and not harming others, because of their intrinsic rightness. The best-known deontological system is that of Immanuel Kant, who argues that all rational beings (which includes human beings) have absolute worth, and have an obligation to treat each other always as ends in themselves, never merely as means.

Deontological intuitionism. The doctrine that what is right, as well as what is good, can be known through intuition.

Descriptive metaphysics. Non-speculative metaphysics, which attempts to determine and explain what human beings know and can know, how knowledge is possible and the limits of human knowledge, but which, unlike speculative metaphysics, does not attempt to penetrate to the nature of ultimate reality.

Design argument for the existence of God. One of the traditional arguments for the existence of God, which points to similarities between the world/features of it and objects designed and made by human beings, and argues that, as the effects are similar, the causes must also be similar.

Determinism. The doctrine that every event has a cause, which, when applied to what are held to be voluntary human actions, suggests that they are not actually free.

Deus sive natura. Spinoza's view that everything is either God or nature, as God and nature, creator and creation, are aspects of the same and sole substance.

Dialectic(s). In Plato's philosophical system, a process of discussion and argument that enables those following it to gain access to the intelligible world and to see the form of the good (see below).

Differential calculus. Method of calculating the rate of change of a quantity using symbols.

Divine right of kings. The doctrine, associated with hereditary monarchy, that the monarch is chosen, and given authority to rule, by God, and is accountable only to God. Therefore, those who challenge, or rebel against, the monarch, defy God's will. The doctrine was widely accepted in England until the seventeenth century, when it was frequently invoked by the Stuart monarchs, but disappeared after the Glorious Revolution. The associated doctrine of non-resistance held that monarchs should be obeyed, not resisted.

Doctor of the Universal Church. Title given by the Roman Catholic Church to those theologians, teachers and writers whose work has been of particular benefit to the Church.

Doctrine of the mean. Aristotelian doctrine that there is a mid-point between the vices of excess and deficiency, and that virtue is finding the mean between these two vices.

Dualistic view of reality. Any doctrine which distinguishes different levels or types of reality, such as Plato's distinction between the intelligible world of the forms and the one we experience through our senses; Descartes' between mind and body; or

Kant's between *noumena* (things-in-themselves) and *phenomena* (things as they appear to us).

Efficient cause. A cause that is capable of producing a particular effect.

Emotive function (of ethical language). The function of ethical language in expressing and/or arousing emotions. See Ethical emotivism below.

Empirical world. The world we learn about through our senses and in relation to which we determine what is true or false on the basis of experience and observation.

Empiricism. The philosophical view that human beings do not have any innate ideas, so experience/observation is their main or only source of knowledge of the world.

Encyclopédie. Eighteenth-century encyclopaedia, edited by Denis Diderot, which brought together articles containing innovative and anti-clerical ideas on a range of philosophical, scientific and other subjects.

End-in-itself/ends-in-themselves. Things or beings that are worthwhile in themselves, and which should not be regarded/treated (merely) as means to an end. According to Kant, human and all rational beings are ends-in-themselves.

Enlightenment (the). Term used to describe the spirit of free enquiry, rationalism and scepticism (about religious dogmas), which characterized the intellectual life of the eighteenth century, and is associated with such writers and thinkers as Diderot and Voltaire.

Epicureanism. See Glossary of Philosophers and Thinkers entry for Epicurus.

Epistemology. Theory of knowledge, theories about what human beings know, how they know what they (claim to) know and the limits of human knowledge.

Esse est percipi. To be (exist) is to be perceived, which is the essence of George Berkeley's subjective idealism.

Essence. The essential nature of something, that which makes something what it is, and without which it would not be what it is.

Ethical descriptivism. Metaethical theory, associated with G. J. Warnock and others, which holds that moral judgements are determined by their content, not their form, and that morality is logically grounded in human needs.

Ethical emotivism. The metaethical theory, associated with A. J. Ayer and C. L. Stevenson, that the function and meaning of ethical terms, such as 'good' and 'right', and the propositions in which they appear, is to express or arouse emotions, not to state something which is true or false.

Ethical intuitionism. The metaethical theory which holds that the truth of propositions about things being good or bad in themselves can only be known through intuition (mental awareness/apprehension); the truth of such propositions cannot be proved or disproved.

Ethical naturalism. The metaethical theory which holds that 'good' should be defined by reference to a natural object, which is an object of experience, such as pleasure/happiness, or that such a natural object should be the criterion for deciding what is good.

Ethical non-cognitivism. The metaethical theory, which includes ethical emotivism, which holds that ethical utterances cannot be true or false, because there is no objective criterion to determine their truth or falsity.

Ethical non-naturalism. The metaethical theory that 'good' cannot be defined by reference to a natural object.

Ethical (universal prescriptivism). The metaethical theory, associated with R. M. Hare, that the meaning of moral language is to be found in certain rules of moral reasoning, and that moral judgements are prescriptive (they guide choices) and universalizable (an action described as 'morally right' must be so for all people in comparable situations).

Ethical subjectivism. The metaethical theory that the rightness of actions and the goodness of ends should be defined in terms of the feelings of approval they elicit.

Ethical supernaturalism. Metaethical theory which relates the meaning of moral terms to the (perceived) will of God, or a normative ethical theory which holds that we should always obey God's commands, whatever they may be.

Ethical symbol. Ethical terms, such as 'good' or 'right'.

Ethics/ethical. Terms generally used interchangeably with morality/moral; set of moral principles that tell us what is good or bad, right or wrong; the (philosophical) study of what is good and right.

Eudaimonia. The Greek word for 'happiness' or 'prosperity', which, according ro Aristotle, is the goal of ethics.

Eudaimonistic ethical theory. A moral theory, originating with Aristotle's *The Nicomachean Ethics*, which views happiness as the goal of ethics, and holds that it will be achieved through a way of life that combines rational activity and virtue. See Virtue ethics below.

Eugenics. The study of ways of improving, or the view that attempts should be made to improve, the qualities of the human species. It can be divided into negative eugenics, which seeks to discourage breeding by those with genetic defects, or who are considered likely to transmit undesirable qualities, and positive eugenics, which seeks to encourage breeding by those thought likely to transmit desirable qualities. The eugenics movement had strong support in the United States and Britain during the late nineteenth and early twentieth centuries, but was accused of racism and class bias, and was discredited by Nazi eugenics experiments during the Second World War.

Exemplar of faith. According to Kierkegaard, Abraham is the model of faith in, and obedience to, God.

Existence is not a predicate. A point made by Kant, in his *Critique of Pure Reason*, that existence is not a concept of something that can be added to the concept of a particular person or thing. To say that a particular thing 'is' or 'exists' does not add a new predicate or attribute to it, but just affirms the existence of the person or thing with all its predicates or attributes.

Existential proposition. Propositions which state that something does, or does not, exist.

Existentialism. Generally, a philosophical approach which holds that, as the world lacks (or appears to) an ultimate purpose and does not offer human beings a clear set of beliefs, values or purposes, individuals must choose these for themselves, and are capable of doing so.

Experience. What relates to the empirical world (see above) and the way human beings experience things.

Extension. In relation to physical objects, that they are extended and occupy space.

External world. The world outside ourselves, which (it is believed) exists independently of us/our perception of it, and contains persons other than ourselves. See also Solipsism/solipsistic position below.

Faith (religious). This can be simply belief in God (which involves going beyond the empirical evidence) or trusting belief in God and his goodness and being willing to obey his commands, whatever they are.

Felicific or hedonic calculus. In his *Introduction to the Principles of Morals and Legislation*, Jeremy Bentham explains how to calculate the quantity of pleasure or pain that a particular action will produce, and thus to decide whether it is the right one. The main factors to be taken into account are intensity, duration, certainty/uncertainty and propinquity/remoteness. In fact, this apparently scientific approach does not remove the difficulty of working out the consequences of actions over time.

Female equality/women's suffrage. In Britain, women were not given full political rights until the Representation of the People Act, 1928, or the right to equal pay for similar work until the Equal Pay Act, 1970.

Final cause. A cause in the sense of the (ultimate) purpose of, or reason for doing something, as opposed to the action which brings it about.

Five ways. The five proofs of God's existence that Aquinas puts forward in the *Summa Theologica*, which argue from our experience of the world to God's existence.

Form of life. The setting, made up of a complex of, for example, historical, cultural or scientific factors, and so on, within which a language is used and from which it derives its meaning. See also Language-game below.

Form of the good. In Plato's philosophy, the form of the good has the same relation to intelligible objects in the intelligible world as the sun has to visible objects in the visible world, and it is the source of reality, truth and goodness.

Forms (Platonic). According to Plato, individual things in the ordinary, visible world, which we experience through the senses, acquire their identity by being, in some way, copies of the unchanging forms or archetypes of these things in the intelligible realm, to which only our minds can give us access.

Free will/freedom of the will (the issue of). Whether or not human actions are actually free. The three main philosophical

responses to the issue are hard determinism, soft determinism and libertarianism (see below).

General categories of thought. See *A priori* concepts/categories
of the understanding above.

General happiness/greatest happiness of greatest number.
Utilitarianism is not concerned only with promoting the
agent's own happiness, but with promoting general happiness, that is, the greatest happiness of the greatest number
of people.

General ideas. See Process of abstraction below.

General will. Rousseau's idea of the will of all the people in a
state, as expressed through the state, which is distinct from
both the individual wills of its members or the will of the majority of them, and which unifies them and seeks their good.

Glorious Revolution (1688–9). The events that led to the removal
of James II from the throne of England, and William III and
Mary becoming king and queen; and which involved recognition of the liberty and rights of subjects (Bill of Rights) and a
degree of religious toleration.

God. The Christian God, who is believed by Christians to be/
have the attributes of being all-powerful (omnipotent), all-
knowing (omniscient), infinitely benevolent/loving, and to
have created the universe and all it contains from nothing.

Golden Rule. Jesus' teaching, in the Sermon on the Mount
(Matt. 7.12): 'So whatever you wish that men would do to
you, do so to them'.

Guardians. Plato's term for the ruling class of the ideal state,
whose philosophical knowledge equips them to govern.

Happiness/pleasure. Utilitarianism is concerned with promoting happiness, but this can mean different things to

different people. Jeremy Bentham identifies happiness with pleasure, and his concern is with the maximization of pleasure: so, the right act is the one that produces the greatest quantity of pleasure. However, John Stuart Mill's conception of happiness is more like Aristotle's *eudaimonia*, and is to be found in a well-balanced life, in which a variety of sources of pleasure, including intellectual pursuits and positive relationships with family and other people, are present, and from which pain and absence of liberty are absent.

Hard determinism. The doctrine that the causal connection between human motives and actions rules out genuine human freedom.

Harm principle. See Principle of liberty.

Hegelianism. The philosophical ideas of Hegel, which had a major impact on the development of nineteenth-century philosophy. See also Absolute idealism and Monism.

Homosexual Law/Sexual Law Reform Society. Organization founded in 1958 to campaign for changes in the law to give homosexuals more/equal rights in the United Kingdom, and which contributed to the passing of the Sexual Offences Act 1967.

Hypothetical imperatives. Kant distinguishes (*Groundwork of the Metaphysics of Morals*) between the imperatives of morality, which are always categorical, and hypothetical imperatives, which do not command absolutely, but only as a means of achieving another purpose.

Idea(s). The term used by early empiricist philosophers to refer to anything that is immediately known, ranging from sense-data to things that are remembered or imagined.

Ideal observer (theory of). Idea proposed by Adam Smith and others that correct moral judgements are most likely to be made by those who do not stand to gain/are not affected by the outcome.

Idealism (philosophical). The view that reality is, in some sense, mental/in the mind.

Immaterialism. The view maintained by, for example, George Berkeley that there are no material objects which exist independently of minds. See also Subjective idealism.

Immortality (of the soul). The idea that the soul (see below) does not die but lives on for ever.

Impassibility. The divine attribute of being incapable of emotion.

Incarnation. The Christian teaching that, in Jesus Christ, God became incarnate (took on human form), in order to redeem human beings.

Induction/inductive reasoning/inductive generalizations/inductive principle. Inferring general principles or propositions from particular instances/inferring probable conclusions from premises based on experience.

Inference. Concluding one thing from something else.

Innate ideas. Inborn ideas, ideas which are known to the mind independently of experience. This doctrine is accepted by rationalist philosophers, but rejected by empiricists, who hold that knowledge is derived from experience.

Intellectual intuition. Ability to have immediate intellectual awareness/apprehension of things, as when metaphysicians claim to have intuitive knowledge of facts that cannot be known from sense experience. See Metaphysics below.

Intelligible world. The world of Plato's forms, to which, unlike the ordinary, visible world (see Empirical world), only our minds, not our senses, can give us access. See Forms and Form of the good above.

Intercessionary prayers. Prayers to God on behalf of others, asking for their needs to be met.

Intuitive knowledge. See Intellectual intuition above.

Invisible hand (theory of). Adam Smith's term to describe the way in which, through competition and the law of supply and demand, a free market in goods and services works in a way that benefits all members of society, even though it is not operated for that purpose and those running businesses are pursuing their own interests.

Is/ought gap. David Hume (in *A Treatise of Human Nature*) raises the question of the relationship between statements of fact ('is') and statements of value ('ought'), and appears to suggest that a move from one to another is logically flawed, as no evaluation (what we ought to do) follows from any factual statement. However, the interpretation of the passage is disputed.

Jansenism. Theological position associated with Cornelius Jansen (1585–1638), which taught predestination and the need for self-denial.

Judaeo-Christian concept of God. See God above.

Justice. Fairness in the context of how individuals or groups are treated in relation to other members of a larger group or community, whether it is (for example) a family, those convicted of crimes, or society as a whole.

Kantian ethics. In his *Groundwork of the Metaphysics of Morals*, Kant expounds a deontological system of morals, which treats certain actions as being right or wrong in themselves, and not because of their consequences. Although morality is completely independent of God, as moral laws must be obeyed for their own sake, Kant argues (*Critique of Practical Reason*) that God needs to be postulated if obedience to the moral law is to be rewarded with happiness.

King-in-Parliament/Queen-in-Parliament. The concept of constitutional monarchy, which developed in England (and subsequently in Great Britain/United Kingdom, following the Acts of Union with Scotland and Ireland), whereby laws are enacted, and government is carried on in the name of the monarch (who formally assents to legislation), but the legislative and executive functions are exercised by parliament and by ministers responsible to parliament.

Kingdom of ends. The moral kingdom, which humans, as rational beings, can create by always following the categorical imperative, and treating themselves and others always as ends, never merely as means.

Knowledge by acquaintance. When we are directly aware of things, as of the sense-data (colour, hardness and so on) which make up the appearance of an object, such as a table.

Knowledge by description. Knowledge that derives from truths about something which are related to things with which we are acquainted. For example, we are not directly acquainted with a table as a physical object, but our knowledge of it as a physical object is connected to our acquaintance with the sense-data that make up its appearance. We can then formulate a description that applies to only that one object.

Labour theory of value. The theory put forward by Adam Smith and David Ricardo that the value of goods and services is determined by the amount of labour employed in producing/providing them.

Language-game. The context within which language is used, such as to discuss the existence of God or to set out the rules of tennis, and within which its meaning is determined. See also Form of life above.

Glossary of Terms

Law of contradiction. See Law of non-contradiction below.

Law of the excluded middle. This states that everything is either x or not-x: for example, something is either a chair or not a chair.

Law of identity. This states that x is x and not something else (here x stands for any entity): for example, a chair is a chair, not a table, a cupboard or anything else.

Law of non-contradiction/principle of contradiction. This states that nothing can be both x and not-x: for example, nothing can be both a chair and not a chair.

Laws of logic. See Laws of thought and Modern logic below.

Laws of nature/natural laws. These are generalizations, based on experience, and so it is logically possible that (if nature changes) they may be disproved by experience.

Laws of thought. The three basic logical principles, the laws of identity (see above), non-contradiction (see above) and excluded middle (see above), which were enunciated by Aristotle.

Legal positivism. The view that laws are commands of the sovereign power in a state (the monarch or government), which has the ultimate authority to decide the state's laws and the rights of its citizens. It rejects the view that laws are not valid unless they conform to the principles of natural law or that citizens have natural rights, which the state must respect.

Libertarian/libertarianism. The view that the human will is free, and must be so if human beings are to be held responsible (and punished) for their actions.

Linguistic philosophy/ordinary language philosophy. The approach to philosophy which focuses on careful analysis of the language in which philosophical problems are expressed and debated, in order to eliminate any confusions which may arise from misunderstanding of/ambiguity in the language used or differences between the way words are used in a philosophical context and their ordinary use.

Literally meaningful/significant. The view associated with logical positivism (see below) which links the meaningfulness or significance of propositions to their being either analytically true (tautologies) or capable of being empirically verified. See Verification/verifiability below.

Logic. Science of inference or reasoning.

Logical atomism. The theory, associated with Russell, and Wittgenstein during the early part of his career, that language can be analysed into elementary propositions, which are collections of names, and that these basic atoms of language denote objects, the basic elements of reality.

Logical constant. Terms in logical systems which have fixed meanings.

Logical construction. Something that is defined logically (according to the rules of logic) in terms of something else, as a material object is in terms of sense-data.

Logical entailment. When the conclusion follows necessarily from the premises.

Logical positivism. The doctrine that the criterion of verifiability should be used to distinguish between metaphysical utterances and genuine synthetic propositions.

Logicism. The view of Russell and Frege, that mathematical truths are truths of logic, capable of being deduced from logical axioms, a set of basic or fundamental propositions. Thus, mathematics is identical with, and reducible to, logic.

Logos spermatikos. In Stoic philosophy, the active principle or principle of reason in the universe, which gives nature its order, in which human beings share, and in accordance with which they should live their lives.

Glossary of Terms

Marxism. Theory associated with Karl Marx (1818–83) and Friedrich Engels (1820–95), which interprets history in terms of economic and class relationships, and holds that ultimately capitalism and bourgeois domination of society will be swept away by a revolution of the oppressed industrial classes (the proletariat), which will result in a classless society, in which private property will be replaced by common ownership.

Master and slave moralities. The Nietzschean distinction between master morality, which associates what is good with power, pride and nobility and disdains empathetic feelings, and slave morality, which values pity, kindness and helpfulness, the qualities most likely to improve the lot of slaves or sufferers.

Materialism. See Physicalism below.

Matter. The collection of all physical objects (things that occupy space, have mass and shape, and so on) in the universe; matter (it is believed) is distinct from mind, exists independently of our perceiving it, and is something of which we become aware through sense-experience.

Metaethics. Study of the nature of moral argument and the meaning and use of such moral terms as 'good' and 'right'.

Metaethical debate of the twentieth century. The debate between the proponents of different ethical theories, such as (ethical) intuitionism, emotivism, universal prescriptivism and descriptivism, which occupied moral philosophers during a large part of the twentieth century.

Metaphysics. Study of what is after (beyond) physics, and which cannot be investigated by ordinary empirical methods; and, as speculative metaphysics (see below), the investigation of what really exists, of ultimate reality, including philosophical systems which attempt to explain its nature, and for which, although they may be coherent, there is little or no empirical evidence. As this activity claims to provide knowledge which transcends the world of science and common sense, and as metaphysical propositions are not analytical truths of logic or mathematics, or capable of being empirically verified, it is dismissed by empiricists (see above) and logical positivists (see above).

Mind–body dualism. See Cartesian dualism above.

Miracle. An event that cannot be accounted for according to established laws of nature, which it appears to break, and which is attributed to God/supernatural causes.

Modern logic. The major developments in logic, during the second half of the nineteenth and early twentieth centuries, associated with Frege, Peirce, Russell, Whitehead, Wittgenstein and others.

Mode(s) (of existence). The modifications of substance, or that which exists in, and is conceived through, something other than itself, i.e. substance. See also Substance below.

Monad/monadism. Leibniz's theory that God has designed the universe, such that it consists ultimately of conscious and volitional entities, or monads, which develop and operate independently of each other.

Monism. The philosophical doctrine, held by Spinoza and others, that reality is made up of one fundamental substance. The opposite of pluralism (see below).

Monopsychism. The theory that there is a universal intellect, which all human beings share.

Moral argument for the existence of God. One of the traditional arguments for God's existence, which (in the version associated with Kant) holds that God is a necessary postulate of morality, or that there is no basis for morality/moral standards, unless there is a God.

Moral law. In Kantian ethics, the *a priori* (see above) moral principles, discovered by the reason, which should govern the actions of all rational beings (see below).

Moral philosophy. Branch of philosophy concerned with moral issues and the general principles of morality.

Moral status. The standing of an individual or groups of individuals in relation to moral principles, and whether he, she or they meet the criteria of personhood, or fulfil other criteria, such that it is accepted that (to a greater or lesser extent) moral principles should govern their treatment. Thus, while it is generally accepted that animals have lower moral status than humans, and can be used to serve human needs, this does not mean they should be treated with indifference or cruelty.

Natura naturans/Natura naturata. Terms used by Spinoza to indicate two different ways of viewing nature: the first identifies the active and creative aspect of nature, the second its passive aspect; but both are part of God or nature.

Natural law. The ethical theory which holds that certain ethical principles and courses of action are good or right, because they are consistent with the nature of human beings and the natural order, but that others are not. For many Christians, particularly Roman Catholics, natural law is the way that human beings, as rational beings, participate in the eternal law, by which God governs the universe, and they must base their ethical principles and decisions on it, in order to achieve their proper end as human beings, made in God's image.

Natural rights. Rights, such as the basic freedoms of liberty, opinion and speech, which people are held to possess on the basis of their humanity, and which reflect their intrinsic dignity and worth.

Natural theology. What human beings can find out about God through the use of their reason and from experience, without the help of revelation.

Naturalistic account of the world. An account of the world/universe which does not involve God as its ultimate cause/explanation.

Naturalistic fallacy. The fallacy of which G. E. Moore accuses Bentham and Mill: that of confusing good or right with/defining it as a natural property or object, such as pleasure.

Necessary being/existence. Something/a being which must exist/cannot not-be/cannot be thought not to be/whose existence cannot be separated from his essence: God.

New philosophers. The new breed of Nietzschean thinkers, who, unlike academic philosophers, will not just study and expound moral values, but will lay down and enforce a new set of moral values for society.

Normative ethics. This concerns the objects or ends, which we regard, or should regard, as good, and the rules or principles that we adopt, or ought to adopt, to govern and/or assess our conduct.

Noumenon(a). Things as they are in themselves, as distinct from how they appear to us.

Omni-benevolence (of God). In Christian teaching, God is believed to be all-loving.

Omnipotence (of God). In Christian teaching, God is believed to be infinitely powerful.

Omniscience (of God). In Christian teaching, God is believed to have infinite knowledge.

Ontology. The branch of metaphysics concerned with being and what (ultimately) exists.

Ontological argument for the existence of God. One of the traditional arguments for the existence of God, put forward by Anselm of Canterbury in his *Proslogion*, which argues from the concept of God to his existence.

Open question argument. Moore's view that, whatever is said to be good, it is always an open question (it can be asked intelligibly) whether it is good, so nothing can be good by definition.

Pantheism. The view that God is everywhere/is (in) everything, as in Spinoza's philosophy.

Paradox of faith. In Kierkegaard's writings, the apparently absurd and self-contradictory aspect of faith, which holds that the single individual is higher than universal ethical precepts.

Parallelism of mind and body. The doctrine that mind and body do not interact with each other, but operate separately under the direction of God, thus solving (by eliminating it) the problem, which Descartes was unable to answer satisfactorily, of how, if mind and body are distinct substances, they can interact.

Parliamentary reform. Until the early nineteenth century, the right to vote in Britain was restricted to those who met certain property-related criteria. The existence of 'rotten' boroughs meant that there was no clear correlation between the population/number of voters in a constituency and whether or not it was represented in parliament, while in 'pocket' boroughs, the MPs were chosen by the individuals or families who owned the land where they were situated. Reform (representation of the people) Acts of 1832, 1867 and 1884 extended the franchise, and redistributed seats on the basis of population. The Ballot Act (1872) introduced the secret ballot, helping to eliminate bribery and intimidation from elections. An Act of 1918 gave the franchise to women over 30, and it was extended to all women in 1928.

Perception/problem of perception. The (problem of) the relationship between sense-data and the physical objects which (it is believed) give rise to them, and how sentences about the latter relate to sentences about the former.

Phenomenalism. The doctrine that the external world/ material things are to be understood and expressed in terms of actual and possible sense experiences.

Phenomenon(a). Things as they appear to us, due to the way we experience them, as opposed to things as they are in themselves.

Philosophy. Literally, love of wisdom, which involves the study of ultimate reality, what really exists, the most general principles of things.

Philosopher-rulers/philosopher-kings. Plato argues that the ideal state can only be created if philosophers become kings, or those who currently rule become philosophers.

Philosophy of religion. Application of philosophical methods to religious concepts, beliefs and arguments.

Philosophical analysis. See Analysis above.

Physicalism. The doctrine that nothing exists apart from, or everything that exists is explicable in terms of, matter.

Picture theory of meaning. Wittgenstein's doctrine, expounded in the *Tractatus*, that language is meaningful because its logical form pictures that of reality.

Pluralism. The doctrine that reality does not consist of one substance, but many.

Pluralism (philosophical). The view that reality is not one substance, but many: the opposite of monism (see above).

Postmodernism. A way of describing the philosophical approach of, for example, Derrida and Foucault, which embraces such ideas as poststructuralism (see below) and deconstructionism (see above).

Poststructuralism. A philosophical outlook which involves a scepticism about attempts to generalize about human beings or human behaviour, or to apply explanatory 'laws' to them, and which questions the existence of objective or scientific truths. See also Deconstructionism and Poststmodernism above.

Postulates of the practical reason. According to Kant, a necessary condition of morality and the possibility of attaining the highest good. The three postulates are freedom (see Libertarianism above), the immortality of the soul and God.

Practical reason. Reason in its practical use, as it concerns morality/the moral law.

Predicate-in-subject principle. Leibniz's principle that the content of any individual subject always includes all its predicates, such that, with perfect understanding of the concept of the subject, there would be knowledge of all its predicates.

Primary and secondary qualities. The view, propounded by Locke and others, that objects in the world have primary qualities (such as extension, shape and motion), which underlie the secondary ones (such as their smell, colour or taste); it is the latter which produce sensations in us, and which we perceive.

Principle of contradiction. See Law of non-contradiction above.

Principle of identity of indiscernibles/Leibniz's Law. The principle that two substances may not be identical, but differ numerically.

Principle of liberty/harm principle. Mill's principle that the only purpose for which society can rightfully exercise power over one of its members, against his or her will, is to prevent harm to others/their interests; his or her own good, whether physical or moral, is not sufficient justification.

Principle of plenitude. The principle that, under God's direction, there is the greatest possible order, variety and perfection in the world, and that things cannot be otherwise than they are.

Principle of pre-existing harmony. The principle that the appearance of causal relationships in the world is in fact produced by God who harmonizes everything.

Principle of sufficient reason. The principle that no fact can exist, or statement be true, unless there is a sufficient reason why it should be as it is, and not otherwise.

Principle of utility. Utilitarian principle of evaluating actions on the basis of the extent to which they maximize pleasure and diminish pain.

Privatio boni. The doctrine that evil is the relative lack of goodness that is an inevitable feature of finite creatures.

Probability. Probability theory is the mathematical/statistical analysis of how likely an event is to occur. In the sense that it is used by, for example, Butler, it refers to rational judgement about the evidence for particular beliefs, such as the occurrence of miracles.

Problem of evil. The problem that arises from the apparent contradiction between the presence in the world of natural and moral evil, and the belief that the world was created by an infinitely powerful and loving God. The issue is summed up in a question attributed to the Greek philosopher Epicurus: is God willing to prevent evil, but not able? Then he is impotent. Is he able, but not willing? Then he is malevolent. Is he both able and willing? Whence then is evil?

Process of abstraction. The empiricist doctrine that general ideas of things are formed by a process of abstraction from our experience of particular instances.

Pyrrhonian doubt. See Scepticism below, Cartesian doubt above and Pyrrho of Elis in Glossary of Philosophers and Thinkers.

Glossary of Terms

Quantifier. In general use, a term for expressions ('some', 'lots', 'many', 'every', 'a few'), which indicate the number of objects, or the number of times an object occurs, in a particular context or domain of discourse. In logic, the important quantifiers are the universal quantifier: 'all/all things are'; and the existential quantifier: 'there is/there exists', which are represented by symbols.

Ramsey theorem. Theory developed by Frank Ramsey that, in any given situation, contrary to what may seem to be the case, complete disorder is impossible.

Rational beings. Any being who possesses reason, and who therefore has moral status: in Kantian ethics, the moral law would apply to any rational being, not just to human beings.

Rationalism. Philosophical doctrine that reason, rather than (sense) experience is the (principal) source of knowledge.

Realism (philosophical). The view that reality is not in the mind, and that the external world/material things really do exist. See also Idealism above.

Redemption (Christian doctrine of). The belief that Jesus' life and death set human beings free from the debt of sin.

Referential theory of meaning. The theory that the meaning of language derives from that to which it refers in the world (an object or referent) or the relationship between words and their referents.

Reformation (the). The period, during the sixteenth century, when the protests of Martin Luther (1483–1546), Huldreich Zwingli (1484–1531) and John Calvin (1509–46), in Germany, Switzerland and France, against the theology and practices of the Roman Catholic Church, led to the establishment of Protestant Churches in Europe. Although not necessarily the intention of the reformers themselves, breaking the authority of the Roman Catholic Church ultimately weakened restrictions on thought and discussion about religious matters, and made an essential contribution to the establishment of intellectual freedom, at least in Protestant (northern) Europe.

Religious toleration. When different religions/religious groups are allowed (or allow each other) to co-exist without discrimination or persecution, which was not fully achieved in Britain until the nineteenth century, when legislation repealing the seventeenth-century Corporation and Test Acts, designed to exclude non-Anglicans from municipal and government office, and the Catholic Emancipation Act were passed in 1828 and 1829.

Representationalism/representative theory of perception. The empiricist doctrine that what we perceive are sense-data, which arise from/represent to us objects in the external world.

Resurrection. The teaching that, after death, the body remains in the grave until the end of the world, when it is raised. See also Soul below.

Revelation/revealed religion. What God chooses to disclose to human beings about himself and/or how he wants them to worship him or conduct themselves through, for example, prophets and holy scriptures.

Romantic movement. The movement in thought, literature and the arts generally, of which, for example, Johann Wolfgang Goethe (1749–1832), William Wordsworth (1770–1850) and Percy Bysshe Shelley (1792–1822) were part, which reacted against what was perceived as the over-emphasis on reason during the eighteenth century, and which brought human feelings and passions, and the beauty of the natural world, to the fore.

Glossary of Terms

Russell's paradox. The paradox, identified by Russell, that, if the class of all classes which are not members of themselves, is a member of itself, it is not a member, and vice-versa. See also Theory of types below.

Scepticism. Doubting everything (Pyrrhonian or Cartesian doubt), or refusing to accept non-empirical sources of knowledge.

Scholastic philosophy/scholasticism. The Christian-centred philosophy, taught in medieval universities, of which Aquinas was one of the leading exponents.

Secondary moral principles. Moral principles or rules, such as those prohibiting murder or theft, which are based on, or derived from, a first moral principle such as the categorical imperative or the principle of utility.

Sense-content(s). An alternative term for sense-datum/data.

Sense-data/datum. That which is given by the senses/is immediately known in sensation, such as colours, sounds and so on.

Sensitive knowledge. Knowledge that comes from experience/the senses.

Sermon on the Mount. Jesus' ethical and religious teaching, which includes the Beatitudes and the Lord's Prayer, collected in Matthew 5—7, and presented in the form of a sermon delivered by Jesus on one occasion.

Social contract/covenant. The long-held theory, particularly associated with John Locke and Jean-Jacques Rousseau, that society originated in a contract between ruler and ruled, which defined citizens' rights, their obligations to each other, and the powers and responsibilities of government. As no such agreement was ever actually made, it is a hypothetical event, but what are held to be its terms provide criteria for measuring justice, and/or identifying its absence, in a particular society.

Soft determinism. The doctrine that determinism and human freedom are compatible, and that human beings are free (and responsible and punishable for their actions) unless subject to external compulsion.

Solipsism/solipsistic position. Believing that only onself exists, arising from the view that one has access only to one's own experiences, not those of other people.

Soul. The spiritual element within human beings, which is held to be the seat of personality and individual identity, which lives on after death, and which, according to Christian teaching, will be reunited with its body at the general resurrection.

Speciesism. Treating one species, in particular human beings, more favourably than others.

Speculative metaphysics. See Metaphysics.

State of nature. The situation of human beings, and how they behave towards each other, when (or before) there is an organized society with a government and laws. See Social contract/covenant above.

Stoics/stoicism. See Glossary of Philosophers and Thinkers entries for Zeno of Citium, Cleanthes of Assos and Chrysippus of Soli.

Sub specie aeternitatis. Under the form of eternity: Spinoza held that our reason enables us to understand that everything in the universe happens necessarily, and thus to perceive them in their eternal or essential reality.

Subjective idealism. The view that the objects we perceive, which we think have an independent existence, exist only in that we perceive them. See *Esse est percipi* and Immaterialism above.

Substance. The fundamental entity(ies) or form(s) of being which exist in the universe. Since the time of Aristotle, a substance has been defined as that which can exist/be conceived by itself, and which does not depend/is not conceived in terms of anything else. What substances exist in the universe, and their nature, has been a matter of debate among philosophers.

Substratum of matter. The underlying substance or 'something' of which material things are made.

Suprasensible reality. A world/reality that is beyond/transcends the ordinary physical world that we know about through experience/the senses.

Surface grammar. Statements or expressions that use similar words and parts of speech may seem to have much the same meaning, but similarities in their surface grammar may conceal significant differences in their meaning.

Syllogism. A form of reasoning, in which, from two propositions or premises, a third can be inferred.

Synthetic (proposition). One which gives actual information. Generally, it is held that synthetic propositions are also *a posteriori*, that is, they derive the information they give from experience.

Teleological argument for God's existence. Argument from the apparently purposeful behaviour of even non-rational and inanimate beings in the world to an intelligent being who directs them towards their end.

Teleological suspension of the ethical. Kierkegaard's way of describing the setting aside of universal and generally accepted ethical precepts (including, for example, those prohibiting murder), in order to serve the higher purpose of obeying God's commands.

***Telos*/teleological view of the world.** The view that everything in the world, including non-rational and inanimate things, has a *telos* (end or purpose), determined by its nature which it does/ought to aim at.

Theism. Belief in God, usually monotheism.

Theodicy. In Christian theology, arguments that attempt to reconcile belief in an infinitely powerful and all-loving God, who made the world, with the fact that the world contains evil and suffering.

Theological determinism. The doctrine that events are pre-determined or predestined by God, which features particularly in monotheistic religions, where God is believed to be omnipotent and omniscient.

Theology. Setting out the beliefs and teachings of a religion in a systematic way; academic discipline concerned with the study of religion/religious beliefs.

Theoretical reason. Pure reason, as opposed to practical reason (see above).

Theory of definite descriptions. Russell's theory that a sentence(s) containing a definite descriptive word/symbol or phrase can be translated into one(s) that does not contain that expression, but which does have a sub-sentence asserting that one and only one object possesses a certain property, or that no object does. For example, 'the round square cannot exist' is equivalent to 'no one thing can be both square and round', which makes it clear that there is no (special or metaphysical) sense in which a round square exists.

Theory of forms. See Forms (Platonic) above.

Theory of knowledge. See Epistemology above.

Theory of types. Russell's theory which resolves his paradox (see above) by proposing a hierarchy of sets, with those at a lower level being ineligible for inclusion in those higher up.

Third way. The third of Aquinas' five ways (see above), which argues from the contingent or finite nature of the world and all it contains (things that can not-be), to an infinite, necessary being (one than cannot not-be), on which the contingent things depend and which is the explanation of why they exist at all.

Thomism/thomist. The school of philosophy, which is particularly important within Roman Catholicism, which follows the philosophical and theological ideas of Thomas Aquinas.

Traditional logic. See Aristotelian logic above.

Trinity. In Christianity, God exists in three co-equal parts, Father, Son and Holy Spirit (Ghost): the Trinity. However, this does not mean that God is divided into three or there are three Gods. God's unity is preserved, because the three persons are of one substance (of one being) and so God is three in one.

Tyranny of public opinion. Public opinion, directed against minorities or individuals, whose beliefs or way of life society regards as unacceptable or unorthodox.

Ultimate reality. The object of traditional metaphysics, which is to discover the nature of reality, what actually exists, and to know all there is to know about things as they are in themselves, as opposed to how they appear to us.

Universal declaration of human rights (1948). Adopted by the General Assembly of the United Nations in 1948, it enumerates human rights, based on affirmation of the intrinsic value of individual human beings.

Universal ethical precepts. Moral laws or precepts which apply without exception to all human beings, who must obey them.

Universals/universal ideas. Properties or qualities, such as whiteness or triangularity, where particular instances have the quality in common, or relations, such as in, before or between, which obtain between particulars, qualities or other relations.

Utilitarianism. A consequentialist ethical system, which holds that acts are not right or wrong in themselves, but only to the extent that they promote pleasure/happiness and prevent pain. Utilitarians differ as to whether the principle of utility should be applied directly to decisions about individual actions (act utilitarianism) or used as a basic principle against which to measure secondary moral principles and decide conflicts between them (rule utilitarianism).

Valid and invalid arguments. Ones where the conclusion does or does not follow from the premises.

Verifiability/verification. The view, argued by A. J. Ayer in *Language, Truth and Logic,* that a genuine proposition must be either a tautology, the truth of which can be discovered analytically, or an empirical hypothesis, the truth or falsity of which can be determined by an actual or possible sense-experience.

Verification principle. The logical positivists' principle that a genuine synthetic proposition must be conclusively verifiable in experience.

Vienna Circle. The group of logical positivist philosophers, led by Moritz Schlick, which met to discuss philosophical issues. See Logical positivism above.

Virtue(s). Generally, moral excellence, a positive character trait that makes someone morally good and admirable.

Virtue ethics. Ethical system based on virtue(s), rather than an idea of what is good (at which we should aim) or right (what we ought to do), and which derives from *The Nicomachean Ethics.*

Weak verifiability. The view that a proposition is genuinely factual if any empirical observations are relevant to its truth or falsehood.

Whigs/Whig Party. Political party established by Anthony Ashley Cooper, first Earl of Shaftesbury (see Glossary of Philosophers and Thinkers), which challenged the exercise of the prerogative powers of the monarch by Charles II and James II and supported the Glorious Revolution in 1688–9 and the Hanoverian succession in 1714. The party of government during the eighteenth century, it introduced the Great Reform Act of 1832, and, after fusion with the adherents of Sir Robert Peel (the Peelites included W. E. Gladstone: see Glossary of Philosophers and Thinkers) following the split in the Conservative Party over the repeal of the Corn Laws (1846), became the nineteenth-century Liberal Party, and remained one of the two main political parties until after the First World War.

World of sense. The world of the *phenomena*. See *Phenomenon(a)* above.

World of understanding. The world of the *noumena*. See *Noumenon(a)* above.

Index

Index

Index

Index